P9-CBX-198

ss Medi

cattle-food hormone
emission Ecolo-G Organic F

ENDANGERED SPECIES ba

Du Pont

Water energy cris
SWORDFIS
Air Detergents
Supersonic Polluti
Transport Breakfa
Cereals

Consumeris

clean-air
Population Growth

Doubling of world's population
seen by 2000 if trend continues

water

ups Ask Ban on Chemicals CORVAIR

lorophene Packagi

The Disaster Lobby

The Disaster Lobby

**Prophets of Ecological Doom and
Other Absurdities**

Melvin J. Grayson
Thomas R. Shepard, Jr.

𝒻 Follett Publishing Company/Chicago

ACKNOWLEDGMENTS

American Jewish Committee. Page 224: Reprinted from
Commentary, by permission. Copyright 1972 by the
American Jewish Committee.

Ballantine Books. Pages 126, 127, 136: From *The
Population Bomb*. © 1968, 1971 by Paul R. Ehrlich.
All rights reserved. Reprinted by permission of
Ballantine Books, Inc.

Funk & Wagnalls Publishing Co. Page 250: From *President
Nixon and the Press*, by James Keogh. Copyright ©
1972 by James Keogh. With permission of Funk &
Wagnalls Publishing Company, Inc.

Grossman Publishers. Page 146: From *Unsafe at Any
Speed*, by Ralph Nader. Copyright © 1965 by Ralph
Nader. Reprinted by permission of Grossman Publishers.

Hamish Hamilton. Pages 32, 35: From *Since Silent
Spring*. Copyright © 1970 by Frank Graham, Jr. Hamish
Hamilton, London.

Houghton Mifflin Co. Pages 32, 35: From *Since Silent
Spring*, by Frank Graham, Jr. Reprinted by permission
of Houghton Mifflin Co.

Nash Publishing Corp. Pages 253, 254: From *The News
Twisters*, by Edith Efron, published by Nash Publishing
Corp., Los Angeles. Copyright © 1971 by Edith Efron.

New York Times Co. Excerpts from *The New York Times*
© 1971/72 by the New York Times Company. Reprinted
by permission.

University of Chicago Press. Page 247: From *A Free
and Responsible Press*, edited by Robert D. Leigh.
Copyright 1947 by The University of Chicago. Reprinted
by permission.

Contents

The Disaster Lobby...

Those prophets of doom whose preposterous activities have brought harm to the people of this nation by depriving them of the right to buy, to own, to use and to benefit from many of the miracles of modern science and technology, including some that are of proven value in saving human lives.

Our criticism is not directed at the skilled professionals who have worked so hard and so effectively to create a better environment, to help the consumer and to improve relations among various segments of the American society. Nor is it directed at the responsible citizens who have supported and aided those professionals.

We therefore dedicate this book to the great majority of Americans—young and old, male and female, black and white, urban and rural, rich and poor, blue collar and white collar, at all levels of education and of all political parties —who, despite the alarms and the threats and the blandishments, were too rational to join the Disaster Lobby and too intelligent to be taken in by it.

ONE "The Worst of Madmen..."

On a morning in late September in the year 1962, a window dresser employed by the Doubleday and Company retail branch at Fifth Avenue and 56th Street in New York City, acting on instructions from the store manager, carried several newly published and recently delivered books to the window area facing Fifth Avenue. Careful not to disturb the merchandise already on display, he placed one of the new volumes in a prominent, up-front position customarily reserved for best sellers and for late releases that had received an unusually large allotment of advance publicity.

In such a way was the book *Silent Spring*, by Rachel Carson, introduced to a segment of New York's window-shopping public. And at such a moment was born a period in American history that might be described as the Age of Unreason. For at no other time—not even during the aberrant decades following the Civil War and World War I—have so many Americans succumbed so thoroughly to the influences of illogic, of unreason and of sophistic nonsense as they did in the 1960's and early 1970's.

It is, of course, an exercise in literary license to date an era from a specific event. Still, the historians persist in doing it. As a result, the Protestant Reformation is said to have begun at the very moment on October 31, 1517, when Martin Luther fastened his ninety-five theses to the door of Wittenberg Palace Church. And to the extent that the start

1

of an era can be pinpointed that precisely, a strong case can be made for positing the onset of the Age of Unreason in America at the instant when Rachel Carson's *Silent Spring* was unleashed on a moderately happy and justifiably tranquil populace.

There was little occurring in the United States in the late summer of 1962 to presage the abrupt and sweeping transition that was about to take place: the metamorphosis from the frolicsome Fifties to the simple-minded Sixties. Earlier that year, John Glenn had become the first American to orbit the Earth, regaining for this nation some of the prestige it had lost when the Russians beat us into space. And then in June of 1962, just three months before Miss Carson's book came out, the Supreme Court of the United States had decreed that the recitation of official prayers in the schools of New York State was henceforth unconstitutional. The Cuban missile crisis was still a month in the future, and the assassination of John F. Kennedy was not to occur for more than a year. And halfway around the world in Vietnam, the war was just beginning to heat up.

So America was more or less coasting along at the time Miss Carson rocked the boat. And while the prerelease publicity had hinted that something out of the ordinary was on the way, there was nothing in the comments to indicate the scope and depth of what was about to happen.

Actually, there was little in the book itself to warrant the shock waves it set off. They were the product, apparently, of what might be termed bibliogenetic chemistry. The reading public, for some reason, was primed to go off half-cocked on the subject of ecology, and *Silent Spring* was a book on ecology made to order for half-cocked readers.

In essence, the Carson opus was an impassioned, one-sided and largely unscientific denunciation of the growing use of chemical pesticides, particularly DDT. It warned that unless man stopped using these insect killers on the scale they were being used, he would poison the fish, the birds, the reptiles, the fur-bearing animals, the vegetation and eventually himself. But there was more to *Silent Spring* than a mere thesis on chemicals. By implication so thinly veiled that it deceived few, it was an attack on many of the concepts and institutions that had caused the nation's intellectual community to seethe, in most cases covertly, for many years.

It was an attack on the business Establishment, since it was businessmen who manufactured and used and condoned the use of chemical pesticides.

It was an attack on scientific and technological progress, since it was science and technology that had developed the pesticides in the first place.

It was an attack on the United States, which made most of the pesticides and exported them for use throughout the world.

And most of all, it was an attack on man himself. For it was man who was spewing out those insidious chemicals in flagrant disregard for the welfare of other creatures. In *Silent Spring*, man was the enemy of nature, and Miss Carson was head cheerleader in the nature rooting section.

To the left-wing academic brigade, with its command posts in Berkeley and Cambridge and New Haven and Madison and its message centers in New York City, Chicago and Los Angeles, *Silent Spring* was reveille and the cavalry charge rolled into one. And thousands and thousands of professors and graduate students mounted for the assault. For some time, they had been disenchanted with American society and outraged by its leaders. Now at last they had a *cause célèbre*. They also had a standard-bearer. They had a nice lady author who wasn't a Communist or even a parlor pink and who couldn't be accused of antiscience prejudice since she claimed to be a scientist. And they had her book—a scholarly-sounding, well-written book that could be exploited splendidly since it seemed to offer the American public a clear-cut choice between rebelling or expiring. And as any good proselytizer knows, nothing works quite so well on a prospective convert as his belief that the only alternative to joining is death.

So millions of Americans joined. They bought the foolishness of *Silent Spring* as avidly as the buxom hausfraus of Bavaria had bought the garbage of Adolf Hitler, and for much the same reason. The propaganda was impassioned and inescapable. Night and day, week in and week out, the public was pelted with anti-DDT statements from Ivy League pedants, from overnight ecologists and from the scores of nature-worshiping environmental organizations that had been trying for years to alert the nation to the danger of allowing human beings to become too healthy or too comfortable. It wasn't good for the birds and the fish, they kept pointing out.

The news media—the television and radio networks, the magazines and the big metropolitan-area newspapers—did their part with talent and zeal. Since the 1940's, these organs of information had been tilting further and further to the left as their conservative owners shifted their focus from editorial content to business survival. Caught in the crunch of fiscal matters, they had stopped supervising the material that went into the newscasts and the talk shows and the feature stories, and into the vacuum they left flew a gaggle of ultra-liberal editors who soon began to shape all journalistic output in their own slanted image. The war against DDT was a natural for them, and they waged it with single-minded ruthlessness.

Inevitably, the outpouring of antipesticide propaganda infected a sizable portion of the populace, and when a sizable portion of the populace is infected, you can see rashes breaking out on every politician from city hall to Congress. Before you could say "A public office is a public trust", back-to-nature bills drawn up by environmental faddists were being introduced in Congress and in many state legislatures to ban or limit the use of insect-destroying chemicals.

And that started the snowball downhill. Encouraged by all of this cogent evidence of incipient careening mindlessness the entire corps of save-the-world do-gooders marched forth. Some waved the banners of ecology. Others garbed themselves in the shining raiment of consumerism. Still others cried out against population explosions or male chauvinism or police brutality or the persecution of everybody from black militants to gay pacifists. But whatever the specific windmill might have been, the tilters all had one attribute in common. They were doomsday-oriented. Visions of catastrophe danced in their heads. It was their contention that unless the government acceded to their demand for, let us say, vitamin-enriched breakfast cereals, the sky would fall and the United States of America would perish under a cloud of empty calories.

Because of their impact on American life, these unhappy warriors merit their own niche in the country's sociopolitical lexicon. They deserve a special place alongside The Robber Barons and The Muckrakers and The Four Hundred, and no appellation suits them quite so well as "The Disaster Lobby."

For Disaster Lobby is what they were. Singly and in awesome phalanxes, by mail or in person, wheedling or threatening or alternating between the two, they unfurled their predictions of calamity and shook them in the faces of both lawmakers and constituents. Again and again and again, with the patience and determination of a nearsighted needle-threader, these self-anointed saviors of humanity clamored for new laws, new rules and new guidelines to govern what must—or must not—be made, sold, bought and used in the United States. And all too often they got what they clamored for.

Although their numbers were never very large, the Disaster Lobbyists exerted an inordinate amount of influence because they were quickly joined by millions of sincere, dedicated but hopelessly ill-equipped rank-and-file Americans who accepted the faulty research, innuendos, and implications as truths and who, alarmed by what they heard, embraced the most fatuous causes as their own. Compounding the problem were the nuts and the almost-nuts. From the dimly-lit rooms of back-street boarding houses, from the depths of the stacks in college libraries, from the park benches and the skid-row bars and the all-night movie palaces, there emerged the people Theodore Roosevelt once called "the lunatic fringe"—the hot-eyed men and women with bulging briefcases under their arms and tales of terror on their lips who, in normal times, remain hidden but who, when the times grow fey, come out to peddle their manic wares. Since they had originated the idea that the world was coming to an end—in that sense, the Rachel Carsons were plagiarists—they felt right at home with the Disaster Lobby folks. It was like a reunion of peanut butter and jelly.

So there they were: the activists out front, the concerned but ill-informed reform groups following along and the borderline and all-out paranoiacs bringing up the rear. And instead of laughing them or defeating them into oblivion, as the nation had done in other eras with its Aimee Mc-Phersons and its Carry Nations and its John Browns, a beguiled America embraced them and their theories in what amounted to a coast-to-coast outbreak of galloping myopia.

It should be noted, for it is highly significant, that most Disaster Lobbyists were what you might call "sometimes reformers." Sometimes they were against fraud and pollution and sometimes they weren't. It all depended on who did the defrauding or the polluting. If the culprit was a big industrial company with fat profits, the Disaster crowd went for the jugular like starving vampires. If, however, the sin had been committed by some nonprofit agency, there was rarely a peep of protest. And since nonprofit agencies are responsible for much of the deception and most of the pollution in this country—in the typical city, for example, the chief sources of air and water pollution are municipal incinerators, buses, and sewage lines—the sometimes reformers were invariably attacking the wrong targets. They were shooting at rabbits while the elephants ran wild.

With the advent of the Disaster Lobby, the basic rules of living that had been hammered together over centuries of trial and error and were accepted because they proved to be the only practical way for civilized men and women to exist together in reasonable comfort and security, these fundamental concepts began to give way under wave after wave of epidemic hysteria.

Thou shalt not steal became, at the insistence of certain factions of the Disaster Lobby, thou shalt not steal *unless your need is, in your mind, greater than that of the person from whom you are stealing.*

Thou shalt not commit adultery became simply thou *shalt* commit adultery, because sex is a groove.

And honor thy father and thy mother was transmuted into honor thy son and thy daughter because, as everybody realized in the Age of Unreason, children were a whole lot smarter and more sincere than their parents. Youth worship was an integral part of the thinking of the period. Because of this genuflection toward the young, theories about schooling underwent major surgery in the America of the 1960's. University students demanded the right to establish their own curricula, to set the standards for grading, to select textbooks and to hire and fire their own teachers. A bizarre proposal, to be sure, but not too bizarre for the presidents of several major universities, who gave in to the demands.

As the decade of the Sixties drew to a close, one of America's most highly regarded authors on education went one step further. He came out in favor of a school system in which there would be no formal classes, no official teachers, no enrolled students, no examinations, no grades and no semesters. Anyone would be able—indeed, encouraged— to walk in off the streets and to teach or be taught, depending on his whim of the moment.

But youth madness was not the primary syndrome of Disaster Lobbyism. If any one factor could be singled out as dominant in the thinking of the Disaster people, it was the belief that man must subordinate his own health, his own comfort, his own pleasures and, if necessary, his own life to the health, comfort, pleasures and lives of other animals as well as to the purity of the environment.

This was the folly that caused so many Americans to petition for a ban on DDT. The fear was that while DDT admittedly had saved millions of human lives and while its abolition would destroy millions of human lives, the continued use of DDT might possibly damage some fish and some birds. And given a choice between man and fish, the Disaster Lobby and its disciples opted for the fish.

This was also the rationale behind many of the air pollution and water pollution measures that were rushed through state legislatures and the national Congress in the 1960's and 1970's. In aggregate, these clean-air and clean-water bills represented an expenditure of hundreds of billions of dollars in public funds and in higher prices for consumer goods—money that would have to come from the pockets of American citizens at a rate of thousands of dollars per year per family.

Was this legislation essential to the health and well-being of the people of the United States? Not in the least. At the time it was enacted, our nation's drinking water was eminently safe, the quality of the air over virtually every major city in the country was better than it had been for many years and neither water pollution nor air pollution posed a substantive threat to human life anywhere from Maine to Hawaii.

Yet the public was willing to support these exorbitant environmental measures because, somewhere along the way, it had become convinced that—regardless of the cost in terms of money or effort or loss of freedom—the environment must be made pristine pure. It had to be cleansed of every last speck of pollution even though it had never been totally pollution-free since the earliest ancestor of man crawled out of the sea.

The conviction that man should take a back seat to nature was also the force behind the bans and would-be bans on such items as household detergents, no-return bottles and the supersonic transport. The detergents, while a boon to housewives, were a potential menace to fish. The no-return bottles, a time-saving convenience for shoppers, might clutter up the landscape. The supersonic transport, an aid

to travelers in a hurry, could add moisture to the stratosphere.

And to the Disaster Lobby, the fish, the landscape and
the stratosphere were far more important than housewives,
shoppers and travelers. After all, housewives, shoppers and
travelers were people, and people rated far down the
scale in Disaster Lobby society.

The social structure of the period deserves special
mention. Through it ran a pronounced strain of egalitarianism, but it was a peculiar egalitarianism indeed. To the
exponents of the philosophy most widely accepted in the
1960's intellectual circles, everybody was equal to everybody else, with several notable exceptions. As already
mentioned, man was not the equal of fish. In addition,
American man was inferior to foreign man, especially to
foreign man in underdeveloped nations. Wealthy American
man was inferior to poor American man. And wealthy
American businessman was inferior to every other living
thing on the face of the earth.

(This was the evaluation that prompted much of the
intellectual community's protest over the Vietnam war. None
of the protesters had agonized very much when America sat-
uration-bombed Nazi Germany during World War II. The
Germans, after all, were white, mainly Protestant, Saxon and
relatively affluent. But when America began bombing North
Vietnam for the same reason—like Germany, North Vietnam
had invaded its neighbors—there was a concerted cry of outrage. For now the bombing victims were brown-skinned,
Buddhist and poor, so our actions were indefensible.)

And it was not, by a long, long shot, the kind of egalitarianism preached by the founding fathers of this country. They
had subscribed to the idea that all men were created equal
and that all men should have an equal opportunity under
law to achieve what they were capable of achieving. But
this wasn't good enough for the heavy thinkers of the
Age of Unreason. They wanted everybody to own and enjoy
the same things, regardless of differences in individual

capabilities, regardless of differences in individual ambitions.

Thus came school busing, and at a time of monumentally preposterous concepts, this was perhaps the most preposterous concept of all. At saner moments in American history, the true liberals—the men and women of good will and clear minds—had fought vigorously for the right of all people to be judged and treated solely on the basis of ability. They had denounced, and properly so, the infamous quota system under which religious and racial minorities received arbitrary ratios for admission to schools and colleges and jobs. The only criterion for such admission, the true liberal insisted, should be an individual's performance as a student and as a prospective employe. Not so, shouted the new liberals of the silly Sixties. Religious and racial minorities *should* be singled out for special treatment, they said. Only this way would everybody wind up with the same education, the same jobs and, presumably, the same income and the same possessions.

To expedite the coming of this even-Steven Utopia, they proposed that each school be required to have the proper mixture of blacks and whites, Jews and gentiles, rich and poor. (They never got around to explaining just what this proper mixture was, or why it was proper.) The schools were to achieve the desired balance by busing students out of their own neighborhoods and into other neighborhoods miles away. In any other era, the proponents of school busing would have been tarred, feathered and prodded out of town with long sticks. In the Age of Unreason, they became presidential candidates.

There was one rather hilarious offshoot of this emphasis on contrived equality. It was known as Women's Liberation, and it was predicated to some extent on the belief that all people were not only equal but identical. According to the more outspoken advocates of Women's Lib in the early 1970's, women were much more than just as good as men. They were the *same* as men. Therefore, said the bra burners, women should work as stevedores, pipefitters, bus drivers, truck drivers and, presumably, baritones. They should be drafted into the armed forces and assigned to combat duty. And they should stop having babies—or at least so many babies—since men do not have babies.

Women's Lib brought with it another curious attribute of the period: an obsessive preoccupation with words. The Women's Libsters became incensed at what they regarded as the male chauvinism of the English language. They objected specifically to words like "manpower" and "mankind" and phrases like "she took it like a man", and they recommended these words and phrases be changed to "humanpower", "genkind" and "she took it like a person."

Ridiculous? Of course. But because this was the Age of Unreason, reputable newspapers and magazines dutifully began referring to female heads of committees as "chairpersons" and employing the other fatuous expressions as well.

This tendency to bow to the most asinine logomachical pressures, so long as they were exerted on behalf of social change, was never more apparent than in the area of race relations. It was during the 1960's, for example, that militant Negroes issued the pronouncement that all members of their race should be known as blacks. Prior to that time, many Negroes regarded the term "black" as opprobrious. But the militants cowed the press, and the word "Negro" was expunged from the media vocabulary.

There was a time during the middle and later 1960's when all it took to get the most innocuous word banished from a newspaper was a couple of irate letters from some two-desks-and-a-telephone group claiming to represent the voice of social justice.

On the other hand, there were some words whose usage became *de rigueur*—almost mandatory. The expressions "relevant", "meaningful" and "dialogue" were so popular that they constituted a sort of verbal Trinity. The promoter of a public event could guarantee maximum media coverage by offering a confluence of these three magical "in" words. All he had to do was to bill his affair as an occasion for "a meaningful dialogue on relevant issues."

The search for meaningful relevance extended into all

facets of the entertainment business. Stage shows and motion pictures were no longer reviewed on the basis of their ability to make people laugh or cry or sing along but on their awareness of pressing social issues. A Broadway extravaganza could incorporate the best lyrics since Porter, the best music since Gershwin and the best choreography since de Mille and still get panned by the first-nighters. It just didn't mean a thing if it didn't have that relevance.

By the early 1970's, the most trivial divertissements were generating Lincoln-Douglas-type debates on the question of whether they made a positive contribution to social progress. An amusing television comedy called "All in the Family" drew angry rebukes from many critics, including Laura Hobson, author of *Gentlemen's Agreement*, not because it wasn't funny, not because it wasn't entertaining, but because, in their opinion, it did not go far enough in condemning religious and racial prejudice. It made its bigoted leading character appear humorous, said author Hobson, and there is nothing humorous about bigotry.

There was nothing humorous about most entertainment in the Age of Unreason, especially the comedies. The ability to laugh at ourselves—an essential attribute in comedy— seemed to vanish as ethnic, racial and religious organizations mounted campaigns to outlaw humorous references to the members of ethnic, racial and religious groups. The villains in dramas of the period had to be clearly identified as white Anglo-Saxon Protestants, since that was just about the only sect in the country without an anti-defamation league.

While the advocates of drastic social change professed a desire for equality among men, they were a negation of their own credo. They did not, in fact, believe in equality. They believed in an intellectual elite. They regarded themselves as superior in intelligence to the masses of Americans, and by virtue of that superiority, they demanded the right to dictate to their fellow citizens the ground rules for living.

This elitism of the intelligentsia was at the very foundation of almost every major movement of the period. The ecology crusade was predicated on the right of an intellectual minority to deny to the majority the comforts and health benefits of science and technology. Consumerism, as personified by Ralph Nader, was nothing more than the usurpation by a select corps of "experts" of the consumer's rights to determine what is made and sold and bought and used in the United States.

It was the conviction of many thought leaders that if a consumerist elite believed long yellow convertibles were impractical and a waste of money, Detroit should stop making long yellow convertibles. And never mind how many Americans wanted that particular type of automobile.

There was also abroad in the years of the Disaster Lobby a strong element of masochism. We had sinned, cried the intellectuals, and we should pay for our transgressions. We had sinned against the birds. We had sinned against the fish. We had sinned against the sky and the oceans and the flowers and the fields. We had sinned against the blacks. We had sinned against the young. We had sinned against the poor. We had sinned against the North Vietnamese.

In the eyes of the self-flagellators, it was not enough for us merely to stop sinning. It was not even enough if we tried to redress the wrongs we had perpetrated. What we had to do was suffer. What we had to do was deprive white Americans of jobs and college admissions in order to give preferences to the blacks we had treated so badly in the past. What we had to do was not merely get out of Vietnam, as President Nixon was doing, but get out in a disorderly retreat while admitting our guilt for being there in the first place. We had to endure a measure of agony, it was said, in order to advance the cause of social justice.

Ah, social justice, that was the catch phrase. That was the "Eureka" and the "Excelsior" of the Age of Unreason. But what passed for social justice in these mixed-up times was reminiscent less of Jean Jacques Rousseau than Lewis Carroll. Only Alice could have understood, let alone coped with, the strange theories and programs that bubbled from the mouths of textbook paranoiacs and were promptly dignified beyond all reason by praise from New Left scholars,

New Left news commentators and New Left government officials.

So when a crime was committed, it became important to know who committed it. If the culprit was a wealthy, old, white, Anglo-Saxon Protestant American businessman, the intellectual community cried out for stern retribution. If, however, the wrongdoer happened to be poor and young and black, he could count on a nationwide campaign for leniency. And it mattered not one whit how grave or how despicable his crime might have been.

In Disaster Lobby America, equal justice became anathema. The leading thinkers of the period spat on equal justice. What they insisted on was unequal justice, with the scales weighted heavily on behalf of the poor, the young and the black, since it was obvious that if you were poor and young and black, it was society—and society alone—that was responsible for your misbehavior.

Thus it came to pass in the 1960's that "law and order" was something not to respect but to sneer at. "Law and order" had meant arresting and trying and punishing *everyone* guilty of a statutory crime, regardless of his age, race or economic status. "Law and order" had meant holding *everyone* to account for his own deeds. "Law and order" had meant the right of *every* human being to be secure in his person and in his possessions. So "law and order" had to go. And to the everlasting discredit of the opinion molders, it went. In city after city, scores of cruel, amoral, recidivist hoodlums were acquitted of heinous crimes simply because they had the presence of mind to commit those crimes in the name of some currently popular cause.

Underlying the trend toward leniency was the Lockean philosophy of the New Left, which held that all human beings were essentially good and decent to begin with and that if some of them turned out bad it had to be society's fault. This kind of Disaster Lobby reasoning led to a growing conviction in the 1960's that whenever something went wrong the culprit had to be the system itself or the inanimate products of the system. Thus in seeking to reduce the number and severity of highway accidents, the crusaders of the period overlooked the primary cause—with very few exceptions, the primary cause of a highway accident is a careless, reckless, inebriated or poorly trained driver—and fastened the blame on mechanical defects in the automobiles. And whenever some hoodlum shot a policeman in New York City, the finger-pointers would scatter their censure in all directions. *The New York Times* would blame the suspect's ghetto upbringing. A student faction at Columbia University would blame police brutality. A neighborhood tenants' association would blame the lack of street lights. A lady in Scarsdale would blame violence on TV. And the mayor of New York, who had a fixation about gun controls, would blame the pistol. Aside from the assistant district attorney in charge of the case, nobody—literally nobody—would blame the punk who pulled the trigger.

Nor was the cigaret smoker, the glutton or the drug addict responsible for his actions. According to the molders of popular opinion, cigaret smoking was caused by television commercials and the companies that put them on the air. Overeating was due to the proliferation of high-calorie foods on supermarket shelves. And the reasons for the increase in drug abuse among teenagers were social pressures and the availability of drugs. There was an astounding reluctance to fix the blame where it most often belonged: on the individual smoker, eater or junkie.

In the Age of Unreason many Americans seemed to have difficulty in separating the good guys from the bad guys. They kept abusing lawmen like J. Edgar Hoover while eulogizing convicted criminals like Malcolm X. They vilified the defenders of South Vietnam, who happened to be our allies, while lauding as patriots the aggressors from North Vietnam, who happened to be our enemies. They assailed American officials who impounded secret information to protect this country, and they placed on a pedestal the Xerox aficionado Daniel Ellsberg, who revealed those ·secrets. They called for the blood of businessmen whose investments and skills were the *sine· qua non* of a a free enterprise system that had made America the envy of the world, and they hero-worshipped the Ralph Naders and the Betty Furnesses and the Esther Petersons whose largely factitious charges were threatening to destroy that system.

The decade of the Disaster Lobby: a time of involuted social ferment, with the good elements being sucked under and the bad stuff rising to the top. A time of mind-jarring flip-flop in the logical order of things—of inside-outness, of upside-downness, of day-is-nightness. A time of eerie happenings made all the more eerie by the stature of the people involved and by the matter-of-fact, not-worth-a-raised-eyebrow attitude of the millions of Americans who saw what was going on and did nothing to stop it.

The Age of Unreason. Those astounding years when . . .

• An Associate Justice of the Supreme Court of the United States of America declared, without a trace of a smile, that he had arrived at a point where he preferred fish to people.

• The Mayor of the City of New York, at a time when hundreds of American soldiers were dying each week in Vietnam, told an audience of cheering college students that the real heroes of that period were the youngsters who had burned their draft cards and run off to Canada.

• A United States Senator from Connecticut likened the police of Chicago, who had bopped a few foul-mouthed, rock-throwing rioters over the head with nightsticks, to the police of Nazi Germany, who had put millions of innocent human beings into gas ovens.

• A United States Senator from Maine introduced and campaigned for legislation that would clean up the nation's waterways at a cost estimated at more than two *trillion* dollars—or approximately $10,000 for every man, woman and child in the country. Human health was *not* a significant factor in the proposal, since the state of the waterways represented little or no threat to people.

• A prominent physicist from the University of Arizona touched off a flurry of scare headlines by testifying in Congress that a fleet of supersonic transports would produce up to 10,000 cases of skin cancer in the United States. He then attributed New York City's power failures to the arrival of flying saucers from outer space.

• Another prominent physicist leaped to the first physicist's defense, saying his views on flying saucers might be unorthodox but they *were* courageous.

• Both scientists were quoted as experts by a United States Senator from Massachusetts, who happened to be opposed to the supersonic transport project.

• The President of Yale University announced, with newspaper and television coverage, that he was convinced no black revolutionary could get a fair trial anywhere in the United States.

• The President of Yale University was proved correct when courts throughout America proceeded to acquit almost every black revolutionary brought to trial.

• The curator of the Adirondack Museum in New York State complained that too many people were visiting his mountain and were threatening it with "overuse." He neglected to say just what it was he was saving the mountain for.

• The most widely quoted environmentalists in the United States agreed that Lake Erie was "dead" as a result of industrial pollution. Somebody apparently forgot to tell the fish. Each year, more fish were being caught in "dead" Lake Erie than in the other four Great Lakes *combined.*

• A former member of the Federal Communications Commission made a speech in which he said world population was growing so rapidly that the number of Earthlings would double by the year 2000. He then said pollution was getting so bad that Earth might become uninhabitable by the year 2005. In other words, he managed to warn about overpopulation and underpopulation in the very same speech.

• The youth of America decided to show their individuality and their contempt for conformity by adopting a rigid code of dress and hair style, to which almost all individuals conformed.

• To dramatize their break with the ultra-conservative

past, young male Americans started wearing the kinds of beards and sideburns last seen during the administration of William Howard Taft, an ultra-conservative.

• In a year when the automobile highway death rate had reached its lowest point in history—only 5.3 fatalities per hundred million miles traveled—a man who was to be hailed as the nation's foremost consumer advocate wrote a book denouncing the automobiles as being *Unsafe at Any Speed* and implying that American cars were becoming more and more hazardous.

• Aroused by the book, pressure groups demanded and got Federal mandates for new "safety" devices. The value of these devices, which cost the public billions of dollars, was questionable at best. The 1960's were the first decade since the National Safety Council began keeping records in which there was no decrease in the automobile highway death rate.

• America's participation in the war in Vietnam—participation that had cost this country thousands of lives, many billions of dollars and untold suffering; participation that had gained us and could gain us nothing but grief, humiliation and scorn; participation that was impelled by a desire to defend a country whose borders had been violated by a ruthless invader—this participation was almost universally denounced by American liberals as "immoral." The definition of the word "immoral" was one of the most puzzling aspects of this puzzling period. It came to be used as a handy description for anything to which the speaker was opposed.

• The same critics of the war who denounced South Vietnam's President Thieu for being "a puppet of the White House" also complained that he was pulling the strings at the White House.

• The most enthusiastic advocates of freedom of speech, press and action—academicians who insisted on everyone's inalienable right to harass the police, destroy government records and fly the flags of this nation's military foes—these crusaders for liberty in all its aspects succeeded in virtually

burying the work of two distinguished behavorial psycholo-
gists because their findings on inherited characteristics were
at variance with the New Left position.

  • Well-fed, luxuriously-clothed, comfortably-housed
Americans who were living twice as long as their great-
great-grandparents, working half as much and enjoying an
infinitely richer and healthier existence kept insisting that
things had been better back in the good old days before all
of this industrial development.

In years to come, historians may well ponder the mood
and events of the 1960's and 1970's and wonder why. Why
did so many of the people of the United States listen so
attentively, indeed respectfully, to the voices of the Disaster
Lobby? Why did they endorse new plans, new laws and new
movements that were soon to cost them so dearly in terms
of lost money and lost health and lost comfort? Why did
they fail to recognize illogic and unreason for what they
were?

The answer may well be that in this curious period,
illogic and unreason came in an unfamiliar guise. In eras
past, eccentrics looked and dressed the part. They wore
exotic costumes and they let their hair become disheveled
and they stood on street corners waving hand-lettered signs
about the imminence of doomsday. You knew who they
were, and you could give them a wide berth, tapping your
forehead as you went.

In the Age of Unreason, the men who predicted a quick
end to the world wore business suits, combed their hair
neatly and appeared on the Johnny Carson show. It was
truly difficult to sort them out from the real people.

It should be noted, in all fairness, that the members of the
Disaster Lobby were essentially kind and good-hearted.
Their goals were, for the most part, admirable. They wanted
a better world inhabited by happier and healthier human
beings. But their altruism, their selflessness, their worthwhile aims, none of these things mitigated in the slightest
the lunacy of the period or the harm it ultimately produced.

It was Alexander Pope who, in his *Imitations of Horace*, so aptly described the dangers inherent in the efforts of zealous, dedicated men and women who want desperately to help mankind but who are not equal to the task. "The worst of madmen," wrote Pope, "is a saint run mad."

TWO The Book That Killed

In the year 1961, there were only 110 reported cases of malaria in the island republic of Ceylon, and for the first time in the memory of Ceylon officials, there were no malaria deaths. None. Then in 1968, seven years later, there were *two and a half million* cases of malaria in Ceylon and *more than 10,000 malaria deaths*. There are many who believe that those millions of new cases and those thousands of deaths—along with untold numbers of pathological casualties elsewhere in the world—can be attributed in large measure to the influence of a best-selling book that was published in the United States in 1962, and acclaimed by many as the salvation of mankind.

The book was *Silent Spring*. The fact that anything so potentially destructive could be so warmly received—its author received award after award for her efforts on behalf of our species—is evidence of the spirit of boundless irrationality that gripped America in the time of the Disaster Lobby.

This tale of paradox begins back in 1874, when an obscure German chemist combined sulfuric acid, monochlorbenzene and the sedative chloral hydrate to produce a new chemical compound called dichloro-diphenyl-trichloroethane. His achievement received little public attention because nobody, not even the discoverer, knew what to do with dichloro-diphenyl-trichloroethane.

21

Then, in 1939, a young Swiss scientist named Paul Mueller found that the strange substance with the long name could be used to kill insects. In fact, its unique properties—it was cheap to make, harmless to humans and domestic animals and absolutely lethal to many of the pests that cause disease in man and damage to crops—made it by far the most valuable insecticide the world had ever known. For his experiments and findings, Paul Mueller received the Nobel Prize for physiology in 1948.

The first practical test of dichloro-diphenyl-trichloroethane came several months after Mueller made his announcement. A horde of Colorado potato beetles had infested large areas of Switzerland in the summer of 1939, and the new insecticide was sprayed over the affected farms with gratifying results.

But it took the United States Army to make dichloro-diphenyl-trichloroethane a household word—or, to be more precise, a set of household initials. In February of 1944, units of the American Army were stationed in Naples, Italy, when a typhus epidemic struck. Immediately, Army medical officers rounded up both soldiers and civilians and had them dusted with the new pesticide from Switzerland. Body lice—the carriers of typhus—were destroyed, the epidemic was halted in record time and the glories of DDT, as the Army called its new weapon, were broadcast to the world.

And the world responded. For thousands of years, humanity had endured in helpless silence the bites and the illnesses and the crop devastation caused by insects. Flea-borne plague had ravaged whole continents. Malaria-infested mosquitoes had made huge areas uninhabitable. Sky-blackening swarms of locusts had turned farmland into deserts. Entire civilizations had succumbed to disease and famine that came on the wings of insects. Now, at last, man had something to defend himself with, and he used it as gratefully and enthusiastically as a drowning swimmer would use a life preserver.

In just one country, the United States, the output of DDT soared to more than 100 million pounds in 1947 and to 600 million pounds by 1960. Other nations made their own, and those that did not imported thousands of tons of the stuff from America.

The results of DDT usage were almost beyond comprehension. In many parts of the world it was as though a decree had been issued against suffering. Certain ailments were wiped out almost overnight. Others were brought under control. And the word "famine" abruptly disappeared from newspaper headlines and the vocabulary of international welfare workers.

For a number of reasons, the miracles wrought by DDT got relatively little publicity in the United States and in other highly developed nations. There, malaria and typhus and plague were afflictions you read about in books. There, starvation was something that happened to other people. So there, DDT has always been more of a convenience than a necessity. It was employed to boost farm production and to hold food prices down. It was sprayed on shade trees to conquer the leaf-munching gypsy moth. And it was welcomed by homeowners as a device for keeping their lawns bug-free and for warding off the flights of gnats and flies and mosquitoes that might otherwise ruin a backyard cookout.

But in Asia and Africa and South and Central America it was a different story. In those less fortunate sections of the world, DDT killed the killers of humanity. In those places where most of mankind lives, DDT became a gift of life.

Estimates differ, but the most conservative guess—that of the World Health Organization—puts the number of human lives saved by DDT at *five million* in just the first eight years of its use. Over 100 million illnesses were prevented by DDT in that same brief period, WHO reports, adding that DDT is so safe that it has never killed or permanently harmed a single person, not even any of the men and women employed as sprayers.

Other health experts have been less moderate in their praise of this extraordinary insecticide. Dr. Joseph W. Still, former director of the Bucks County, Pennsylvania, Health Department and an ex-lieutenant colonel in the United States

Army Medical Corps, where he observed the use of DDT first-hand, has estimated that "there are one *billion* human beings living today healthy who would be either sick or dead without DDT." According to Still, the pesticide has protected huge portions of the earth from contamination by such diseases as malaria, plague, typhus, yellow fever, diarrhea and sleeping sickness.

And Walter Ebeling, professor of entomology at the University of California in Los Angeles, has stated that "probably no other compound, not even penicillin, has saved as many lives."

This, then, was the situation when, in the late 1950's, a shy, slender, blue-eyed, best-selling author named Rachel Louise Carson became interested in DDT and other chemical killers of pests.

In assessing the labors of Rachel Carson, one should know something about her background. It is important to understand, for example, that while the public regarded her as a scientist, the only science degree she ever received was an honorary one, from Oberlin College. Significantly, *Current Biography* listed her in its 1951 edition as "author, scientist," the word "author" coming first. In 1964, after her death, the descriptive line in *Current Biography* was "writer, scientist." The difference between "author" and "writer" is an elusive one, but the fact that each of them preceded the word "scientist" is revealing.

Much of Miss Carson's life was spent shuttling between careers in biology and literature. The uncertainty became evident when she was a student at the Pennsylvania College for Women, in Pittsburgh. After having enrolled as an English major, she switched to science, but it was a Bachelor of *Arts* degree that she received in 1929.

After teaching science subjects at the summer school of Johns Hopkins University and receiving her Master of Arts degree in biology, she became a member of the zoology staff at the University of Maryland. She did additional postgraduate work at the Marine Biological Laboratory at Woods Hole, Massachusetts, and in 1936 became an aquatic biologist with the United States Bureau of Fisheries, later to be renamed the United States Fish and Wildlife Service. Miss Carson remained with the government until 1952, but during her tenure she began writing about the ocean and its denizens and after 1952, she devoted all of her time to writing.

"Ever since childhood," she told a book reviewer for the *New York Herald Tribune,* "I've been fascinated by the sea and my mind has stored up everything I have ever learned about it."

Her mind soon was to disgorge its treasures. Her first book, called *Under the Sea-Wind* and subtitled *A Naturalist's Picture of Ocean Life,* was published in 1941. But it was her next book, *The Sea Around Us,* published in 1951, that catapulted her into the public eye. Previewed by *The New Yorker* in three instalments and given further impetus by its having been tapped as an alternate selection of the Book-of-the-Month Club, *The Sea Around Us* quickly became a national best seller. And unlike many best sellers, it won the praise of the most acerb critics.

Although Rachel Carson always was to reject the description of her as a "nature-lover", everything she did and said and wrote indicated, if not a love of nature, at least a remarkable affinity for it. So it is easy to understand why she became concerned when, in the late 1950's, she began to hear reports from friends and colleagues about damage to wildlife caused by the increased use of pesticides.

It is noteworthy that Miss Carson's response to these reports was to plan a book rather than a scientific study project.

Having left her job with the Fish and Wildlife Service, she was able to direct all of her attention to this new venture. And with the triumph of *The Sea Around Us* to attest to her skill as a writer, she had no difficulty in getting a publisher interested. Houghton Mifflin gave her a handsome advance payment, and in 1958, Rachel Carson began work on the book that was to be known as *Silent Spring.*

Because of recurring spells of illness, she was unable to

proceed on the book as rapidly as she had hoped, and it wasn't until the summer of 1962 that the manuscript was delivered to the publisher. Meanwhile, news of the upcoming literary event had leaked out—*The New York Times* ran a feature article on July 22, 1962, headlined "Silent Spring Is Now Noisy Summer" and filled with talk about the furor the book was about to stir up—and, as a result, virtually all of the nation's ecology freaks, nature fanatics and assorted other members of the Disaster Lobby set were primed to fire when Miss Carson was ready.

Publication date for *Silent Spring* was September 27, 1962. By September 28, thousands of Ceylonese were already under a sentence of death.

What was this book that did so much to harm the very people it was designed to help? In a brief sentence, it was an exposé of the dangers of chemical pesticides. In Miss Carson's opinion, the various insect poisoners that were being used in increasing amounts were not only destroying bugs but were threatening with extinction many species of birds and fish. Some of these chemicals, she charged, posed a grave danger to man himself through their tendency to accumulate in the fatty tissues of the human system. And she added a dialectical clincher. She wrote that many insects had built up a resistance to chemical pesticides, so that the bug killers were now almost useless as well as dangerous.

While Miss Carson denounced all of the popular insecticides, she reserved her sharpest barbs for DDT.

It was DDT that was the apparent villain in "A Fable for Tomorrow," the opening chapter in *Silent Spring*. "A Fable for Tomorrow" begins with a reference to "a town in the heart of America where all life seemed to live in harmony with its surroundings. Then," wrote Miss Carson, "a strange blight crept over the area and everything began to change."

The change included "mysterious maladies" that killed the chickens, a sickening of the cattle and sheep and a number of unexpected and unexplained deaths among human beings. Meanwhile, the birds disappeared, the streams became lifeless and the vegetation withered and turned brown.

What was responsible for this desolation, this bleakness, this silent spring? Miss Carson leaves no reader in suspense. On the roofs of the houses, she wrote, there could be seen patches of "a white granular powder" that, a few weeks earlier, had fallen from the skies.

As might be surmised, a common form of DDT is a white granular powder, and it is frequently applied from the skies by crop-dusting airplanes.

While Miss Carson admitted that "this town does not actually exist," towns just like it might very well exist. She said each of the disasters had actually occurred at one time or another in one place or another, and she added that "this imagined tragedy" might someday become a reality for all Americans.

That is all the Chicken Lickens of the Age of Unreason needed to set them off. Huge, fluttering flocks of them headed out, to the town halls, to the State Houses, to the Congress of the United States, clucking and squawking for help. The sky was falling, the sky was falling, and America's prophets of doom wanted it pasted back in place.

Adding fuel to the flames of irrational panic was the critical acclaim accorded *Silent Spring* by a sympathetic press. To those newsmen and commentators with a knee-jerk affection for anything that might embarrass Big Business and the Establishment, the issue was clearcut. DDT was manufactured by Big Business. DDT was used by farmers who had become Big Business. DDT was sanctioned by the Establishment. *Silent Spring* was against DDT, so let's hear it for *Silent Spring*.

And hear it America did.

Soon after its publication, the awards began to settle on Rachel Carson's book like some white granular powder. Among the first to come in was the Schweitzer Medal of the Animal Welfare Institute, named after the humanitarian, Dr. Albert Schweitzer. Its being presented to Rachel Carson was tantamount to giving Captain Ahab the Save-the-White-

Whale Medal. There was Dr. Schweitzer doing everything in his power to help the victims of tropical diseases, and here was a book that did more to foster the spread of tropical diseases than anything since the hatching of the first tse-tse fly.

Other honors heaped on *Silent Spring* and Miss Carson included the Constance Lindsay Skinner Achievement Award of the Women's National Book Association, the Award for Distinguished Service of the New England Outdoor Writers Association, the Conservation Award for 1962 of the Rod and Gun Editors of Metropolitan Manhattan, the Conservationist of the Year Award of the National Wildlife Federation, the Annual Founders Award of the Izaak Walton League, a citation from the International and United States Councils of Women and—another curiosity in view of the disparate objectives of the donor and recipient—the 1963 Achievement Award of the Women's Division of the Albert Einstein College of Medicine.

But this was just the overture to the symphony of hosannas for *Silent Spring*. The book reviewers were even more ecstatic than the awards committees.

"*Silent Spring* is a devastating attack on human carelessness, greed and irresponsibility," said *Saturday Review*.

"Miss Carson's cry of warning is timely," said *The New York Times*. "If our species cannot police itself against over-population, nuclear weapons and pollution, it may become extinct."

"May well be one of the great and towering books of our time," said *The Chicago Daily News*.

"Certain to be history-making in its influence upon thought and public policy all over the world," said the *Book-of-the-Month-Club News*.

And Stewart Udall, then Secretary of the Interior, added a few words of his own. "A great woman," he said, "has awakened the nation by her forceful account of the dangers around us. We owe much to Rachel Carson."

With praise like that, there was a great deal of publicity, which snowballed into still more praise and ever more publicity. The book soon went into its second and third and fourth printings—it ultimately topped twenty printings in paper back and reached eleven in hard cover—and sales zoomed over the million mark and, eventually, the two million mark.

And throughout this country and other countries where translations were available, the monumental good achieved by DDT since 1944 was quickly forgotten, and its reputation for helping mankind was swept away on a wave of anti-pesticide sentiment that had all the scientific soundness of a voodoo rooster-plucking ceremony in Haiti.

The Toledo, Ohio, Public Library, responding to Rachel Carson's suggestion that good insects be used to kill bad insects, sent to California for a huge supply of ladybugs in the hope that ladybugs would prove as effective as DDT in keeping aphids off the library's shrubs. They were not.

Scores of candidates for public office wrote to Miss Carson, asking her to tell them what stand to take on pesticides. This is roughly akin to asking a turkey, just before Thanksgiving, what stand to take on axes.

And in state legislatures across the nation, lawmakers fell over each other introducing bills that would restrict or ban entirely the use of chemical pest-killers. By the end of 1962, more than forty such measures had been adopted while hundreds of others were under active study.

But the most ominous response of all came from the White House. President John F. Kennedy, who had read *The New Yorker* series, asked his Science Advisory Committee to look into the charges drawn up by Miss Carson. This was the first step on the Federal level, and it triggered a chain of moves that led first to a gradual compulsory phaseout of DDT usage in the United States and later to a total ban mandated by the Environmental Protection Agency under President Richard M. Nixon.

Of course, neither President can be blamed very much for what he did. Neither President had much of an alternative. In each instance, the drumbeat of demands for the abolition of DDT and other pesticides was too loud and too persistent to ignore. As early as the spring of 1963, every major conservation group in the United States was exerting pressure to outlaw DDT, and when it comes to exerting pressure, a steam cooker could take lessons from an aroused conservation group. Official Washington quickly got the message.

There is no mystery about the posture taken by conservationists on the DDT issue. They acknowledged the possibility that DDT was beneficial to human beings, but they contended that it wasn't doing the birds and the fish any good. Whenever the interests of mankind come into conflict with the interests of other species, America's conservation lobby has almost always sided unhesitatingly with the other species.

In the past, such a preposterous attitude had been treated with the proper amount of disdain by the public at large. In the Age of Unreason, it was warmly applauded by a substantial portion of that public. The inmates had taken over the asylum and the welcome mat was out for kooks of all persuasions.

America's daffiness was contagious. Other countries, experiencing their own symptoms of Disaster Lobbyism, began to share in the growing hysteria over chemical pesticides. Norway, Finland, Sweden and half a dozen other nations instituted restrictions on the use of DDT, and those nations that did not outlaw the compound became extremely gunshy in employing it. A member of the staff of the Ceylon Embassy in Washington, who asked that his name not be used, recalled in the spring of 1972 the DDT episode in his country.

"There was once a great amount of malaria in Ceylon," he said. "We had as many as two or three million people afflicted with it at one time. Then we began spraying the mosquito areas with DDT and by 1960 we had reduced the cases to almost zero. Then three years later we heard about the dangers of DDT so, with malaria almost gone, we stopped spraying. The mosquitoes came back and malaria came back, so we have begun spraying again."

Would Ceylon have stopped using DDT in the mid-1960's

if there had not been so much adverse publicity about it? The Embassy man shrugged his shoulders. "Possibly not. *Probably* not. But there *were* those bad reports."

Members of the World Health Organization have been less guarded in their appraisal of the Ceylon situation. Several of them have said flatly that it was *Silent Spring,* and *Silent Spring* alone, that persuaded the Ceylonese to abandon DDT.

In evaluating the book and its effects, the objective observer keeps running up against two uncontested facts. Most certainly—and not even Stewart Udall would dispute the statement—many, many people are alive today because DDT was used. And just as certainly, if you can believe the World Health Organization and officials of such concerned nations as Ceylon, many, many other people are dead today because the use of DDT was discontinued.

Even so, those deaths might be justified if Miss Carson's basic premises were true—if DDT does, indeed, pose a critical threat to all of nature, including man—if DDT does, in fact, do more harm than good. In that case, the abolition of DDT would be warranted. In that case, the hysteria whipped up by *Silent Spring* had a legitimate basis.

That, however, was *not* the case.

Unfortunately—no, *tragically*—Miss Carson made many serious mistakes in her book, and each mistake was compounded by erroneous inferences and outlandish assumptions emanating from the back-to-nature, Disaster Lobby factions that thrived in the 1960's.

First of all Miss Carson erred in assuming, if she did assume, that her readers would carefully analyze her entire book and would then adopt a scientist's attitude of reserving judgment until all the facts were in. (She did state in *Silent Spring* that she was *not* in favor of a blanket ban on pesticides. "It is not my contention," she wrote, "that chemical insecticides must never be used." Instead, she urged extensive testing to see whether these insecticides were as harmful as she believed them to be.)

But as might have been expected, most of her readers did

not maintain their equilibrium, such as it was. What they did was fly into a collective tizzy of such magnitude that all chemicals, no matter how benign, became anathema. In the homes of some Carson converts, aerosol cans containing the most innocuous substances were hurled into garbage containers in what amounted to a quasi-religious rite of antichemical catharsis.

Miss Carson may have planned it that way. Although she often dissociated herself from irresponsible movements stemming from *Silent Spring*—her friend Shirley Briggs once said, "Rachel was mortified when nutty little publications praised her book, generally for all the wrong reasons"—the book itself did much to encourage these movements. Even her admirer, Frank Graham, Jr., who in 1970 wrote a book called *Since Silent Spring* that might be regarded as a 333-page eulogy, admitted that "in style and content, Rachel Carson designed *Silent Spring* to shock the public into action against the misuse of chemical pesticides."

You need go no further than her chapter headings to find examples of this intent to shock: "Elixirs of Death", "Needless Havoc", "Rivers of Death" and "Beyond the Dreams of the Borgias" are a few samples.

Shocking the public has never been considered an act of cool, scientific detachment, and *Silent Spring* was anything but cool or detached—or scientific, for that matter.

A case in point was Miss Carson's opening section on the imaginary town that didn't exist but might have. It was the sort of thing you might expect from a Mary Shelley writing about the construction of a monster in some castle in Transylvania. It was not what you would expect from a woman who billed herself as a scientist.

There was also little of the scientist in Miss Carson's careful selection of facts to be included in *Silent Spring* and her even more diligent eschewal of facts that tended to militate against her conclusions. Thus, she kept hammering away at the possibility that DDT would eventually prove harmful to human beings because of its long-term buildup in body tissues, citing medical reports of the existence of DDT in various organs of people exposed to it. What she failed to do was point out that single doses of five grams of DDT—and even more—have been administered to human beings in the successful treatment of barbiturate poisoning, according to Walter Ebeling, U.C.L.A. And, notes Professor Ebeling, *five grams of DDT are roughly four times as much as the average American will assimilate in a 70-year lifetime.*

It would seem likely that, if a person can accept without ill effects five grams of DDT in one spoonful, we should all be able to tolerate one-fourth of that amount over a 70-year span. But Miss Carson neglected to incorporate this interesting item in her book.

She also failed to make logical inferences *in favor* of DDT from the facts she did use. For example, after noting in *Silent Spring* that scientists don't know how much DDT can be tolerated by the human body, she reported that the amount of DDT in the bodies of individuals with no unusual exposure ranged from 5.3 parts per million to 7.4 parts as a result of normal dietary intake. Agricultural workers have 17.1 parts per million in their bodies, she said, and workers in insecticide plants have as much as 648 parts per million.

The almost too obvious conclusion to be drawn from these figures—although Miss Carson never drew it—is that if factory workers with 648 parts per million of DDT in their bodies are not killed or made ill by it, then the average American with only one-hundredth that amount in his tissues should be a hundred times safer. And the fact is that no one, inside or outside of an insecticide plant, has ever suffered permanent injury as a result of environmental exposure to DDT.

Miss Carson also referred repeatedly to disappearances of fish and birds from their usual haunts, attributing this phenomenon to ingestion of DDT that has been sprayed on vegetation or dumped into streams. In many instances, however, these disappearances proved to be temporary or to have been the result of dislocations that had nothing to do with DDT or any other pesticide.

In a 1971 article in *Life* magazine, Franklin Russell, a natural historian, declared that "Rachel Carson's terrifying description of the disastrous overdose of DDT in New Brunswick's forests, which killed just about all insects, birds and fish in some areas, did not include the fact that two years later nearly all life systems there appeared back to normal."

Miss Carson preferred to leave her readers with the impression that the birds and fish were gone forever—that the "silent spring" would remain silent until man abandoned his use of chemical poisons.

Russell had his own interpretation of Miss Carson's methods: "Alarmism is apparently used by intelligent and responsible people like ... Carson out of desperation and the feeling that conventional methods of communication have failed."

An understandable emotion on Miss Carson's part, perhaps, but hardly conducive to accurate comprehension of the problem.

In reporting on declines in population of certain species—such as the peregrine falcon and the bald eagle—Miss Carson tended to heap the entire blame on pesticides. She ignored all data that would refute her theory.

There is no mention at all in *Silent Spring* of the findings of scientists like Dr. Gordon Edwards, entomologist at San Jose State College, who has attributed bird population declines to the construction of roads and buildings on breeding grounds—not to pesticides.

Dr. William Hazeltine, another California entomologist, regards pesticides as one of the *least* important causes of avian dislocation. The chief culprits, he says, are hunters, trappers, campers and the general encroachment of human beings into nesting and feeding areas.

Furthermore, states Hazeltine, the reports of the imminent extinction of species like the peregrine falcon and the bald eagle are without foundation. Both species are on the numerical increase at many of their favorite retreats, he has found.

And several other eminent scientists have noted that, since the beginning of life on earth, over 100 million species of animals and plants have become extinct. With the exception of a few dozen, all of them disappeared long before the advent of chemical pesticides. To blame DDT for a process that has been going on for millions of years, say these scientists, would be ridiculous.

Miss Carson was equally unprofessional in contending that DDT was no longer of much value in fighting insects since the insects had developed an immunity to it. According to *Silent Spring*, the resistance to DDT of both houseflies and certain types of mosquitoes dates back to World War II, soon after the American Army began spraying against malaria-carrying mosquitoes in Italy. A year later, states the book, houseflies and certain types of mosquitoes displayed evidence of immunity to the pesticides, and the level of immunity has risen since that time "at an astounding rate."

In his sequel to *Silent Spring*, Frank Graham echoed the resistance theme. "Strains of malignant malaria continue to frustrate medical science," he wrote in *Since Silent Spring*. "Furthermore, at a recent W.H.O. conference in Geneva, the organization admitted that the program to eradicate malaria in West Africa had bogged down because of widespread insect resistance to DDT."

The implications were plain, and a bemused America understood them. DDT and its fellow insecticides were destroying wildlife and vegetation and, very probably, man himself. To make matters worse, they were no longer killing insects, so let's abolish them. And off went the letters to the Congressmen.

By the early 1970's, almost the only creatures on earth unaware that DDT had stopped destroying insects were farmers, scientists and the insects themselves.

On February 12, 1971, several months after Frank Graham's book came out and almost nine years after Rachel Carson's did, the World Health Organization issued a special report praising DDT as an eminently safe and tremendously effective means of destroying houseflies and malaria mosquitoes. It said DDT had freed "over a billion people" from the risk of malaria in the past twenty-five years and added that spraying was still necessary to protect 329 million more people from the disease.

"Even temporary lack of DDT for malaria control can seriously jeopardize the gains achieved at such great cost," said WHO scientists, who apparently had not read Graham's book.

Meanwhile in Ceylon, where government leaders had heard that resistance line before, spraying continues against mosquitoes that do not seem to realize they're supposed to be immune.

But is was Miss Carson's suggested remedy for the insect dilemma, perhaps more than anything else, that clinched the case against her in the eyes of bona fide scientists. After having condemned chemical pesticides on the ground that they had not yet been adequately tested with regard to their long-range effects on man and beast, she blithely proceeded to offer as alternatives a potpourri of programs that have not been tested at all—or that have been tested much less than has DDT.

Among her solutions: sterilization of male insects by radiation; the use of insect venoms on other insects; spraying with various bacteria, such as bacillus thuringiensis, which causes "a fatal septicemia in the larvae of the flour moth"; and spraying with "a solution containing a virus obtained from the bodies of caterpillars that have died because of infection with [an] exceedingly virulent disease."

In *Since Silent Spring*, Graham chips in with this remedy: dropping sterilized pink bollworm moths on cottonfields to mate with the moths already there, thus preventing propagation. The moths would be sterilized, he said, through exposure to cobalt-60 irradiation.

Nowhere did Miss Carson or Graham express any concern about the possible effects on the so-called "chain of life" of these alternatives to DDT. What happens when moths irradiated with cobalt-60 are set loose? What effect might there be, not only on the insects they are supposed to destroy, but on the entire ecological framework? And how about those "exceedingly virulent disease" bacteria let loose on the world? Would they kill only the caterpillars or would they go on to destroy other living things?

DDT, which has been around for more than a quarter of a century without harming a single human being except through accidental misuse, was regarded by Miss Carson as undertested and potentially dangerous. How much testing should go into the release of cobalt-irradiated moths and disease bacteria? Another twenty-five years? And meanwhile, of course, we clamp a ban on DDT and the people of Asia and Africa and Latin America go on dying.

While books like *Silent Spring* and *Since Silent Spring* were received with limitless enthusiasm by the anti-Establishment factions of a befuddled America, the real-life scientific community was less than overwhelmed. Several highly regarded scientists were actually underwhelmed, and said so.

It was unfortunate, but characteristic of the period, that many prominent and influential Americans swallowed everything Miss Carson had to say and paid no attention whatsoever to the scientists.

No headlines were made when Dr. Frederick J. Stare, of the Department of Nutrition, Harvard School of Public Health, said, "Miss Carson flounders as a scientist in this book" or when he added, "Dispassionate scientific evidence and passionate propaganda are two buckets of water that simply can't be carried on one person's shoulders."

Becoming specific, Stare stated: "Residues of DDT do build up in stored fat in human beings but not to harmful levels and they are not permanent. If you'll accept that scientific fact, then you will have to discount many of Miss Carson's most hair-raising examples from which she makes possibility projections."

Dr. William J. Darby, nutritionist at the Vanderbilt University School of Medicine, had this to say: "Her ignorance or bias on some of the considerations throws doubt on her competence to judge policy. For example, she indicates that it is neither wise nor responsible to use pesticides in the control of insect-borne diseases."

And there was this from C. G. King, president of the Nutrition Foundation: "The problem is magnified in that publicists and the author's adherents among the food faddists, health quacks and special interest groups are promoting her book as if it were scientifically irreproachable and written by a scientist."

In the years following the publication of *Silent Spring*, more and more authoritative testimony and hard factual evidence have cast increasing doubt on the validity of Miss Carson's views.

Contrary to her suggestion that chemical pesticides like DDT might be a cause of cancer—she had written that "in laboratory tests on animal subjects, DDT has produced suspicious liver tumors"—experiments in the late 1960's indicated that DDT may actually inhibit the growth of malignant tumors. Reporting on the results of a study involving workers exposed to high levels of DDT for ten to twenty years, Dr. Edward R. Laws, Jr., of Johns Hopkins University, stated: "It is noteworthy that no cases of cancer developed among these workers in some 1,300 man-years of exposure, a statistically improbable event."

Laws went on to say that, of eighty-nine DDT-fed mice inoculated with tumor cells, seven did not develop cancer. All of the eighty-seven mice inoculated with tumor cells but not DDT *did* develop cancer. Although all cancerous mice died, those with DDT in their systems lived significantly longer.

"DDT," concluded Laws, "may have an anti-cancer producing potential."

One of the most outspoken defenders of DDT has been U.C.L.A.'s Professor Ebeling. "DDT," he wrote in a letter to *The Los Angeles Times*, "is one of mankind's major triumphs. It has been the principal insecticide in the control of insect vectors of yellow fever, typhus, elephantiasis, bubonic plague, cholera, dengue, sleeping sickness and dysentery."

Dr. Guzman Garcia-Martin, chief of the Malaria Eradication Program, Pan American Sanitary Bureau, stated in 1969 that "since 1955 DDT has been the main weapon in the worldwide malaria eradication program. Research has continued for the development of other methods of attack against malaria and for the development of alternative insecticides. To date, there is no insecticide that could effectively replace DDT."

Similar statements were issued at frequent intervals in the past decade by the World Health Organization, which, despite Frank Graham's remarks, is now and always has been thoroughly pro-DDT. Far from giving up on DDT because of the alleged resistance to it of malaria mosquitoes, WHO made this announcement in January of 1971:

"It is obvious that the withdrawal of DDT would indeed be a major tragedy in the chapter of human health. Vast populations of the world would be condemned to the frightening ravages of endemic and epidemic malaria."

The health organization added that after testing more than 1,400 compounds, it had found only two that might qualify as DDT replacements. Each was far more expensive than DDT—prohibitively so for use in underdeveloped nations where tropical diseases are most prevalent.

World Health Organization scientists stated that these same tests had proved to their satisfaction that DDT was absolutely harmless to human beings, even when used indoors as a spray against flies and other household pests.

About the same time, Dr. Still, the former Pennsylvania health official and ex-member of the Army Medical Corps, unleashed a stinging attack on the "so-called environmental protectionists" who, on the basis of vague theories and unproved charges, had aroused public opinion against DDT.

"Although the exaggerated charges have been exposed by competent authorities," said Still, "these refutations in many cases have not even been mentioned by the mass media which presented the original scare stories. As a result of the anti-DDT hysteria, we are now at the point where politicians may ban the most beneficial chemical known to man because a big publicity campaign has succeeded in giving DDT an image completely false."

A call to action against those who would abolish DDT was

issued by Dr. Thomas H. Jukes, Professor of Medical Physics in residence at the University of California. "We must not allow millions of people to sink back into disease and misery," he said. "We must defeat this campaign."

Dr. Earl Butz, a member of the Purdue University Research Foundation and soon to be named United States Secretary of Agriculture, declared in 1970 that without chemical pesticides, 60 million Americans would starve. It was these pesticides, he said, that made it possible to harvest bumper food crops year after year.

And then, on November 8, 1971, there came a defense of DDT that not even the most Carsonophilic newspaper or the most Disaster Lobby-minded television commentator could ignore. The source happened to be Dr. Norman E. Borlaug, winner of the 1970 Nobel Peace Prize, and the forum for his statement was the 16th Governing Conference of the United Nations Food and Agriculture Organization, held in Rome.

In a bitter, slashing speech, Dr. Borlaug denounced *Silent Spring*, which he said was responsible for "the vicious, hysterical campaign against the use of agricultural chemicals."

He condemned the activities of "the moving forces behind the environmental movement," and he identified them by name as the Sierra Club, the National Audubon Society, the Izaak Walton League and "the new legal arm of the movement," the Environmental Defense Fund.

He stated flatly and unequivocally that, if the campaign to ban DDT and other chemical pesticides were to succeed, the world would be doomed to starvation.

Much of Borlaug's talk was devoted to a protest against what he described as "the current crusades of the privileged environmentalists in the United States." These were the people who wanted DDT outlawed by the American government, he said, and once DDT was banned in this country, there would be an immediate demand for its abolition worldwide.

"This must not be permitted to happen," Borlaug told the

U.N. conference, "for no chemical has ever done as much as DDT to improve the health, economic and social benefits of the people of the developing nations. If agriculture is denied the use of these chemicals because of unwise legislation that is now being promoted by a power group of hysterical lobbyists who are provoking fear by predicting doom for the world through chemical poisoning, then the world will be doomed, not by chemical poisoning but from starvation."

What effect has this logic had against the misleading, emotional and simplistic arguments advanced in *Silent Spring?* So far, the impact has been limited entirely to foreign countries. Regulations against DDT have been rescinded in most of Scandinavia. And those governments that had discontinued their own spraying programs — Ceylon is one of them — have now resumed them.

Only in the United States, home of the Disaster Lobby, has hysteria prevailed in the face of reason. In response to petitions by various environmental groups, the Federal government began in 1969 to issue orders prohibiting the use of DDT in specified instances. The first bans covered DDT spraying of shade trees, tobacco plants and household surfaces. In 1970, the prohibition was extended to fifty other uses. Then in June of 1972, the Environmental Protection Agency announced that beginning December 31, 1972, the use of DDT would be permitted only on three minor vegetable crops in certain geographic areas under severely restricted conditions.

In issuing the announcement, EPA Administrator William D. Ruckelshaus, who in 1971 had said DDT did *not* represent "an imminent hazard", told newsmen that the pesticide posed "an unacceptable risk to man and his environment." His new stance and his actions were at complete variance with the findings of Federal examiner Edmund S. Sweeney, an Interior Department officer designated to look into the DDT controversy. In April 1972, after seven months of hearings and 8,900 pages of testimony, Sweeney said there was "a present need for the essential uses of DDT" and added that the benefits of DDT far outweighed the risks.

The Ruckelshaus edict also ran counter to the recommendations of EPA's own Scientific Advisory Committee, which had found DDT to be extremely useful in controlling disease-bearing and crop-damaging insects and had tacked on this statement:

"DDT has a very low acute toxicity to man and his domestic animals, and exposure to high doses for short periods of time does not appear to cause any irreversible damage. There is no evidence that DDT exerts a teratogenic [mutation] effect. The probability of tumoragenesis and carcinogensis is low."

And Ruckelshaus disregarded the pleas—and the hard evidence—of the Agriculture Department. Emphasizing the importance of DDT in maintaining crop quality and quantity at high levels, Agriculture again and again had noted the absence of reliable information linking DDT with environmental deterioration. "We know of no reports," the Department said on one occasion, "of any endangerment of any species of fish as a result of the use of DDT."

But Ruckelshaus did not listen to the Agriculture Department. He did not listen to his Scientific Advisory Committee. He did not listen to the Federal hearing examiner or his 8,900 pages of testimony. He did not listen to Nobel Laureate Norman Borlaug or U.C.L.A. Professor Ebeling or Johns Hopkins' Edward Laws or the University of California's Thomas Jukes or Harvard's Frederick Stare or the scores of scientists of the World Health Organization. What William Ruckelshaus listened to, intently and responsively, was the Disaster Lobby and its millions of head-nodding followers.

With DDT scarce and becoming scarcer, farmers turned to other pesticides that, according to A. V. Krebs, Jr., a research associate of the Agribusiness Accountability Project, were causing serious illness among farm workers. Krebs cited official reports from California and New Jersey of widespread poisonings in the wake of a shift from DDT to organic compounds. These poisonings, said Dr. Thomas Milby of the California State Health Department, took the form of "a slow, insidious impairment of hand-eye coordination and other neuromuscular functions."

Even *The Washington Post*, as ecology-minded as any newspaper in America, acknowledged in its issue of June 16, 1972, that the substitutes for DDT were "easier on the environment but far harder on the health of those who work in the fields."

And there was the economic impact. Replacements for DDT proved to be much more expensive and much less effective. Barry Commoner, Director of the Center for the Biology of Natural Systems at Washington University, St. Louis, and an outspoken foe of DDT, admitted that the Federal ban on chemical pesticides would add *$290 million a year* to the cost of growing food in the United States. As a result, he said, wheat prices would rise by 12 percent.

But this was the time in America when the cost of food for human beings was not the critical consideration. Neither was the health of farm workers. What mattered in this era of the Disaster Lobby was the well-being of the fish and the birds and the animals of the forest. As long as they were thriving, the environmental groups were happy and so was William D. Ruckelshaus. It was the Age of Unreason, and many Americans in high places had been conditioned to take the side of fish against man and to accept the word of quacks against that of capable scientists. And the most eloquent monuments to this kind of thinking were row upon row of gravemarkers in distant Ceylon.

THREE

Air Today, Gone Tomorrow

As the decade of the 1960's got under way, the average resident of the United States was outliving his Colonial ancestors by more than thirty years. He was eating better food, getting sick less often, working half as many hours, earning twenty times as much in real income, receiving almost twice the schooling, wearing finer clothes, occupying superior homes and enjoying the help and the fun and the convenience of scientific miracles not even dreamed of 200 years earlier—miracles like television, radio, the telephone, electric lights and rail, automotive and air transportation.

Despite this solid evidence to the contrary, it was the prevailing opinion among many left-leaning thought leaders of the period that the nation's citizenry was worse off than it used to be. They pointed to youth rebellions and drug addiction and consumer complaints and racial unrest and, above all, to environmental pollution as symptoms of a progressive deterioration in what they liked to call "the quality of life."

Convinced that ecological doomsday was just around the corner, the heavy thinkers of the Age of Unreason spent much of their time demanding new laws that would stop progress and would deny the American consumer many of the fruits of modern science and technology. The products of our factories, they contended, were fouling up the air and the water and endangering other species.

So the Disaster Lobby went to Washington to get those products banned—or at the very least, stringently regulated. And all too often, it got just what it asked for. One reason was its ability to enlist the support of a sprinkling of scientists with impressive credentials. Prominent among them was Barry Commoner, holder of five university degrees and legitimate claimant to the titles of biologist, botanist, chemist, physiologist and educator. From time to time, Commoner would appear before a Congressional committee or an important civic group and warn that the days of mankind were numbered unless industry stopped injecting gases into the atmosphere and dumping mercury into the oceans. Frequently, he would win over the Congressmen and the civic leaders, and they would add their endorsements to proposed legislation against gas-injecting and mercury-dumping.

By the late 1960's, the concept of a spotless environment had taken on all of the political allure once reserved for motherhood, Mom's apple pie and being born in a log cabin. And while favoring of environmental reforms might not guarantee a political candidate's election, opposing them would most assuredly have guaranteed his defeat.

So persuasive and so persistent were the Disaster Lobbyists that no politician—no matter how powerful, no matter how sensible—could stand up to their pressures, particularly those involving ecological uplift.

After the elections of 1968, men of reason hoped that Richard Nixon, a cool conservative with a strong streak of pragmatism, would be able to stop the madness. They hoped in vain. President Nixon did try for a while to pursue a course of prudence and moderation in dealing with the environment, but in the end, he too bowed to the inevitable. And although he gave in grudgingly, he did give in. He had no alternative. Under our system of government, no individual—not even the President—can ignore the desires of the people, and in the late 1960's, most of the people of the United States, stirred into unthinking passion by the Disaster Lobby, desired an environment clean enough to wipe their white gloves on, and never mind the cost.

The cost was high. During the first three years of the Nixon Administration, more than $4.5 billion of Federal money alone was spent for major environmental programs. That was three times as much as the sum spent on the environment by the Kennedy and Johnson Administrations combined. There is a simple explanation. During the Kennedy and Johnson Administrations, the Disaster Lobby was just beginning to take shape. The insanity had not yet jelled.

To accommodate the econuts, President Nixon established an Environmental Protection Agency, with broad powers to enforce air and water standards set up by Federal law. And for good measure, the President tacked on a new Council on Environmental Quality, a new National Oceanic and Atmospheric Administration and his recommendation for a new Department of National Resources.

An indication of how well the ecology wing of the Disaster Lobby had done its job can be found in the President's State of the Union message of January 20, 1972. He devoted a major section of it to the environment.

"The need for action ... is urgent," said President Nixon. "The forces which threaten our environment will not wait while we procrastinate. Nor can we afford to rest on last year's agenda in the environmental field. For as our understanding of these problems increases, so must our range of responses."

Less than three weeks later, he submitted to Congress a special message on the environment in which he referred to "the environmental awakening" of America.

"It marks a new sensitivity of the American spirit and a new maturity of American public life," said the President. "It is working a revolution in values, as commitment to responsible partnership with nature replaces cavalier assumptions that we can play God with our surroundings and survive. It is leading to broad reforms in action, as individuals, corporations, government and civic groups mobilize to conserve resources, to control pollution, to anticipate and prevent emerging environmental problems, to manage the land more wisely and to preserve wildness ... Toward keeping the momentum of awareness and action, I pledge my full support and that of this Administration and I urgently solicit the continuing cooperation of the Congress and the American people."

Then, sounding more like the industry-baiting president of the Sierra Club than the conservative President of the United States, he proceeded to outline a series of proposals for new laws, including one that would place a charge of 10 to 15 cents a pound on sulfur emitted into the atmosphere by private companies.

While the Disaster Lobbyists of the 1960's and 1970's had many axes to grind, the one they honed most pertinaciously was the specter of mass asphyxiation through air pollution. Again and again they spoke of a continuing degeneration in the quality of air and they issued warnings about the coming day when noxious fumes would replace the oxygen in the atmosphere and human beings would have a choice between breathing from portable containers of filtered air or not breathing at all.

In typical Disaster Lobby style, the prophets of suffocation used every available avenue for the spreading of their doomsday gospel. There was a period in 1968 and 1969 when it was almost impossible to open your metropolitan newspaper or flip through your favorite national magazine or tune in to a newscast or a televised debate on major issues without having the prospect of unbreathable air served up to you in vivid detail.

The propaganda worked. Scared into irrationality, scores of thousands of Americans began badgering their Congressmen and state legislators with demands for mandatory air pollution controls. Either to dramatize their position or in actual fear of being poisoned, some people took to wearing gauze face masks in the streets. Others refused to go out into the streets at all. An acquaintance of the authors was so moved by the mounting hysteria that whenever he ventured outdoors in New York City he obligingly began to cough in a display of what might be described as Chronic Propaganda Bronchitis, or Disaster Lobby Throat.

Such coughing was, indeed, psychosomatic. For the stark, unalloyed truth is that the air pollution panic of the 1960's was almost entirely contrived. Throughout the period, the quality of the air over the major cities of the United States was substantially better than it had been in decades, and it was—and is—improving all the time. The fact that the great majority of Americans believed otherwise, as indicated in public-opinion surveys, is testimony to the effectiveness of the Disaster Lobby and to the general aura of fatuity that pervaded the period.

In Scene I, Act I, of *Macbeth*, William Shakespeare, writing more than 300 years ago about events occurring almost 1,000 years ago, has one of his characters refer to "the fog and filthy air."

And there was fog and filthy air in abundance in Macbeth's Scotland and Elizabethan England. Down through the centuries, historians and diarists have portrayed the cities of Europe as clouded over with an almost permanent mantle of black, choking, soot-filled gook.

The reason was that the common heating and propulsion fuels prior to the late 1800's were wood, peat and coal, and the combustion of wood, peat and coal produces huge amounts of sulfur gases and other pollutants. Then oil and natural gas were gradually substituted for the other fuels, and the air started getting cleaner.

Professor Matthew A. Crenson of Johns Hopkins University took note of the change in fuels when, in an article in *The New York Times*, dated April 20, 1971, he stated that city air in the United States was getting progressively cleaner and not dirtier, despite what the propagandists were saying.

"The available evidence," said Crenson, "indicates that there has been a general decline in sulfur dioxide pollution during the past 30 or 40 years. In some cities, the sulfur dioxide content of the air today is only one-third or one-fourth of what is was before World War II. In some ways, at least, city air is probably cleaner today than it was 30 or 40 or 50 years ago. The city of tenements . . . was probably a good bit dirtier than today's city."

By inserting words like "in some ways" and "probably", Professor Crenson was being a good deal more cautious than he had to be. The long-term trend toward cleaner air is corroborated by scientific study after scientific study. It is totally irrefutable.

In 1931 and 1932, for example, the United States Public Health Service conducted measurements in fourteen cities and found that the average concentration of particulates in the air was 510 micrograms per cubic meter, according to a report in *The New York Times* by Eugene Guiccione, senior editor of *The Engineering and Mining Journal*. Then in 1957, the Department of Health, Education and Welfare began an air-monitoring program and discovered an average particulate concentration of only 120 micrograms per cubic meter. Since then, the air monitoring program has been extended to sixty-four cities and continuing measurements reveal a yearly decrease in particulates. By 1969, the average concentration was down to 92 micrograms per cubic meter.

In individual cities that monitor their own air, the trend invariably has been toward improvement. There are no exceptions.

New York City is a revealing case in point. Throughout the second half of the 1960's, while amateur ecologists and other members of the Disaster Lobby maintained their drumbeat of despair about worsening air quality in the nation's largest city, the air quality was, in fact, getting better month by month, as it had been for decades.

The extent of the improvement can be seen in a booklet entitled *Data Report, Aerometric Network, for Calendar Year 1970,* prepared and issued by the Department of Air Resources, Environmental Protection Administration, City of New York, and signed by Commissioner Robert N. Rickles.

The booklet contains charts and graphs tracing the levels of air pollution in the New York City area back to 1966, when the monitoring program was inaugurated. It shows data for both average and peak-period contamination by all major pollutants, including sulfur dioxide, carbon monoxide, nitrogen dioxide, nitric oxide, aldehydes and suspended particulates.

It reflects the most thorough job of air-pollution measurement conducted by any city in this nation, and its message is loud and clear. New York City's air has been getting cleaner year by year, pollutant by pollutant. Here are the figures for the *maximum* concentrations in *peak* periods:

Sulfur dioxide—down from 1.20 parts per million in 1966 to .50 parts per million in 1970.

Carbon monoxide—down from 35 parts per million in 1966 to 20 parts per million in 1970.

Nitrogen dioxide—down from .48 parts per million in 1966 to .25 parts per million in 1970.

Nitric oxide—down from .20 parts per million in 1966 to .07 parts per million in 1970.

Aldehydes—down from .46 parts per million in 1966 to .16 parts per million in 1970.

Suspended particulates—down from 1,250 micrograms per cubic meter in 1966 to 500 micrograms per cubic meter in 1970.

By 1971, the air over New York City had become so pure that the local newspapers, which had been dutifully carrying the Disaster Lobby warnings for half a dozen years, could no longer ignore the truth.

On May 24, 1971, *The New York Times* published a story quoting Air Resources Commissioner Rickles as saying, "We had the lowest air pollution levels [yesterday] since . . . 1952."

On the same day, the *New York Daily News* ran a piece on air quality in which Rickles described May 23, 1971, as "easily the best day the city has seen in this century."

Although no other city in the nation, with the possible exception of Los Angeles, keeps as detailed a watch on air pollution as does New York, the measurements that are made elsewhere tell similar stories.

On April 13, 1970, *Air and Water News*, a weekly publication of McGraw-Hill, reported on conditions in Philadelphia. Citing official government sources, it listed the following data:

Sulfur dioxide—down from a 1962-1967 average of .085 parts per million to a 1969 average of .075 parts per million.

Sulfation index—down from a 1960-1967 average of 2.35 milligrams per 100 square centimeters to 1.34 milligrams in 1969.

Suspended particulates—down from a 1960-1967 average of 146 micrograms per cubic meter to a 1969 average of 118 micrograms.

In Chicago, authorities reported substantial decreases for the two types of air pollutants measured there: sulfur dioxide and suspended particulates. Sulfur dioxide levels fell from an average of .07 parts per million in 1966 to an average of .03 parts per million in 1970. Concentrations of suspended particulates dropped in Chicago from an average of 138 micrograms per cubic meter in 1964 to an average of 119 micrograms in 1970.

And the situation is equally rosy in Los Angeles, the successor to Pittsburgh as home of the nation's worst pollution problem. According to a publication entitled *Profile of Air Pollution Control, Air Pollution Control District, County of Los Angeles, 1971*, the number of days in which eye irritation was recorded in the Los Angeles Basin diminished from 198 in 1960 to 163 in 1965 to 128 in 1970.

The number of days in which the California standard for total oxidants in the air was equalled or exceeded—the standard is an hourly average of .10 parts per million—dropped from 286 in 1960 to 241 in 1970.

The number of days in which the California standard for carbon monoxide was equalled or exceeded—the standard is 10 parts per million—went from 365 in 1965 to 203 in 1970.

The number of days in which the California standard for sulfur dioxide was equalled or exceeded—the standard is a daily average of .04 parts per million—decreased from 323 in 1957 to 95 in 1970.

While Los Angeles remains a problem area in the context of air quality, the problem is obviously becoming less and less acute. And significantly, the improvement began there, as it did throughout the country, long before the Disaster Lobby started making its lapel-clutching forays into the halls of government.

Of all the ecological ogres conjured up by the alarmists of the era, none was as baseless as the frequently voiced charge that air pollution had led, or was leading, to a reduction in the world's oxygen supply—that the air we breathed today would be gone tomorrow. On June 24, 1970, scientists of the Environmental Science Service Administration and the National Science Foundation issued a report on a three-year study into the composition of air at seventy-eight sites around the world. Their finding: the amount of oxygen in the air in 1970 was precisely the same as the amount of oxygen in the air in 1910.

The study had been conducted because of fears generated by Dr. Lloyd Berkner and Dr. L. C. Marshall, two scientists frequently quoted by the Disaster Lobby. Berkner and Marshall had suggested that as a result of pesticide pollution of the oceans marine plant life was no longer producing enough oxygen to maintain the former levels.

Their apprehension was unfounded. The oxygen content of the air was 20.946 percent by volume in 1910, when it was analyzed by scientists of that period, and according to the 1967-1970 study, it is still 20.946 percent by volume.

In their commentary on the latest research, Dr. Lester Machta of the Environmental Science Services Administration and Ernest Hughes of the National Bureau of Standards declared that not only is oxygen just as plentiful as it ever was, but that "man's burning of coal, oil and gas would not have any appreciable effect on world oxygen supply even if all the known reserves of these fuels were to be consumed."

Needless to say, this unequivocal assurance, backed up by unimpeachable evidence, had no effect at all on the tactics of the Disaster Lobby. Its members went right on talking about the depletion of oxygen and quoting Berkner and Marshall as though nothing had happened.

And they persisted in flaunting the oxygen scare even after research by Professors Leigh Van Valen of the University of Chicago and W. S. Broecker of Columbia University showed that the Earth has never relied on plant photosynthesis for its oxygen.

"The significance of this information," observed Dr. A. L. Jones, a research scientist at Standard Oil of Ohio, "is that the supply of oxygen in the atmosphere is virtually unlimited. It is not threatened by man's activities in any significant way. If all of the organic material on earth were oxidized it would reduce the atmospheric concentration of oxygen by less than 1 percent. We can forget the depletion of oxygen of the atmosphere."

But Disaster Lobbyists had no intention of forgetting any aspect of the air pollution panic they had so diligently concocted. Nothing, least of all facts, could deter them from spreading the alarm. They continued to wail about impending asphyxiation at a time when true scientists were trying to assure the public that it had nothing to worry about. And because this was the Age of Unreason, the doom-mongers were heeded while the scientists were pretty much ignored.

One such scientist was Dr. William T. Pecora, Director of the United States Geological Survey, who devoted more of his time than he could spare to a valiant, but fruitless, campaign aimed at refuting the irresponsible charges of the ecofreaks. Again and again, Pecora attempted to drive home the single most cogent piece of evidence against the concept of man's poisoning of the atmosphere: the largest portion of air pollutants by far originates not with mankind but with nature itself.

In the August 17, 1970, issue of *Industry Week,* he made a remarkable statement that in ordinary times would have quelled all hysteria about air pollution. He noted that more particulate matter and more combined gases were ejected into the atmosphere by the volcanic eruptions of Krakatoa in Java in 1883, Katmai in Alaska in 1912 and Hekla in Iceland in 1947 *than from all of mankind's activities in recorded history.*

"Add to known volcanic activity the normal action of winds, forest fires and evaporation from the sea," stated Pecora, "and we can readily conclude that man is an insignificant agent in the total air quality picture . . ."

The author of the *Industry Week* article went on to analyze the origins of all of the major air pollutants, one by one, starting with the various compounds of sulfur.

"About one-third of the sulfur discharged into the atmosphere," he wrote, "comes from mankind's activities, mostly in the form of sulfur dioxide, while the rest comes from natural sources." In other words, nature is polluting the air with sulfur gases twice as fast as man is.

The author added that once in the atmosphere such gases as sulfur dioxide and hydrogen sulfide are quickly oxidized and therefore pose little in the way of a cumulative threat. They become sulfate aerosol and are removed from the air by precipitation as rain or snow.

Of all of the gaseous nitrogen compounds, said the *Industry Week* report, only nitric oxide and nitrogen dioxide are emitted by man-made devices, at an annual rate of about fifty million tons. By contrast, natural sources emit these nitrogen pollutants at an annual rate of about 500 million tons—or ten times as much.

Hydrocarbons are also produced by nature. "Methane is just one example," the article reported. "It is produced in flooded swampy areas at a rate of 1.6 *billion* tons a year. Pollutant emissions [from man-made sources] amount to only 90 million tons a year."

One major pollutant, carbon monoxide, is primarily a product of mankind, with an estimated 80 percent of the total worldwide emission coming from the internal combustion automobile engine. The article pointed out, however, that carbon monoxide incidence in ambient air in the Northern Hemisphere is about one-tenth of a part per million, while the level fatal for human beings is 1,200 parts per million.

In a speech to the Public Relations Society of America in Cleveland on December 14, 1971, Dr. Jones, of Ohio Standard Oil, effectively exploded the specter of carbon monoxide as a threat to mankind. He observed that this gas does not accumulate in the atmosphere, as indicated by measurements taken at various times both north and south of the Equator.

"Since the ratio of automobiles in the Northern and Southern Hemispheres is nine to one respectively," he said, "it was expected that the Northern Hemisphere would have a much higher concentration of atmospheric carbon monoxide. Measurements show that there is no difference in carbon monoxide amounts between the Hemispheres and that the overall concentration in the air is not increasing at all."

He noted that the highest concentrations of carbon monoxide occurred in rooms in which many people were smoking cigarets, with the levels there sometimes reaching 200 parts per million. Even in cities with the heaviest vehicular traffic, outdoor carbon monoxide levels seldom go above thirty-five parts per million. "If a heavy smoker spends several hours without smoking in polluted city air containing thirty-five parts per million of carbon monoxide," said Jones, "the concentration of carbon monoxide in his blood will actually decrease."

Although members of the Disaster Lobby relied heavily on the human health factor in ramming through sundry ecological reforms, there has never been any scientific evidence that polluted air—except in isolated instances in sharply localized areas—represents a substantive threat to mankind. And with levels of pollution continuing to drop, even those few outbreaks are rarer today than at any time since the beginning of the Industrial Revolution.

One disease the Disaster Lobby always linked to air pollution was emphysema. Throughout the crusade, proponents of stringent ceilings on gas emissions kept citing emphysema as the product of pollutants in the skies over our cities. They noted that the incidence of the disease had been rising steadily in recent years, and they attributed this increase to what they liked to refer to as the deterioration in the quality of urban air.

Their logic was as faulty as their information. Early in 1971, a group of New York State physicians released the results of a statewide study showing that people living in rural areas were more apt to contract emphysema than were residents of the big cities. Indeed, the margin of difference was so pronounced as to cause speculation that there is something in grass, weeds or tree foliage that when inhaled by unusually susceptible persons brings on emphysema.

The irony here is obvious. Apparently, this frequently fatal disease may be the end product not of those noxious fumes in the city air but of the sweet-smelling, chlorophyll-packed, oxygen-releasing greenery so revered by the ecological panic-mongers.

But what of sulfur dioxide, the arch-villain of the cleanup campaigners? In the August 1968 issue of *Environmental Science and Technology,* Dr. Mario C. Batigelli, Associate Professor of Occupational Health, Public Health Service, University of North Carolina, reported that "all attempts to find conclusive evidence of health damage caused by sulfur dioxide at levels normally present in city air have failed."

In the same issue of the same publication, Dr. Gordon J. Stoops, of the Haskell Laboratory for Toxicology and Industrial Medicine, dismissed as without foundation the widely circulated charge that lead emissions from automobiles powered with high-test gasolines constituted a serious health hazard. "There is no evidence," said Stoops, "that the present body burden of lead in the general population is causing any deleterious effect on human health."

Measurement of lead levels in the atmosphere have revealed a broad range extending from a minimum of less than .01 microgram per cubic meter in Thule, Greenland, to a maximum of 2.5 micrograms per cubic meter in New York City. At peak traffic periods in heavily traveled sections of New York City, readings have gone as high as 50 micrograms, but only for very brief periods of time. And despite this unusually high level, city authorities have stated that to their knowledge there has never been a case of human illness resulting from airborne lead. Furthermore, the manufacturers of products containing lead note that workers in their factories remain healthy in spite of continuous readings there of more than 150 micrograms per cubic meter—well over fifty times the average reading for New York City.

The fear that pollutant levels currently found in urban air are a cause of lung cancer—a fear stirred up and kept alive by Disaster Lobby propaganda—also appears to be baseless. Health officials in California, with its Los Angeles Basin containing some of the dirtiest air in the nation, conducted a study there and, on January 15, 1971, reported that "there is no evidence that respiratory cancer is associated with community air pollution in California."

"No evidence," the scientists kept informing a panicky public throughout the Age of Unreason, but the scare went on. Fanning the flames were the news media that, for various reasons that will be dealt with later, latched on to the 1960's ecology movement with all of the fervor of an evangelist in pursuit of a sinner. Newspapers like *The New York Times* were among the first to jump aboard the antipollution showboat and among the last to leave, even when the old tub began springing leaks through the many holes poked by scientific research.

During the late 1960's, the *Times* published scores of articles either reporting or implying that the quality of the air over New York City was degenerating. This was during the period when the city's Department of Air Resources put out annual reports showing that air quality was actually improving.

And even when the *Times* itself started carrying stories on atmospheric amelioration, it managed to keep the stories short and bury them on back pages. Perhaps that is why the newspaper's editorial writers never got the message. They went on into the 1970's lamenting the state of the city's air, apparently ignorant of the very developments the news writers were, at long last, beginning to tumble to.

Thus, on October 31, 1971, five months after the *Times* ran an article calling attention to the fact that New York City air pollution levels were at a twenty-year low and four months after it reported on a 10 percent improvement in New York State air, it published a plaintive editorial decrying the state of the atmosphere.

"Not so many years ago," the *Times* editorial writer rhapsodized, "the appearance of a thin blue haze in the autumn sky, accompanied by calm air and mild temperatures, was typical of one of the year's most pleasant interludes, Indian Summer. Now we have another kind of haze in the autumn sky . . . It is a brown haze, or a yellow one, or a dull gray haze, and it smells of sulfur and carbon dioxide and soot and nitrates and chemical mixtures hard to identify—a smothering blanket on the land . . . Now we have the white man's Smog Summer."

While the *Times* editorial writer was apparently endowed with certain remarkable powers—he could smell carbon dioxide, which is odorless—he nevertheless deserved a failing grade in Current Events. Our charitable assumption, of course, is that he was not aware of the tremendous improvements in air quality. On the other hand, there is always the possibility that he *was* aware of the improvements but, for various reasons, chose to ignore them.

Despite the mantle of holier-than-thou goody-goodness they assumed, many Disaster Lobbyists employed deliberate chicanery in trying to achieve what they regarded as worthwhile goals—those ends that justify any means. To purify the environment, they would never balk at omitting a set of figures or forgetting a pertinent piece of information.

A graphic example of this type of convenient memory lapse appeared in 1970 in an advertisement placed in the New York City regional edition of a national magazine. The ad, signed by an organization calling itself Citizens for

Clean Air, Inc., was headlined, "Your children's chances of dying from polluted air are better than yours." Support for the headline was to be found in the following sentence in the copy block: "The longer you live with New York's polluted air and the worse it gets, the better your chances of dying from it."

The truth, as we have seen, is that New York's air is getting better, not worse, and, as a result, our children's chances of dying from polluted air are *not* better than ours. In fact, the entire advertisement was woven from a skein of outright lies and misleading innuendo. It was the kind of message that, signed by a private corporation, would have evoked howls of rage from the consumerists and lawsuits and threats of lawsuits from the Federal Trade Commission. However, because it was run by a nonprofit organization in the name of sacred ecology, there wasn't even a murmur of protest. Such was the thrust of the Age of Unreason.

The ellipsis technique in environmental reporting was resorted to by *New York Times* columnist Tom Wicker in an article that appeared in late March of 1972. Several days earlier, a special committee of the United States Office of Science and Technology had issued a report urging a re-examination of laws that mandated additional antipollution devices for 1976-model-year automobiles. If the statutes were not relaxed, the committee said, the price of the average 1976 car would have to be increased by $755.

Wicker was outraged. If indeed the new antipollution devices would add $755 to the cost of automobiles, he wrote, that increment should be absorbed not by the car buyer but by the car manufacturer. After all, wrote Wicker, it was the automobile maker who polluted the air in the first place. Therefore, it was the automobile maker who should give up part of his profits to clean up the air.

What ecobuff Wicker neglected to tell his readers was that no manufacturer could swallow the additional cost without going bankrupt. If General Motors, the most profitable car producer by far, had cut its prices by $755 a car in 1969, a typical year as costs and profits go, it would have ended the year with a net *loss* of $3.7 billion. The other companies making cars would have suffered even greater fiscal pains.

It is possible that Tom Wicker was unaware of the facts of corporate life when he made his fanciful suggestion, but only barely possible.

The report of the Science and Technology committee touched on other negative aspects of the ruinous clean-up legislation stampeded through Congress in the ecology panic of the 1960's. Among these was the set of air quality standards imposed on all municipalities by Federal law. Enforcement of these   standards, observed the committee, would cost the various governmental bodies involved an aggregate of $63 billion *more* than the benefits expected to accrue during the decade from 1976 through 1985.

On top of that, the committee said, there was no chance at all that the standards could be met in many urban areas, even if automobiles were somehow made entirely pollution-free. The report implied strongly that the air quality requirements were not only unrealistic but unnecessarily stringent.

As might have been expected, the committee statement elicited anguished cries from sacrifice-or-perish members of the ecology movement. The typical Disaster Lobbyist could not have cared less about $755 hikes in the price of automobiles. He didn't like automobiles in the first place. And he was equally indifferent to the mention of $63 billion deficits in government spending. What he wanted was crystal-clear, simon-pure, totally antiseptic air, and he didn't care what it cost to get it. He didn't even care whether it was, in fact, technologically attainable, or whether it had ever been present on the face of the earth outside of a laboratory.

So consumer advocate Ralph Nader, who dabbled in Disaster Lobbying, termed the committee report a "sellout" to automotive interests. And Senator Edmund Muskie, who made a political career out of catering to the whims and fears of the air-sniffers and water-fanciers, said it "serves Big Business", as if that were an indictment of some kind.

When this book was written, the issue of automobile emissions and municipal air standards was still in doubt. If the law is permitted to stand, the 1976 automobile will not only cost many hundreds of dollars more but will burn about 20 percent more gasoline than its 1972 model predecessor. This increased consumption, due to diminishing engine efficiency, would add more than $150 to the average motorist's fuel bill each year. And performance would suffer at all speeds.

It should be noted that long before the Disaster Lobbying of the late 1960's responsible pollution-fighters both inside and outside the automotive industry had developed an emission-control system that, by 1972, was removing up to 80 percent of all pollutants formerly present in car exhausts. But 80 percent improvement is never good enough for a fanatic, especially a fanatic at large in the Age of Unreason. The Disaster Lobby demanded tougher legislation, and tougher legislation was what it got. Congress passed a law requiring the installation of a device that would cut exhaust emissions by *another* 90 percent. This was the law that would affect automobiles in the 1976 model year. This was the law that would increase the price of cars by an average of $755 and annual gasoline bills by more than $150. This was the law that the Science and Technology committee wanted to see relaxed because, to its members as well as to every other level-headed American who examined it, it made no sense at all.

Of course, if the air really were becoming more polluted and if current and expected levels of pollution actually did constitute a serious health problem, there would have been some justification for a law eliminating car emissions at ruinous cost to the motoring public. But those reasons existed only in the feverish minds of environmental extremists. To the objective observer, it seemed a pity that, come 1976, the people of America would have to start spending an extra $7 billion a year for automobiles and an additional $8 billion a year for fuel, simply because a jittery flock of latter-day Chicken Lickens had succeeded in convincing the Congress of the United States that the sky was falling.

FOUR "...On the Side of the Fish"

Every summer, William O. Douglas, an Associate Justice of the Supreme Court of the United States by profession and a hard-nosed naturalist by predilection, declares a personal recess and adjourns to a mountain clearing near Goose Prairie, Washington. There, in August of 1971, he was tracked down by an enterprising and well-conditioned newspaper reporter, who attempted to get an interview. Justice Douglas declined to discuss court matters or politics, but he did make one public statement, which was subsequently printed in *The New York Times*. "I," said the eminent jurist, "am on the side of the fish now and against people."

It is possible, perhaps even likely, that the statement was uttered at least partly in jest, although the *Times* omitted to say so and Justice Douglas does have stern views about man's contamination of the environment. However, the point is moot. In the context of this discussion, what Justice Douglas did or did not mean is irrelevant, immaterial and of little consequence except inferentially. What is important is the fact that, in regulating the use of water during the Age of Unreason, many Americans were so solidly on the side of the fish and against people that the people almost didn't make it.

Throughout this period, the Disaster Lobby churned up wave after wave of alarm about the state of the nation's waterways and drinking water supplies, and throughout this period the Disaster Lobby got what it wanted. Spurred on by the growing alarm and oblivious to everything but the quest for zero pollution, lawmakers vied with each other for the distinction of having introduced the most costly water purification measure in world history. The front-runner in this regard was United States Senator Edmund Muskie, whose 1971 bill outlawing all discharges into all bodies of water carried a price tag estimated at between two and three *trillon* dollars—or more than $10,000 for each person in this country.

But the payment of money was only one of the sacrifices expected of the public in the name of antiseptic water. Laws were passed in many municipalities barring the sale of certain detergents—invariably they were detergents that had been proven both safe and effective as washday products—and there was a great deal of pressure for legislation outlawing colored toilet and facial tissues.

The irony in this frenetic activity was that virtually all of the measures were unnecessary in terms of protecting human health, and many of them were actually deleterious to human health. But while the advantage to people was either debatable or nonexistent, there *were* a few beneficiaries. In some limited areas of the nation, the fish would be helped. And few Americans publicly questioned the sagacity of spending two to three trillion dollars and giving up washday products and subjecting human beings to a life of dirty clothes and skin rashes just so some fish could enjoy themselves. From Goose Prairie, Washington, to Washington, D.C., the battle lines had been drawn, and from the standpoint of high-level influence, the fish had it all over the people.

Underlying this preposterous situation was a thick layer of ignorance. Unfortunately, hardly anyone who was campaigning for drastic water pollution reforms in the 1960's and 1970's knew anything at all about water pollution. As a consequence, the public was left with the erroneous impression that water pollution was a latter-day phenomenon resulting from the Industrial Revolution, that the problem was at a crisis point and that we were all on the verge of having to choose between dying of poisoned water and dying of thirst.

Nothing could be further from the truth.

Actually, water pollution has been a scourge of mankind for as long as mankind has existed. The Old Testament describes the effects circa 1000 B.C. of a type of water pollution common today. "And all the waters that were in the river," it says, "were turned to blood and the fish that was in the river died, and the river stank."

According to Harold B. Gotaas, Dean of the Technological Institute at Northwestern University, this Biblical occurrence can be attributed to a major bloom of red algae.

In an article in the November 1968 issue of *Industrial Water Engineering*, Gotaas cited other examples of water pollution predating the new industrial age. The Thames River in London was so filthy during the early and middle years of the Nineteenth Century, he said, that wet sheets were frequently hung in the windows of the riverside Parliament buildings to help reduce the smell.

In those years and earlier, diseases brought on by contaminated drinking water—such ailments as typhoid fever and dysentery—were among the leading causes of death, particularly for the young. As recently as 1900, the death rate from waterborne typhoid in the United States was thirty-five per 100,000 population, with the levels in some cities running considerably higher. In Chicago, it was ninety per 100,000 people.

Today, as a result of a gradual and continuing cleanup, involving water treatment plants and the judicious use of chemicals, the death rate from typhoid is below .001 per 100,000 population—or roughly 35,000 times less than it was in 1900.

Gotaas summed it up: "Today in the United States waterborne disease is a very unusual happening. We drink water from public supplies without concern about health problems." He then made this significant statement. "Never in history," declared this expert on the environment, "has the quality of the water supplies for cities been better."

But the Gotaas article appeared only in a trade publication

read by a select group of scientists and industrialists. His message never reached the general public. What did reach the public, through the mass media, were the scare stories of the Disaster Lobby. Day after day, the prophets of ecologic doom were warning their fellow Americans that their drinking water was contaminated, that water supplies were dwindling, that pollutants from factories and homes were destroying our waterways—Lake Erie, they said, was already irrevocably dead and the other Great Lakes were dying—and that the situation had become so grave that even the oceans were affected.

The New York Times Magazine of October 24, 1971, carried an article typical of the period. Written by freelance Michael Harwood and titled "We Are Killing the Sea Around Us," it paints the customary grim picture. And it does it in the customary method: by means of exaggerations, half truths and a liberal dose of carefully worded innuendo.

For example, Harwood quotes Dr. Max Blumer of the Woods Hole Oceanographic Institute as having said, "Lake Erie may or may not be restored within 50 years, but a polluted ocean will remain irreversibly damaged for many generations." Harwood then adds this thought: "And who would care to argue that a dead ocean would not mean a dead planet?"

The dialectical convolutions of the Harwood article are worthy of a Cicero. It should be noted that Blumer had *not* said that Lake Erie is dead, or even ill, yet the quotation leaves the reader with the impression that something is terribly wrong with the lake. Blumer had *not* said that our oceans are polluted or in danger of being polluted, yet the threat is left dangling there, like a Damoclean sword. And Harwood then takes these hypothetical, nonstated perils and carries them to a make-believe-conclusion-once-removed. "A polluted ocean," which has not been postulated, let alone established, is neatly transmuted into "a dead planet," which is not necessarily a consequence of the original unsupported proposition.

One could almost hear an intellectual Chicken Licken

muse that "The sky is not falling, but if the sky did fall, everything would get crushed and we would wind up with a broken Earth."

The logic is undetectable, but logic was not a *sine qua non* for public alarm in the Age of Unreason. And the *Times* article alarmed a sizeable portion of the public.

Conditioned by this kind of doomsday propaganda, many civic-minded Americans could be counted on to respond with the proper mixture of fear and anger whenever they learned of a specific bout of water pollution. They wrote indignant letters to their Congressmen right on cue, in much the same way as Pavlov's dogs salivated.

Such was the case in February of 1969 when an oil well being tapped by offshore drillers in the Santa Barbara Channel off the coast of California sprang a leak and coated the surrounding area with a thick veneer of gunk. It was a classic instance of pouring troubles on oiled waters. The Disaster Lobby and its disciples had a made-to-order culprit and they took maximum advantage of their opportunity. Professional nature-lovers converged on California to have their pictures taken in the company of an oil-soaked bird. *Life* magazine published an article describing the Santa Barbara Channel as "a sea gone dead" and agonizing over the prospect of dead seals "as far as the eye could see." Its sister magazine, *Sports Illustrated*, chipped in with a piece called "Life with the Blob", the "blob" being a reference to the Santa Barbara oil slick. A wealthy Santa Barbaran named Lois Sidenberg became an overnight celebrity by forming an organization called Get Oil Out—the acronym itself was irresistible—and flying around the state in her own air-polluting helicopter to gather evidence of water pollution and to whip up support for antidrilling legislation. And the nation's lawmakers could not help but be impressed.

While cooler heads prevailed in the Congress of the United States, panic set in on the state level. In Delaware, Governor Russell W. Peterson campaigned for, obtained and, in 1971, signed into law a bill barring all heavy manufacturing from locating within a two-mile-wide strip of land along

Delaware's 115-mile coastline. The statute, designed to prevent pollution in Delaware Bay, specifically banned oil refineries and petrochemical complexes and prohibited the construction within the bay itself of marine terminals for transshipment of liquid and solid bulk materials.

Not long after Governor Peterson joined Justice Douglas on the side of the fish, a bill was introduced in the New Jersey Legislature that would bar heavy industry and off-shore transfer facilities from that state's side of Delaware Bay.

With the United States already feeling the effects of a shortage of energy-producing materials, the clear thinkers abroad at the time viewed the Delaware and New Jersey developments with concern. What would happen, they wondered, if all of our coastal states adopted similar measures and thereby cut off much foreign oil that now supplies about one-fourth of this nation's petroleum needs and by 1985 will be supplying over half?

While the seaboard states fretted about oil spills in ocean waters, Federal officials were busy conjuring up new laws to purify our inland waterways. The Nixon Administration, sensitive to Democratic charges that it was lukewarm on ecology, drew up legislation aimed at eliminating 90 percent of all pollutants now being dumped into rivers and lakes. The cost of this cleanup, to be completed by the year 1985, was estimated conservatively at $60 billion.

The drafters of the bill should have known better. In the face of demands for instant perfection, a 90 percent cleanup just wasn't good enough. What the conservationists wanted was a 100 percent cleanup. What they wanted was crystal-clear, table-quality water flowing in every stream in the nation, and they soon found the man who could get it for them. His name was Edmund Muskie, and he was a United States Senator from Maine who had the added clout of having been the Democratic party's candidate for Vice President in 1968 and who appeared for a while to be a shoo-in for his party's presidential nomination in 1972. To further his chances, he was being promoted as another Abe

Lincoln, and coming out in favor of a clean environment had just the right touch of the Lincolnesque.

So a bill marked S. 2770 was introduced by Senator Muskie into the Congress of the United States. In brief, it called for zero pollutant discharge—oh how those Disaster Lobbyists loved the word "zero"—into America's waterways within the next fourteen years.

The White House estimated that the Muskie bill would cost government and industry a total of $316 billion, with most of it to be spent in the 1970's. According to a report in *Newsweek*, "Industry was appalled at the prospect, and the Administration wanted no part of it."

But to oppose any ecology measure in this period called for a level of courage bordering on the Homeric. "The bill," noted *Newsweek*, "was so politically irresistible that it was almost sure to sail smoothly through Congress—and the President would not dare veto it."

One elected official, however, dug a little deeper into the Muskie clean-water bill and was so appalled by what he found that he went on record against it. He was Nelson Rockefeller, Governor of New York, and what he found was that its cost to the nation would be considerably higher than the $316 billion estimated by the White House staff. To take the steps necessary for attainment of zero water pollution would require an expenditure of over $230 billion in New York State alone, the Governor said. He put the ultimate cost for the nation as a whole at a staggering two to three *trillion* dollars.

Testifying at a hearing on the bill before the House Committee on Public Works, Governor Rockefeller observed that, to a prudent man, the costs would seem to outweigh the benefits.

What followed was a widely publicized exchange between the Governor and Representative Bella Abzug, the klaxon-voiced, anti-Establishment gadfly from lower Manhattan.

"Don't you think, Governor," she said, "that the people are way ahead of us in wanting cleaner air and water?"

"Yes," answered Rockefeller, seemingly refusing to play the straight man, "but we are a little ahead of them in collecting taxes."

In the end, of course, the pressures of the Disaster Lobby won out. Despite the overkill implicit in the Muskie bill, despite its preposterous price tag, it was passed by the United States Senate with a vote that reflected the times. The tally was eighty-six for the bill and zero against the bill. Zero against. Not a single Senator—not even the most conservative member of that body—felt confident enough to go on record as opposing a piece of legislation that bore the magic label of ecology. When it came to the environment, it was as though a moratorium had been declared on sanity.

After the House hearing, several amendments were tacked on to the cleanup bill, somewhat modifying its more outrageous aspects. The basic provisions were retained, however, and with those basic provisions, the measure was ultimately enacted.

Even before the Muskie bill was drafted, the United States was feeling the negative effects of environmentalist pressures on the issue of water pollution. The uproar centered around household detergents. According to a variety of activist groups, the ingredients in washday products, particularly the phosphates, were finding their way into the nation's waterways and were polluting them and creating a major health hazard for the fish.

As has been noted, there was a peculiar social order in Disaster Lobby America. First came the fish. Then came the people. So with the fish apparently threatened, drastic measures were introduced in community after community to eliminate the peril. In some cities, such as Chicago, only those detergents containing phosphates were outlawed. In others—Suffolk County, New York, was one—the sale of all detergents was proscribed. And throughout the country, schools of irate fish-worshipers descended on city halls and state houses to demand the immediate abolition of products that made clothes clean, that made household chores less arduous, that were perfectly safe for use by human beings, but that had one, and only one, flaw: they posed a possible threat to a few fish.

At a time when paradox was the accepted order of the day, the Great Detergent Caper boasted what must be regarded as the ultimate irony. For the organization that was most outraged by the effects of phosphate detergents on fish, the group that lamented the loudest about the suffering of the trout and the bass and the other denizens of the deep, was the Izaak Walton League of America, many of whose members are dedicated to the Waltonian sport of impaling fish on barbed hooks and dragging them, squirming and gasping, out of their natural element and into the life-destroying air.

But irony or not, the League and its sympathizers got their way. Many cities and counties adopted laws against detergents containing phosphates. In places where there were no laws, the antidetergent forces persuaded housewives by the millions to use other cleansers. And Federal authorities jumped on the bandwagon by suggesting to soap manufacturers that they come up with alternatives to phosphates.

The soap makers saw the cease-and-desist handwriting on the wall and scurried to develop substitutes. One of these was nitrilotriacetic acid, commonly known as NTA. Another was caustic soda. Supermarket shelves were soon swept clean of phosphate detergents, and their places were taken by new washday products containing the other ingredients. Across America, television sets jumped to hastily written jingles that sang the praises of granules and powders that cleaned "just as well" as the old brands but contained no phosphates.

A report to the shareholders of Procter & Gamble dated October 13, 1970, called attention to the fact that "we have already reduced the phosphates going into our detergents by 90 million pounds per year" and promising that "by March 1972 we will have reduced the phosphates going into our products by approximately 500 million pounds per year." This would have amounted to a 30 percent cutback in phosphate content.

Alert promoters were quick to take advantage of the

obvious trend. One of these was the North American Chemical Corporation, of Paterson, New Jersey, which in July of 1970 went on the market with a nonphosphate detergent bearing the eminently attractive name of Ecolo-G and sold in an outdoorsy, leafy-green box. In an interview for *The Wall Street Journal* of December 9, 1970, Louis d'Almeida, North American Chemical's executive vice president, reported that 70 percent of the nation's supermarkets were already carrying the brand—a saturation level almost unheard of for a new product from a relatively small company. He confidently predicted that sales of Ecolo-G would reach 240 million pounds within its first year.

D'Almeida also took the opportunity to shrug off as "sour grapes" the statements from several established soap companies that substitutes for phosphates had not yet been proven effective as cleaning agents or safe for use by human beings.

Perhaps the chief reason for the phenomenal takeoff in sales of products like Ecolo-G was the enthusiastic support of amateur ecologists. They had been warning their fellow Americans about the perils of insecticides and detergents and other manifestations of the Industrial Revolution. Now some "public spirited" and "ecology-oriented" manufacturers were providing alternatives to these threats to the environment. The least the Disaster Lobby could do was offer its endorsements.

At the time of the Great Detergent Caper, one of the most outspoken Disaster Lobbyists on the hustings was a tall, young, black-mustached attorney named Jerome Kretchmer, who, in January of 1970, had been named Environmental Protection Administrator of the City of New York.

Kretchmer was a friend and backer of New York Mayor John Lindsay. Kretchmer was a devout liberal. Kretchmer was fond of nature. These, such as they are, were Jerome Kretchmer's only qualifications for the job of Environmental Protection Administrator of the City of New York.

An unnamed acquaintance quoted by *The New York Times Magazine* of April 25, 1971, made a little joke of

Kretchmer's flimsy credentials. "Jerry," he said, "knows about air pollution because he breathes, he knows about solid waste disposal because he takes out the garbage, but he doesn't know about the pollution of water because he probably doesn't drink much of the stuff."

But in a way, Jerome Kretchmer was a perfect choice for the job. He knew nothing about the environment at a time in American history when people who knew nothing about all sorts of subjects were making vast amounts of money distributing their lack of knowledge to the populace.

To Kretchmer, the uproar about phosphates in detergents was a welcome development. He had no solid information about phosphates or about detergents or, for that matter, as the *Times* informant had indicated, about water pollution. But one thing Jerome Kretchmer understood very well indeed was a popular issue, and in 1970, the controversy over phosphate detergents was about as popular as an issue could possibly get.

So it was that during the late summer and fall of 1970, Jerome Kretchmer, Environmental Protection Administrator of the City of New York, made the rounds of civic and professional club meetings in the New York Metropolitan Area to espouse the cause—and the sale—of nonphosphate washday products. The authors attended one such meeting, that of the Sales Promotion Executives Association, and recall a brief speech by Kretchmer during which he attacked the big beer manufacturers for marketing their products in throwaway cans and the big soft drink manufacturers for marketing their products in no-return bottles and the big power utilities for messing up the sky and the big soap companies for making phosphate-laden detergents.

The climax of the talk came when the speaker reached into a brown paper bag that he had placed at the foot of the lectern and drew from it a large, economy-size box of Ecolo-G.

"This," said Kretchmer, after a pause for dramatic effect, "is the washday product of the future. This is the answer to one of our major environmental problems—the pollution of our waterways. I plan to spend a lot of time in the next few months telling people about this product and urging them to use it. The name, ladies and gentlemen, is Ecolo-G."

But Kretchmer did not spend nearly as much time promoting the advantages of Ecolo-G as he had planned. In the spring of 1971, several weeks after Kretchmer's s.p.e.a. appearance, the United States Food and Drug Administration seized large quantities of Ecolo-G and ordered it taken off the market until its producers agreed to place on the box the following warning: "Danger. Harmful if swallowed. Avoid contact with skin, eyes and mucous membranes. Keep out of the reach of children."

This, then, was the boon to mankind hailed so enthusiastically by New York City's Environmental Protection Administrator. *"Danger. Harmful if swallowed. Avoid contact with skin, eyes and mucous membranes. Keep out of the reach of children."*

How did this happen? Why was an important official of the nation's biggest city going around telling consumers to stop using products that were safe for human beings to use and urging them to employ instead a product that was a potential menace to sundry parts of the human anatomy?

The answer can be given in one word: ignorance. Neither Kretchmer nor his fellow members of the Disaster Lobby really understood soaps or detergents or their effects on people and the environment.

For one thing, phosphates used in detergents are not pollutants at all. They are fertilizers.

"When phosphorus and other nutrients accumulate in waterways, the water is fertilized," explains a pamphlet of the New York State College of Human Ecology of Cornell University. "This process of fertilization is called eutrophication. Algae grow well in the eutrophic or fertilized water. After algae die, they may wash ashore, decay and cause odor. They may also sink to the bottom as they die; in that case, the decay process uses up oxygen that had been dissolved in the water. Then the fish die. Now the phosphates did not kill the fish. Neither did the other nutrients nor the algae. The fish died from a lack of oxygen, which was one of the consequences of the eutrophication of water."

By far the largest source of fertilizer phosphates in the nation's waterways is nature itself. Phosphates in detergents contribute only a small fraction.

The College of Human Ecology pamphlet noted that phosphates are used in detergents because, without harming human beings, they soften the wash water, increase the activity of the surface wetting agent, provide the necessary alkalinity for cleaning and cut down on the redepositing of dirt onto clothes by keeping dirt particles in suspension in the wash water.

Among the substitutes for phosphates listed in the pamphlet were NTA, carbonates and silicates, but it was emphasized that these substitutes are generally less effective than phosphates as cleaning agents and that they have not been proved safe for usage by people.

Because more than one-third of all phosphates entering rivers and lakes comes from such natural sources as rain, falling leaves and other vegetation, and because another 30 percent comes from livestock manure and agricultural fertilizers, with only 18 percent the result of detergents, most experts have agreed that the elimination of phosphates in washday products would have a minimal effect on the eutrophication of our waterways.

During the late 1960's and early 1970's, many of these experts spoke up in an attempt to discourage the trend toward environmental overkill. In a letter to the Federal Trade Commission in April 1971, Harold E. Hillmer, President of the Wisconsin Environmental Health Association, stated: "It is extremely unlikely that the elimination of phosphates from detergents will result in any significant improvement in the overall eutrophication picture."

Dr. Warren C. Westgarth, Director of the Environmental Quality Laboratories and Technical Service, Department of Environmental Quality, State of Oregon, said, "I doubt that total removal of all synthetic detergent phosphates would stop the nuisance growths."

Dr. Grant K. Borg, of the Department of Civil Engineering, University of Utah, said, "It does not follow that algal blooms and eutrophication will stop if phosphorus only from detergents is removed."

Other scientists were less equivocal. In a letter to *Science* magazine, Drs. John H. Ryther and William M. Dunstan, of the Woods Hole Oceanographic Institution, declared: "If all phosphates from detergents could be eliminated . . . no reduction of algal growth or eutrophication could be expected."

And Dr. Philip H. Abelson, president of the Carnegie Institution of Washington and editor of *Science,* wrote in the September 11, 1970, issue of that magazine that "the elimination of phosphates from detergents would not solve the eutrophication problem. There are too many sources of these chemicals in municipal, industrial and agricultural wastes. The treatment of municipal wastes is of particular importance in minimizing eutrophication. If these were managed properly, phosphates arising from human wastes and from detergents would be simultaneously eliminated."

But to the Disaster Lobby, the idea of having cities improve their sewage systems seemed to lack a certain basic appeal. It did not require the public to sacrifice their comfort and safety in the interest of animals. It did not punish private industry. So the environmental dilettantes kept up their pressures. They got Representative Henry Reuss, a Wisconsin Democrat with an anti-Establishment tilt, to introduce a bill outlawing the sale of phosphate detergents nationally. The stage was set for a total phase-out of safe, effective cleansers when, in April of 1971, the Surgeon General of the United States brought the madness to an abrupt halt with an announcement that dismayed the Disaster Lobby.

Federal health authorities had been investigating the detergent situation since the earliest attacks by the environmentalists. The charges had been so emphatic and had generated so much public alarm that the government's first reaction, as noted before, was to issue a request to soap manufacturers for stepped up activity in finding a substitute for phosphates.

As the manufacturers hastened to comply and as more and more phosphate-free products were introduced, Federal officials intensified their own research. And what they found was what the soap companies had known all along: that phosphates were the only ingredients yet discovered that would clean clothes to a degree of whiteness and brightness the public had come to expect and that would not harm human beings in the process.

The statement by the Surgeon General was clear and explicit:

"In respect to efforts to displace phosphates from detergents, it should be realized that tests conducted thus far indicate that some of the currently used substitutes for phosphates are clearly toxic or caustic and pose serious accident hazards, especially to children. Other substitutes not yet fully tested may also be toxic and/or caustic . . . Let me amplify my concern . . . Such materials measured in quantities as little as a fraction of a teaspoon may cause severe damage to the skin, eyes, mouth, throat, larynx, esophagus or stomach upon contact. Anyone who has gotten lye on his skin will remember that the reaction is virtually immediate and that removal of the offending material requires prompt and vigorous action."

Later in his statement, he referred to various substitutes for phosphates as being so dangerous that anyone using them would run a "serious risk of irreversible loss of sight, loss of voice, ulcerations and blockage of the esophagus, severe skin burns and even death."

It was just about this time that the government issued its order taking Ecolo-G off the market.

But while the Surgeon General's statement merely warned of the hazards of replacing phosphates with suggested substitutes, and while the action against Ecolo-G was limited in both scope and intent, there was nothing ambiguous or circumscribed about the official pronouncement released in September of 1971 by representatives of several Federal

agencies. In a joint news release, they urged American housewives to resume their use of detergents containing phosphates. They said the alternatives they had tested were
unsafe.

As might be expected, the Disaster Lobby was furious.
When it appeared that the nation's fish were in danger, the
Lobby and its followers had demanded remedial action.
Now that the threat was to the health of human beings,
they apparently could see no need for the government to
intervene.

The environmentalist-oriented *New York Times* was especially annoyed. In an editorial that epitomized much of the
fatuity of the Age of Unreason, the *Times* took the government to task.

"The Federal government," said the editorial, "succeeded
last week in undoing several years of public education on
the harm that detergents do to the nation's waters. In an
action as unnecessary as it was sudden and confusing, four
of its top health and environmental officials urged a return
to phosphate detergents on the ground that alternative
cleansers were worse."

The *Times* refused to accept that determination. According to the newspaper, it sounded like some kind of plot
spawned by the soap industry.

"Nothing in the government's explanation justified its
panicky reversal," said the *Times*. "Its explanation, it may
be pointed out, followed closely the line of reasoning advanced by leading elements in the soap and detergent lobby.
Whether or not it was industry pressure that accounted for
the change, people who have been accurately warned of
how much damage phosphates can do to lakes and streams
will find it difficult to take on faith the next warning that
issues from the guardians of the environment."

And *that* was the gravamen of the *Times* complaint. The
environmentalists had been proven wrong about detergents.
There was now a distinct possibility that the public would
question *all* of their conclusions.

But it was the *Times'* own conclusion that underscored

the absurdity of the prevailing viewpoint among thought leaders of the era. The newspaper advised its readers to ignore the warning of the Federal authorities and to go on using substitutes for phosphate detergents.

"Less harm could be done for the time being if housewives continued, with reasonable care, to use so-called caustic sodas, especially in combination with regular soap," said the *Times*, which then appended a bit of reasoning that should be used in all psychology classes as an example of faulty logic. "A nation that suffers the lethal automobile and allows handguns is not likely to be overwhelmed by the presence of washing sodas in the home—along with a dozen other potentially risky substances such as drain cleansers, dangerous drugs or even kitchen matches."

That's not much different from saying that as long as you permit jaywalking at certain intersections, you might as well allow purse-snatching, pocket-picking and arson.

The *Times* concluded its editorial by repeating the recommendation that housewives should go right on using substitutes for phosphate detergents until safer substitutes are marketed. "A holding pattern of this sort, rather than the implausible course the government has chosen, would allow a continuing effort to save the nation's waters without causing more than a minimal risk to health," said the *Times*.

"A minimal risk to health" was the newspaper's euphemism for the list of ailments cited by Federal authorities, including "loss of sight, loss of voice, ulcerations and blockage of the esophagus, severe skin burns and even death."

But in the opinion of the *Times* and other self-appointed guardians of the environment, it was essential that this nation reorder its priorities. And in the shuffle, one of the lowest priorities of all appeared to be the one assigned to people. What did a blocked esophagus matter, as long as "the nation's waters" could be purified?

Actually, the nation's waters were a whole lot purer than the Disaster Lobby people let on. Consider, for example, the much pointed to and worried over Lake Erie, which was to some environmentalists what the Alamo was to Nineteenth Century proponents of a free Texas. "Remember Lake Erie," cried the doomsayers of the 1960's. "It used to be a healthy lake and now it's dead."

This tidbit of pseudo-information, swallowed without question by a public conditioned to ecological scares, would have greatly surprised the organisms most dependent on Lake Erie: the fish residing there. A dead lake would be presumed to contain no live fish. Lake Erie is loaded with live fish. In 1969, the last year for which figures are available, *more fish were harvested from Lake Erie by commercial and sport fishermen than from all of the other Great Lakes combined.*

The obituaries for Lake Erie also astonished Dr. William Pecora, Director of the United States Geological Survey. In the spring of 1971, *Barron's* quoted Pecora as having said, "I come right out of my chair whenever I hear once more on television that Lake Erie is dead. Lake Erie, if anything, is too alive. The western part of the Lake is a natural nutrient trap, an extremely narrow shelf that receives a large amount of natural organic material transported by rivers from the surrounding terrain. That organic material may be green scum to humans, but it means food for the fish."

It is all of this food, he said, that accounts for the unusually high fish population in Lake Erie. "A similar situation, also productive of fish, is found in Lake Michigan's Green Bay, which was so named because of the algae present when man first discovered it," he told *Barron's.*

Pecora omitted to mention, although he might have been tempted to, that the discovery of Green Bay predated the introduction of the first phosphate detergents and that modern man and his Industrial Revolution could not therefore be blamed for the algae or the scum.

Actually, the fish count in the Great Lakes is probably not much different today from what it was a century ago. The tonnage of fish taken from the lakes remains fairly constant from year to year. For example, the Lake Erie catch was 50 million pounds in 1878, when the government began keeping records, and it was 59 million pounds in 1969.

Fundamental to much of the furor over water pollution was a widespread acceptance of a series of baseless myths.

Myth One: the world supply of water is shrinking. The truth, as noted by Dr. Gaylord W. Anderson, Mayo Professor and Director, School of Public Health, University of Minnesota, at the First International Water Quality Symposium in 1965, is that the quantity of water on our planet does not change. "The amount of water for this world," said Dr. Anderson, "is the same as it was centuries ago. And so far as we know, the amount of water that's going to be for the generations that follow us is the same as it is now." The runoff of all streams in the United States outside of Alaska and Hawaii is some 1.2 trillion gallons a day. We are using this water only 27 percent as fast as it is being supplied.

Myth Two: industrial pollution is curtailing the oxygen content of the oceans and is thus altering the life patterns there. Walter S. Broecker, Professor of Earth Science at Columbia University, exploded that one in an article in the June 26, 1970, issue of *Science*. "Were man to dump all his sewage into the deep sea . . . the oxygen supply . . . would last 25,000 years," he wrote. "In conclusion, it can be stated with some confidence that the molecular oxygen supply in the atmosphere and in the broad expanse of open ocean are not threatened by man's activities in the foreseeable future."

Myth three: some large bodies of water have been so severely polluted by mankind that the damage can never be repaired. Scientists from the United States, Great Britain and Canada walked up to that canard in November of 1970 at a three-day Anglo-American Conference on Environmental Control. After the meeting, the conferees issued a report stating that "difficult as some of the [pollution] problems were, there was none that could not be solved, nor any major example of pollution which had been proved irreversible."

Myth four: the water drunk by our ancestors was more healthful than the water we now drink. Sheer nonsense.

The water drunk by our ancestors killed them by the millions. The water we drink is almost completely nontoxic and nonpathogenic. Raymond L. Nace, a hydrologist for the United States Geological Survey, referred to this evidence of progress in a speech. "To improve on the general rains from heaven is really an achievement of which we can be quietly prideful," he said. "We extend the perimeter of water and its uses."

Myth five: where water is polluted, the chief culprit is heavy industry. Also nonsense. Where water pollution exists, the primary factor is almost always municipal sewage. Agricultural runoff is often a close second. Lake Erie is a case in point. It has already been noted that most of what is called pollution in Lake Erie is actually over-fertilization of algae. In the few places where the Lake *is* polluted—the area near Cleveland is one—the source of pollution is raw sewage from population centers and the form the pollution takes is a high coliform bacterial count. "If we put in the proper sewage treatment facilities," Ohio research scientist A. L. Jones told a Cleveland audience in December of 1971, "the Lake will sparkle blue again in a very few years."

Many of the false assumptions about water pollution came together in the huge outpouring of environmentalist protests that followed the Santa Barbara oil-well blowout of 1969. The oil leaking from the offshore drilling site had barely bubbled to the surface when the tantrums began. Terming the incident "an ecological catastrophe," "a disaster of major proportions" and "a crime against nature," among many other things, the outdoor buffs began issuing news releases that told of hundreds of thousands of dead birds and tens of millions of dead fish and a beach stained for all eternity by the thick, black byproduct of human greed.

The California Legislature in Sacramento and the Congress of the United States were urged to prohibit forthwith all offshore oil operations and to shut down those onshore wells close to the Pacific Coast.

So loud and protracted were the arguments of the amateur ecologists that public opinion quickly swung in their favor.

Several regional polls showed ratios in favor of shutting down the wells that ranged from a solid three to two to an hysteria-tinged six to one.

The only thing that saved offshore drilling was the awareness of government officials that to close down the wells would be tantamount to closing down the nation's economy. For by 1969, one-sixth of the world's petroleum was being pumped out of offshore wells. And with the United States already on the brink of a crippling shortage of energy materials, the elimination of this important source would have rendered much of the country cold, dark and immobile.

Then, little by little, the truth began to emerge. It soon became apparent to those Americans interested in facts that the Santa Barbara Channel affair had been artfully orchestrated from the annoyance it actually was into the apocalyptic event it was made to resemble. The Disaster Lobby had created a Potemkin Village in reverse.

When the whole story unfolded, it was clear that Santa Barbara had been the exception rather than the rule. Offshore drilling is a commonplace procedure dating back to 1894, and blowouts of the Santa Barbara type are a rarity. One company, Standard Oil (New Jersey), revealed that it had completed more than 1,500 wells in United States waters and had experienced only three blowouts, all of which were controlled before oil could contaminate the water or the shoreline.

It has been estimated that since 1894 some 20,000 oil wells have been drilled off the coasts of seventy countries.

The effects of the Santa Barbara incident were not nearly so bad as the Disaster Lobby had claimed. The "hundreds of thousands of dead birds" turned out to be 4,000. The "tens of millions of dead fish" added up, in reality, to fewer than you might find at a well-stocked fish market. And the Santa Barbara beach, supposedly gummed up in perpetuity, was quickly restored to its pre-blowout status. It is today as clean and pure as any beach in the world.

In mid-1969, Dr. Dale Straughan, a marine biologist at the University of Southern California, was put in charge of a forty-member team of scientists and asked to conduct a full-scale study of the Santa Barbara blowout. Among the forty men and women assigned to her were instructors and graduate students from u.s.c., the University of California and Johns Hopkins. Their investigation went on for more than a year and resulted in a 900-page report that thoroughly refuted each one of the doomsday charges leveled by the Disaster Lobby. Far from being "a dead sea forever," the Santa Barbara Channel was found, eighteen months after the oil well leak, to be teeming with life.

"Not only had overall damage from the spill been greatly overestimated," said *The Los Angeles Times* in an article on Straughan's study, "but where damage could be documented, nature was returning to normal."

A key reason for the minimal impact was a fact of nature either overlooked or carefully ignored by those who favored drastic environmental reforms. For oil leaks are a natural phenomenon. Each year, far more oil is released into the oceans from seabed fissures than from all of the man-made wells and leaky tankers combined. The Straughan research team revealed that natural leaks in the Santa Barbara Channel had been releasing up to 160 barrels of crude petroleum each day for many centuries, and that crude oil had become a part of the environment long before man drilled his first well there. As a result, most marine species had adjusted to the presence of oil in the water. There was no traumatic injury when the blowout came.

The Los Angeles Times story said Straughan's team was unable to verify any of the accounts of permanent damage.

"No ill effects on animal and vegetable plankton could be discerned," the newspaper said. "The volume of biomass and its distribution did not change significantly between May and October of 1969. No damage from oil pollution could be found on sandy beaches. The channel fish catch was actually found to have been greater in a six-month period following the oil spill than in a comparable period the year before. Moreover, the spill had no apparent effect on whales, and the same held true for seals."

The *Times* added that it had turned up a pertinent footnote to the Straughan study. This took the form of an interview with Ruth Case, manager of the Underseas Gardens, a barge aquarium moored in Santa Barbara harbor. All of the marine life in the aquarium is dependent on water circulated from the harbor and therefore experienced the same conditions as marine life outside the aquarium at the time of the 1969 blowout.

"Throughout the spill," said Mrs. Case, "our loss of life was not greater than we normally have in an aquarium where animals of all kinds feed on one another. The oil floated on top and it didn't seem to poison anything below."

To any reasonable person, it would have been apparent that, in the United States of America in the last half of the Twentieth Century, the pollution of waterways was not nearly as great a threat to fish as were the activities of commercial fishermen and the fishline-casting members of the Izaak Walton League. Studies in Lake Erie and the Santa Barbara Channel had turned up cogent evidence exculpating mankind. The trouble was that in the 1960's this country was undergoing a shortage of reasonable persons. The demands for zero pollution continued.

Some of the favorite targets of the Disaster Lobby were the industrial companies that, because of the nature of their business, pumped large quantities of hot water into whatever lake or stream might be handy. Such pumping, said the econuts, raised the temperature of the surrounding water and did grave harm to the fish that resided there.

In 1971, scientists from the University of Georgia decided to investigate these popular charges. They proceeded to Par Pond, a 2,800-acre lake near Aiken, South Carolina, into which a nearby Du Pont plant pumped a billion gallons of 115-degree water each day. The entire lake contained only 180 billion gallons, so the Du Pont operation had a material effect on water temperatures from shore to shore and from top to bottom. And sure enough, as the scientists discovered, there had been a noticeable change in the fish. Almost to a fish, they were healthier and bigger and longer-lived than the fish in neighboring lakes that did not have the benefit of a Du Pont installation.

The Wall Street Journal carried the report. It quoted University of Georgia biologists as saying that after a month's growth the offspring of largemouth bass in Par Pond were roughly nine times heavier than the month-old offspring of largemouth bass in nearby lakes.

"What's more," said *The Wall Street Journal,* "the Par Pond bass mature and start reproducing in two years instead of the normal three and lay more eggs, thereby presumably enhancing survival of the species. Ecologist Whit Gibbons similarly has found that the yellow-bellied turtles common to the region reach reproductive size in five years at Par Pond compared with a norm of nine years, that the Par females lay nearly three times as many eggs per clutch and that they may even lay three times a year instead of the normal two."

But the pressure groups refused to be turned off by facts. They had got it into their heads that water pollution was exterminating the fish, that water pollution was morally wrong and that water pollution had to go, even if a few people had to go along with it.

Abel Wollman, Professor Emeritus of Sanitary Engineering at Johns Hopkins University, put the matter into refreshingly clear perspective. "With the discovery of the environment in the past five years or so," he said in a signed magazine article in November 1970, "the drive toward a zero risk world has been the characteristic of standard making. In place of tedious scientific exploration, a new philosophy has entranced everyone. Standards should be determined by public acclamation or by plebiscite. No longer is it necessary to measure relative benefits, debits, costs, technological tools or enforceability. The maximum quality of life shall prevail —whatever that is."

To attain this "maximum quality of life," the dilettante environmentalists did indeed abandon all considerations of "benefits, costs, technological tools or enforceability"—especially costs. The multi-trillion-dollar Muskie bill was a case in point. So were campaigns to clean up specific bodies of water, such as Lake Erie and the Delaware River Basin.

In July of 1969, Samuel S. Baxter, Water Commissioner of Philadelphia, observed that the cost of bringing the Delaware River into compliance with new purity standards imposed by an ecology-minded Delaware River Basin Commission would be well over $400 million dollars. "Will there be any benefit that can justify the expenditure?" asked Commissioner Baxter. "The only one I can see is that once every 20 years, during a drought, there will be a 10 percent increase in the amount of shad swimming upstream to spawn. Do we want to benefit a few fish, or build new schools to replace old firetraps?"

He need scarcely have asked the question. The answer was right there for everyone to see. It was perfectly obvious that, at that moment, confused Americans were wholeheartedly in favor of benefiting the fish and letting the school children make do with whatever was left.

Identical judgments were being made on a somewhat larger scale by the would-be caretakers of Lake Erie. Environmental groups from all sections of the country wanted Erie cleaned up totally, thoroughly and right away. And never mind the cost or all of that scientific fiddle-faddle about natural nutrients and algae and eutrophication.

Faced with the very real prospect of a wildly extravagant zero pollution scheme for Lake Erie, Dean Gotaas of Northwestern's Technological Institute, entered a demurrer. He said the lake could be made somewhat cleaner by treating isolated pollution points along the shores, but he questioned the wisdom of trying to restore it to its original condition. "It is doubtful," he said, "that benefits of that degree of restoration would be worth the costs when compared with other needs for pleasant living."

Since the waters of Lake Erie posed no threat to human health, he saw no reason why staggering sums of money should be spent to provide it with a photogenic facelift.

"Emotional and exaggerated rather than logical views of water pollution are common," Gotaas stated. "I'm afraid that we will be spending lots of money for nebulous results unless we put the problem into perspective."

Perspective. There was the magic word. But, alas, to paraphrase the late Fred Allen, among Americans in the Age of Unreason you could put all of the perspective there was into the navel of a flea.

FIVE **Mother Nature Did It**

Throughout the late 1960's and early 1970's, many of the most outspoken and influential of America's amateur ecologists were held in thrall by two obsessions. The first was that as a result of industrial pollution our world was no longer as clean and pure as it used to be. The second was that anything not absolutely clean and pure should be abolished by law.

Both of these quirks came into play during the Strange Case of the Mercury in the Fish, which began making headlines in 1970 and continued to make headlines through much of 1971.

In a sense, the mercury episode was an obvious sequel to the somewhat earlier uproar over water pollution. Then the panic involved charges that mankind was poisoning the fish. Now, according to the Disaster Lobby, the fish were poisoning mankind. But it wasn't simply a matter of poetic justice or piscatorial revenge. Man was still the villain, said the Disaster people, since it was he who had introduced the poison into the fish in the first place by dumping mercury wastes into various bodies of water.

As it ultimately was demonstrated, the source of the mercury was not mankind at all, and the Disaster Lobby was left with a liberal portion of egg on its face.

The Strange Case of the Mercury in the Fish began early in 1970, when some Canadian college students went fishing on Lake St. Clair, a 600-square-mile basin northeast of Detroit, between Lake Huron and Lake Erie. They later analyzed their catch and discovered in the flesh of the fish substantial quantities of the highly toxic metal, mercury. The story was immediately reported in detail—and, as often as not, under big, bold, front-page headlines—by environment-happy newspapers; and the scare was officially launched.

Dr. Bruce McDuffie, a young analytical chemist at the State University of New York in Binghamton, read the news stories and did some analyzing of his own. He studied fish taken from the Chenango and Susquehanna Rivers, near Binghamton, and found mercury in *them.*

"We'd always thought of our rivers as pretty clean," he later told an interviewer from *The New York Times.* "So when I found so much mercury in our fish, I was really upset."

Other New York State chemists analyzed fish from other bodies of water and, lo and behold, more mercury. And, of course, more big, bold, front-page headlines.

By this time, the Disaster Lobby was in full cry. American industry was poisoning the waterways with mercury, and something had to be done right away or we could say good-bye to fish as a menu item. This warning took on added substance when the United States Food and Drug Administration began analyzing samples of fish sold to the public for human consumption and found that much of it, particularly swordfish and canned tuna, exceeded the F.D.A.'s "safe" level of .5 parts of mercury per million of animal tissue.

This fact was released to the press by the F.D.A., and the shockwaves radiated outward to envelop much of the nation. Thousands of consumers stopped eating fish and other thousands of consumers began writing letters to their Congressmen to demand an immediate clampdown on the use of mercury by American manufacturers.

Had such a decree been issued, the effects on the public might have been drastic indeed. Mercury is an ingredient in many essential products, ranging from important medicines to electrical switches and scientific instruments. It is also used in the processing of still other products, including plastics and paper.

For the time being, however, the Federal authorities were content merely to seize 12 million cans of tuna, most of which were later released for sale, and to urge the public to cut down its intake of swordfish. Eventually, the F.D.A. advised consumers to stop eating swordfish in any quantities.

Local and state health officials quickly took their cue from Washington. New York State, for example, issued a warning against the consumption of any fish taken from Lakes Onondaga, Erie, Ontario, Champlain and Saratoga and from the Niagara, Oswego and St. Lawrence Rivers. Specimens of fish from each of these lakes and rivers had shown mercury levels in excess of the .5 parts per million guideline of the F.D.A.

The zealots of zero pollution even took their paranoia to the United Nations. They proposed that the World Health Organization of the U.N. issue an injunction against the marketing of food fish that contained more than .05 parts of mercury per million. This was a level ten times lower than the one prescribed by the Food and Drug Administration, and its adoption would have had cataclysmic repercussions. According to Dr. Thomas Jukes of the University of California, virtually all food fish have higher concentrations of mercury than .05 parts per million and the establishment of that figure as a ceiling "would effectively remove most fish as an article of human diet."

It was during 1970 that Barry Commoner delivered a speech in Chicago at a convention of the American Association for the Advancement of Science in which he strongly implied that industry was the chief culprit in the mercury episode. He said that between 1945 and 1958 manufacturing companies had consumed and processed about 50 million pounds of mercury. About 24 million pounds of that total was "missing and unaccounted for" and had presumably found its way into the environment, he told the Association.

(Dr. Commoner had, of course, resorted to one of the

oldest tricks in the statistics game. To maximize the figures he wanted maximized, he had translated tons into pounds and had lumped together fourteen years of industrial activity. If you convert his data to the kinds normally used, you find that the total emissions of mercury into the environment by United States industry amounted to only 850 tons a year—or the contents of fourteen freight cars. Was Commoner trying to imply that fourteen carloads of mercury were polluting the Atlantic and Pacific Oceans and all of the rivers and lakes in the United States?)

The climax of the hand wringing over mercury pollution came on May 20, 1971, when the Senate Subcommittee on Energy, Natural Resources and the Environment held a hearing in Washington. According to a report the following day in *The New York Times*, "various experts on environmental chemistry told Congress that the ecological harm caused by mercury and possibly arsenic pollution was so grave that it would be decades and probably centuries before the pollutants were dissipated."

The *Times* said testimony by the "experts" indicated that "mercury levels in fish are increasing to the degree that they pose a threat to the entire American fishing industry", that "the first human case in the United States of mercury poisoning from fish has been discovered on Long Island" and that "another species of fish—striped bass—has been found to have hazardous levels of mercury in its flesh."

Dr. John M. Wood, Associate Professor of Biochemistry at the University of Illinois, startled the assembled Senators by stating that "there is now from 50 to 100 times as much mercury in fish from the St. Clair River as there was in 1935."

Dr. Roger C. Herdman, of the New York State Department of Health, supplied the details about "the first human case in the United States of mercury poisoning from fish." He identified the victim as a "Mrs. N. Y.", who, he said, became ill after having eaten ten ounces of swordfish each day for several years beginning in 1964. Her symptoms included dizziness and difficulty in walking and Herdman stated that "the best medical judgment must be that 'Mrs. N. Y.' suffered an episode of methyl mercury poisoning subsequent to the ingestion of swordfish."

So lugubrious was the testimony of the Disaster Lobbyists that Senator Philip A. Hart, a Michigan Democrat who had given more than token support to the Disaster Lobby, was impelled to deliver himself of a poignant comment. "Every day you hope to get up in the morning and hear that something good has happened," he said after the Subcommittee hearing, "but it doesn't seem to go that way."

There was a good deal of truth in what he said. During the Age of Unreason, it was almost impossible to hear that something good had happened, primarily because much of what was heard originated in the mouths of people like Senator Hart. And Senator Hart was convinced that the world was going to hell in a defective capitalistic handbasket.

Following the news reports of the Subcommittee session, the mercury poisoning hysteria climbed to a new peak. For if the witnesses were to be believed, American industry was spewing mercury into the environment so rapidly that the mercury content of at least some fish had increased up to 100-fold in only thirty-five years. The peril had reached the point, presumably, where a human being had been infected and millions of other human beings were obviously in grave danger.

The Disaster Lobby was poised to strike, to demand an immediate cessation of mercury processing by industry, when one by one the facts—the cold, hard, unemotional facts—began to emerge from source after source after source.

Actually, some clues had surfaced even before the Senate hearing. On December 30, 1970, New York State Environmental Conservation Commissioner Henry L. Diamond advised fishermen against eating anything taken from Lake George because samples of lake trout, rainbow trout and smallmouth bass caught in the lake had revealed mercury contents in excess of .5 parts per million. There was nothing unusual about the warning—similar injunctions were being released across the nation—but what was unusual was the remark accompanying the warning.

"It is a great mystery to us where the mercury came from," Diamond said, "because there are no known discharges of mercury into the lake."

So there was the first tiny hole in the Disaster Lobby's case. There were no factories anywhere near Lake George or its tributaries using mercury, let alone dumping mercury. How did the fish acquire the metal?

Then on May 20, 1971—by coincidence, the same day as the Senate Subcommittee hearing—Commissioner Diamond bored another small hole in the indictment against American industry. He rescinded all previously issued warnings on the eating of fish, with three exceptions. Lake trout from Lake George, muskellunge from the St. Lawrence River and all fish from Lake Onodaga were still on the proscribed list. In revoking the previous warnings, he said they had been based on incomplete evidence.

"We erred on the side of health," the Commissioner declared.

He also noted that his error "on the side of health" had frightened people so much that many were afraid even to swim in the lakes and rivers cited by his department. He belatedly pointed out that swimmers were in no danger at all, even when mercury levels in fish were extremely high.

But it was another public announcement from Commissioner Diamond that began unraveling the ball of circumstantial evidence, wild guesses and irrelevancies that had been put together with such care by the Disaster Lobby. He reported that fish caught prior to 1930 and preserved as trophies had been revealed to have mercury levels more than twice as high as the .5-parts-per-million ceiling established by the F.D.A. What is more, the fish had been caught in Long Pond and Boyd Pond, high up in the Adirondacks and scores of miles from the nearest factories.

The news staggered the purveyors of doom. If forty-year-old fish had more mercury in them than today's fish, how could you insist that mercury poisoning was a current phenomenon stemming from stepped-up industrial activity? How could you support the thesis, as delivered at the Senate Subcommittee hearing, that fish today contained up to a hundred times as much mercury as fish thirty-five years ago? And since the New York State fish were former residents of bodies of water remote from any factory, how could you inculpate industry at all?

While the Disaster Lobby took time out to mull over these questions, additional embarrassments cropped up.

On August 8, 1971, the Smithsonian Institution revealed that samples of fish pickled almost a century ago contained as much mercury as fish being caught in 1971. This was the lead paragraph of a United Press International dispatch datelined Irvine, California:

"Tuna caught off the Pacific and Atlantic coasts beginning in 1878 and preserved by the Smithsonian Institution have been analyzed by Dr. Raj Kishore and Professor Vincent Guinn at the University of California at Irvine. They found that salt water contamination by mercury, a poisonous metallic element, ranged from .3 to .6 parts per million of tissue. The government recently has been recalling shipments of fish containing mercury levels of more than .5 parts per million."

The plot obviously was beginning to thicken. According to the University of California scientists, Nineteenth Century fish were the repositories for just as much mercury as Twentieth Century fish. Obviously, then, Americans have been eating mercury-laden fish for many decades. And they have been eating such fish without experiencing any ill effects, since "Mrs. N.Y." of Long Island was identified at the Senate hearing as the first American ever to have developed mercury poisoning from the ingestion of fish.

Kishore left little room for the Disaster Lobbyists to maneuver in when he stated, "The increase of mercury contamination in the oceans since 1878 probably is negligible."

The case against the industrial Establishment, which had appeared so watertight just a few months before, was now

leaking at every seam. But for the defamers of modern industry, the worst was yet to come. On December 27, 1971, Dr.
Edwin Wilmsen, Curator of the Museum of Anthropology
in Ann Arbor, Michigan, delivered a paper at the annual
meeting of the American Association for the Advancement
of Science in which he reported the discovery of "high levels
of mercury" in the remains of fish that lived *2,000 years ago.*

Wilmsen told his fellow scientists that he had examined
catfish and fresh water drum fossils at sites near Saginaw,
Michigan, and Apple Creek, Illinois, and the remains of
anchovies and tuna dug out of the ground in southern Peru.
Using a process known as neutron activation analysis, he
was able to compute the mercury levels in these specimens.

"Our data," he said, "suggest that mercury concentration
in prehistoric fish was of the same order of magnitude as that
in [present-day fish]. Two of the samples, both from Peru,
approach the highest levels of mercury ever detected in
marine fish."

The Peruvian specimens, said Wilmsen, were dated about
1200 A.D., while those from Michigan and Illinois had lived
in the period from about 100 B.C. to 400 A.D.

Needless to say, Wilmsen's findings caused considerable
consternation in the ranks of America's factory-haters. For
the implication was inescapable. If there was all that mercury
in the environment hundreds of years ago, American industry
could not possibly be responsible. The villain must have been
—and you could almost hear the jaws dropping on amateur
ecologists all over the United States—*Mother Nature herself.*

Still the evidence rolled in. A letter to *The New York
Times* from Dr. Leonard J. Goldwater, Professor of Community Health at Duke University and an authority on
mercury poisoning, disputed the Senate testimony of Herdman about the illness of "Mrs. N. Y." Herdman had ascribed
her condition to "mercury poisoning subsequent to the
ingestion of swordfish." According to Goldwater, the symptoms as related at the Senate hearing would appear to rule
out mercury poisoning.

"Poisoning by methyl mercury compounds," said Goldwater, "has been characterized by the permanence and irreversibility of the injury to the nervous system. The fact that 'Mrs. N.Y.' spontaneously recovered almost completely means that her case is at least atypical and at most not methyl mercury poisoning at all."

He noted that "Mrs. N. Y." had been eating swordfish in an attempt to lose weight, and he wondered whether she had employed other reducing methods at the same time.

"It is well known," he said, "that a number of widely used reducing pills with and without prescription contain mercury and depend on the diuretic action of mercury. Ingestion of these drugs even ten years ago would raise the level of mercury in her system."

Goldwater said Herdman had apparently based his diagnosis largely on the fact that the Food and Drug Administration regarded the mercury content of swordfish as excessive. The swordfish actually eaten by "Mrs. N. Y." had never been analyzed, the Duke University professor pointed out, and he added that "I question the validity of the F.D.A. standard."

His reservations about the Federal crackdown on food products containing mercury in excess of .5 parts per million stemmed from the belief that some mercury might be essential to all living organisms. At an international symposium on mercury sponsored by the University of Michigan, Goldwater presented evidence of the existence of mercury in one form or another in all types of soil and in all kinds of food.

But it was the University of California's Thomas Jukes who provided the definitive data in the Strange Case of the Mercury in the Fish. In the late summer of 1971, he announced that various studies had placed at about 100 million tons the amount of mercury now present in the oceans. Of that total, he said, "less than 1 percent is the result of all human activities since the beginning of time." The rest was put there by nature itself.

Currently, said Jukes, factories around the world are adding about 5,000 tons of mercury to the oceans each year through emissions into the air and into various waterways. Natural sources account for another 5,000 tons annually. In the opinion of Jukes, the combined increment is insignificant when compared with the huge quantity already there.

In a paper presented at a joint meeting of the California and Nevada Dietetic Associations in Las Vegas on April 19, 1971, Jukes expressed the belief that certain species of fish have always contained high levels of mercury and that human beings have been eating these fish without ill effects for many thousands of years.

"We will have to establish a tolerance for mercury and make a mental adjustment to it," he told the dieticians, "for mercury, like all the elements, is naturally present in all living organisms."

He cited swordfish and tuna as two species of fish with an apparent affinity for mercury. This affinity, he said, is probably based on biological characteristics. Tuna, for example, have a higher respiration rate than most other edible fish and, as a result, pass exceptionally large amounts of seawater over their gill surfaces. The more water they pass, said Jukes, the more mercury they absorb.

He said environmentalists who blame industry for the mercury content of fish ignore the fact that mercury levels of 1 to 2 parts per million have been discovered frequently in fish caught hundreds of miles from any source of industrial contamination. But while Mother Nature is obviously the guilty party, there is a widespread reluctance to put the finger on her, said Jukes, who thereby put his own finger on a key feature of the Disaster Lobby era.

"Condemning nature is unpopular," he declared. "The dogma of the environmentalists seems to be that 'only man is vile'."

Yet the deeper the investigation went, the less culpable man seemed to be. When the United States Geological Survey examined water samples at 720 sites covering all fifty states, the District of Columbia and Puerto Rico, it found only two places where a combination of dissolved mercury and mercury attached to suspended particles ex-

ceeded .005 parts per million. Neither was in or near an
urban center or an industrial complex, although most of the
samples were taken from these heavily populated areas. The
highest concentration—.0068 parts per million—was discovered in the south fork of the Coeur d'Alene River in Idaho
and the second highest—.006 parts per million—was in a
specimen taken from the Merced River near Yosemite
National Park in California. And while there is some industrial activity in the vicinity of the Idaho test location, the
California site ranks among the most unspoiled and pol-
lutant-free in the world.

Eventually, the evidence accumulated to the point where
even *The New York Times* seemed to be at least partially
convinced. One of the first newspapers to accept and pub-
licize the theory that the mercury in the fish came from
industrial pollution, it now executed a halfhearted about-
face. In an article on the release of impounded tuna stocks by
the F.D.A.—the agency said it had seized the tuna because it
thought 23 percent was contaminated, but actually only 3.6
percent exceeded the .5-parts-per-million guideline—the
Times offered this somewhat lame explanation for its own
readiness to blame industry:

"When high mercury levels were discovered last year in
fresh water fish, California sea lions and Alaskan fur seals,
it was at first believed that the contamination was due to
industrial pollution. But many scientists appear now to have
swung over to the belief that the presence of the metal is a
result of its concentration in the food chain.

"The theory is that the metal is present in microscopic
amounts in the bodies of small marine animals, such as
plankton. After eating the plankton, larger forms of aquatic
life are eaten in turn by still larger varieties. During this
process the mercury is seldom excreted but remains in the
flesh and is increasingly concentrated in the food chain."

So the Strange Case of the Mercury in the Fish ended, not
with a bang, but with a series of muted whimpers from those
who, a short time earlier, had been all too ready to jump up

and down on American industry with the hobnailed boots of blind bias.

Unlike the DDT episode, this one precipitated a few relatively minor inconveniences rather than a major tragedy. Millions of housewives were unable to buy canned tuna for a while, but the product is now back on the supermarket shelves. Some fainthearted vacationers missed out on a summer of swimming in their favorite lakes and rivers, but if they ran across that news item about swimming being perfectly safe, their sacrifice was shortlived.

Of course, the swordfish industry both at home and abroad suffered a crippling blow. Prior to the F.D.A. warning on May 6, 1971, the United States had consumed more than 25 million pounds of swordfish a year, with 15 million pounds coming from Japan, 7 million imported from Canada and over half a million pounds supplied by America's own fishermen. The figures are now sharply lower.

What is even more regrettable, the millions of Americans who enjoyed an occasional meal of swordfish will no longer find many dealers or restaurants offering it for sale. This highly nutritious, low-calorie, low-cholesterol delicacy became a scarce item in most communities after the demand for it fell off. The same is true of fish species not mentioned by the F.D.A. All of that talk about mercury poisoning scared off many fish-eaters and deprived them of this source of medically endorsed nourishment.

In issuing its warning on swordfish, the Food and Drug Administration had bowed to the pressures of the Disaster Lobby while ignoring both hard evidence and common sense. The hard evidence showed that swordfish have *always* contained the levels of mercury they now contain. Common sense should have made it clear to the F.D.A. that since human beings have been eating swordfish-cum-mercury for thousands of years without becoming ill—even the celebrated "Mrs. N.Y." was only *suspected* of having been a victim—the ingestion of swordfish could not possibly be regarded as a substantive threat to human life.

But hard evidence and common sense, like perspective, were more likely to be shunned than embraced among Disaster Lobbyists. For this was the time when some of the nation's heaviest thinkers were spreading the word that any contamination was too much contamination, that any risk was too much risk, that zero pollution and zero jeopardy were not only essential but attainable and that the only thing standing in the way was American industry, that fountainhead of all contamination, all risk and most of the other evils of this life. In pursuit of its Unholy Grail, these reformers were willing—make that "eager"—to slap a ban on everything in sight, and pesticides, high-powered automobiles, household detergents, colored toilet paper, offshore oil wells and swordfish were just the opening salvo. In this rich land, there was oh so much to be prohibited, and the Disaster Lobby had just begun to fight.

SIX

The $12 Lawsuits

Since 1802, the Corps of Engineers of the United States Army has been busy helping to carve a dry, safe, habitable environment out of the savagely hostile wilderness that once was America. In these past 170 years, it has built 9,000 miles of levees and flood walls, 350 reservoirs, 22,000 miles of navigable waterways and 7,500 miles of improved channels, and it has maintained these facilities in reasonably good operating order. It could accomplish all of this because, until the mid-1960's, it enjoyed the cooperation and good will of virtually all Americans.

But then came the ecology mania of the Age of Unreason, and suddenly the Army Engineers were the bad guys. Indeed, Supreme Court Justice Douglas, with a display of prejudice and intemperance rarely encountered in one of his calling, took it upon himself to describe the Engineers as "public enemy number one." What was their crime? They were guilty of meddling with Mother Nature—that sweet old lady who year after year slaughters millions of human beings with her floods and her droughts and her earthquakes and her diseases—and for that reason the Army Engineers had to be stopped.

And the Army Engineers *were* stopped. At one point in 1972, a total of fifteen major Engineer construction projects involving billions of dollars in appropriated public funds were bogged down in lawsuits and other dilatory procedures set in motion by the self-appointed guardians of nature in the raw.

These are the projects, and some of them would never survive the ecologists' harassment: New Hope Reservoir, North Carolina; Cross-Florida Barge Canal; Tennessee-Tombigbee Waterway; West Tennessee Tributaries; Gillham Dam, Arkansas; Cache River Flood Control Project, Arkansas; Oakley Reservoir, Illinois; LaFarge Reservoir, Wisconsin; Cooper Lake and Channels Project, Texas; Laneport Dam, Texas; Wallisville Dam, Texas; Gila River Channelization, Arizona; Lower Granite and Asotin Dams, Washington; East Fork Lake, Ohio; and Tocks Island Dam, between Pennsylvania and New Jersey.

Several of these projects were designed primarily or coincidentally to inhibit floods. If they had been permitted to proceed on schedule, how many lives might have been saved in the early 1970's when floods killed hundreds of Americans? Had the victims been fish or birds, the outrage of the Disaster Lobby would have known no bounds. Because the victims were merely people, hardly an angry voice was raised. And the flood control projects continued to gather dust in various Federal courts and regulatory agencies.

In most of the suits tying up construction of this type, the plaintiffs were the big national conservation groups. The same names cropped up again and again: the National Wildlife Federation, the Izaak Walton League, the Audubon Society, the Sierra Club. And a frequent litigant in the later years was the Environmental Defense Fund, which was established in 1967 for the limited purpose of obtaining injunctions against the use of DDT on Long Island, and which later branched out in other ecological directions.

Although these organizations liked to picture themselves as poor little Davids trying to save the world from the mighty Goliaths of the military-industrial complex, the truth lies in the opposite direction. In reality, *they* were the Goliaths. There wasn't a private company in the United States that could set aside funds or legal talent to match the clout of the nature lobby. In 1972, just one arm of that lobby, the

Sierra Club, employed a full-time paid staff of 102 and had a budget of $3.5 million devoted entirely to blocking projects of the Army Engineer variety. (By contrast, the International Telephone and Telegraph Company, America's eleventh largest corporation in terms of 1970 sales, has only one full-time lobbyist in Washington, as the Jack Anderson-Dita Beard story revealed in 1972.)

Actually, the conservation people didn't need a great deal of money or talent to do what they had set out to do. That point was made clear by John H. Gullett, a Washington, D.C., attorney who specialized in environmental cases—as counsel for the defense.

Declared Gullett: "You shouldn't be able to go in and stop 10 years of work in 20 minutes with a $12 lawsuit." The $12 figure was a reference to the cost of filing the necessary stop-work papers in any United States District Court.

This was all it took to halt many mammoth public welfare projects in the 1960's, including the Cross-Florida Canal, which would have traversed the Florida peninsula between Jacksonville and Yankeetown and slashed 600 miles from the journey between ports on the Atlantic Ocean and those on the Gulf of Mexico. In both economic and military terms, the value of the 125-mile waterway would have been immense. But just about every conservation group in America opposed it on the ground that it would interfere with the happiness of the birds and alligators occupying central Florida. So intense was the sentiment and the public protest it engendered that the White House ultimately stepped in and killed the project. At the time of the first court decree holding up work on the Cross-Florida Canal, twenty-five miles had already been excavated at a cost well in excess of $50 million.

It was a putative threat to fish that halted the $69 million Tellico Dam project in Tennessee after $35 million had been spent. Work on the dam began in 1967 under the direction of the Tennessee Valley Authority. On completion, Tellico would have converted a thirty-three-mile stretch of the Little Tennessee River into a 17,000-acre lake and supplied power for industries turning out products worth $76 million a year. But a lawsuit was filed by the Environmental Defense Fund, which argued the dam constituted "a threat to seven rare or endangered species of fish which live in the Little Tennessee River." On January 13, 1972, a Federal judge in Tennessee ordered the T.V.A. to discontinue all operations at Tellico.

Even on those rare occasions when the conservationists lost out in court, they were usually able to delay the target projects for so long a period of time that the sponsors would pack up their blueprints and look for another site. Or they would quit entirely.

A typical case involved the Consolidated Edison Company, the biggest supplier of power to New York City and its suburbs to the north. In 1963, Con Ed announced plans to build the world's largest pumped water storage plant. It was to be erected on the west bank of the Hudson River, just south of Cornwall, New York, and, according to company spokesmen, it would provide a means of "increasing the reliability of electricity in New York City and Westchester County." Such a goal was eminently worthwhile. If there was one thing lacking in New York City's electricity during the 1960's, it was reliability. In summer, with millions of air conditioners straining to overcome the heat, hardly a week went by without a power failure due to equipment overloads. In fall and winter, the need for additional lighting created similar problems. The roof fell in on the night of November 9, 1965, when 80,000 square miles in the Northeastern United States, including metropolitan New York, were blacked out. Only heroic efforts by utility and government workers, combined with a monumental amount of good luck, prevented a major catastrophe.

So rational human beings in the New York area welcomed the announcement by Con Ed. But this was the Age of Unreason, and rational human beings were maintaining a low profile. A suit against the Consolidated Edison project was filed by the Wilderness Society, the Izaak Walton League, the National Audubon Society and the Sierra Club. Seemingly indifferent to the plight of power-starved people—to

the needs of hospitals and schools and homes and businesses
—the plaintiffs argued in their brief that the proposed plant
might kill some fish. They said it would suck up so much
water from the Hudson River that ocean water would be
drawn upstream and the fresh water fish would succumb
to the salt water environment.

For years, the case shuttled from hearing to hearing and
from court to court, but Con Ed refused to throw in the
towel. That storage plant was indispensable, and there were
no other feasible sites. The litigation finally arrived in Washington, and on June 19, 1972, the Supreme Court of the
United States rejected the complaint of the conservation
groups and gave the project its blessing. The vote was eight
to one in favor of Con Ed, and it wouldn't take a clairvoyant
to figure out which Justice filed the dissenting opinion. William O. Douglas was still "on the side of the fish . . . and
against people."

The Supreme Court ruling did not, unfortunately, end
the matter. In the fall of 1972, officials of the big New York
City utility said the project was still tied up in seemingly
endless miles of procedural red tape that was being manipu-
lated artfully and effectively by the nation's pro-fish groups.

For some reason, apparently the production of energy and
energy materials seemed to infuriate many environmentalists
more than any other activity of mankind. Although they
opposed most kinds of progress, they reserved their best
efforts for those projects connected with the generation of
power. Oil fields, coal mines, gas pipelines, electric power
plants, all were special targets of the Disaster Lobby. And
the more severe the nation's power shortage became in the
1960's and 1970's, the greater were the pressures against the
kind of expansion that might have relieved the shortage.

When fossil-fueled generating plants were virtually the
only sources of electricity, the Disaster crowd objected to the
building of additional plants on the ground that they would
pollute the air through the emission of coal smoke. Then
atomic reactors were introduced, and the environmentalists
had to come up with a brand new bogeyman. Atomic reac-

tors do not emit smoke. But the National Wildlife Federation and the Sierra Club and their colleagues were equal to the challenge. They began by claiming that hot water pumped by atomic energy plants into adjacent lakes and streams was hurting the fish. When various scientific studies revealed that the fish thrived on hot water, the complaints tacked off in a new direction. Next the charge was that radiation emissions from the plants and the possibility of explosions constituted a threat to human life. While the regard for people rather than animals represented a refreshing change, the effects were no less damaging.

On November 16, 1970, Sherman R. Knapp, President of the Atomic Industrial Forum, Inc., speaking at his organization's annual conference in Washington, D.C., expressed grave concern about the spreading rash of lawsuits against companies seeking to build atomic energy plants. In addition, he said, there were many construction delays brought about by harassment through the Atomic Energy Commission's licensing procedures, which he described as "hopelessly vulnerable." A combination of the two—lawsuits and licensing deferments—had been resorted to by the antipower environmentalists in a successful attempt to block construction of a nuclear facility at Monticello, Minnesota, said Knapp. The applicant, Northern States Power Company, had been prevented from starting on the project "for a long, long time," he declared, adding that a plant in Michigan had been held up for five months by similar proceedings at a cost to the investors of nearly $15 million.

The cases he cited were not unique. Many desperately needed plants were being litigated to death all over the country, while perhaps scores of others were being abandoned in the embryo stage by promoters unwilling to undergo the delays and money risks involved. Even after a plant got the green light from courts and regulatory agencies, the harassment continued. In the spring of 1972, the National Wildlife Federation and the Sierra Club were co-plaintiffs in a suit that forced the Atomic Energy Commission to re-study the environmental impact of an atomic power plant at Calvert Cliffs, Maryland.

The real pity of it all was that, at this critical juncture in mankind's development, atomic energy was the best hope—perhaps the *only* hope—for continued progress and fulfillment. Without a steady supply of energy, civilization as we know it would fall apart. Cars could not move. Airplanes could not fly. Machines would grind to a halt. Homes would grow cold and dark. Hospitals and schools would cease to function.

Until recently, the primary sources of energy were fossil fuels, but the supply of fossil fuels is finite. Already, the United States is feeling the pinch of a petroleum shortage. Each winter, the demand for natural gas grows and the amount available dwindles. Coal is more abundant but not even coal can be mined forever. One significant advantage of nuclear energy is the durability of source material. And when the nuclear fusion of hydrogen is perfected, the supply of fuel will be virtually inexhaustible.

Another advantage is cleanliness. There is no smoke from atomic plants, and no liquid pollutants. Furthermore, despite doomsday warnings circulated by the Disaster Lobby, the production of atomic energy is safe. It is safe for human beings and safe for the environment.

In his Washington speech, Sherman Knapp said he could not understand the reason for the "sudden hysteria" about environmental effects of nuclear power plants. He noted that there were then seventeen nuclear power plants in operation and "there has not been a single case of the thermal emission seriously damaging the ecology."

Dr. Chauncey Starr, Dean of the U.C.L.A. School of Engineering and Applied Science, was even more enthusiastic about the potential for nuclear power.

"The more I study the problem," he wrote in *Look* magazine in August of 1971, "the more I am convinced that we really have something great for mankind. [Nuclear power production] has unique clean air qualities. It's unique in several aspects. It does not involve combustion. We don't have to bring air in to handle the fuel. The amounts of material that feed into the plant as fuel or that come out of the plant as waste products are very small and easy to handle."

Starr rejected as groundless the talk about potential hazards through radiation leaks.

"The nuclear plant contribution [to radiation] is now so small that even projecting future growth, the total impact is a negligible part of the normal population exposure to other sources of radiation," he wrote in *Look*. He said the average American picked up much more radiation through medical X-rays and through cosmic rays than he could possibly encounter from atomic energy plants.

"For nuclear power," he wrote, "the radiation level to which the public is exposed is one-thousandth to one-tenthousandth as high as the levels which have proved harmful in long-term studies of animals, through low-level continuous radiation.

"The hazard to the public of nuclear accidents is less than the hazard of continuous exposure, which is already trivial. There has not been in this country a single nuclear power station that's had an accident that's released damaging radioactivity to the public."

But nuclear power still has limited applications in our society. The United States continues to depend on fossil fuels for most of its energy requirements, and because it does, the Disaster Lobby continues to do everything it can to impede the flow of those fuels.

Petroleum is a prime example. In 1970, the United States was using 15 million barrels of petroleum each day—and producing only 10 million barrels. The remainder was imported. By 1980, consumption of petroleum in this country will exceed 20 million barrels a day, but production will have leveled off at 11 million barrels. Again, the rest will have to be imported. As a result of the growing gap between domestic use of petroleum and domestic production of petroleum, this nation will, by 1985, be importing well over half of the fuel we depend on to power our cars, trucks and airplanes.

What compounds the problem is the fact that almost all of the oil imported by the United States comes from nations in the Arab bloc. And some Arab bloc nations have been known to nationalize their oil fields and to shut off the flow of export oil at the drop of a treaty or trade agreement. Such actions in the 1980's, with America relying on foreign suppliers for most of its petroleum, could bring this country to its knees, both economically and militarily, in a matter of weeks.

So there is a pressing need for more domestic production. Unfortunately, most attempts to increase production are met with furious antipetroleum campaigns by the far-out environmentalists. The dismal projections for domestic oil output —the total is expected to increase by only about 1 percent a year—are the result of Disaster Lobbying against the oil depletion allowance (it was reduced in 1969, and exploration for oil immediately fell off), against off-shore drilling, against the drilling of new wells on land sites and, most recently, against development of the massive North Slope oil fields in Alaska.

When oil was discovered on the North Slope in the 1960's, there was rejoicing not only by the petroleum industry but by large numbers of American consumers who like to have heat in their homes in the winter and gasoline in their automobiles. It was estimated that at full production the new Alaska wells would pump out two million barrels of crude oil a day, thus making a significant contribution toward abatement of the nation's energy crisis.

Enter the Disaster Lobby. The obstructionists could do nothing to prevent the Alaskan wells from being drilled, but they could keep the oil from reaching the American consumer. All they had to do was block construction of the proposed $2.5 billion trans-Alaska pipeline, through which petroleum would be transmitted from derricks deep inside the Arctic Circle to refineries in states to the south.

First to file suit against the pipeline was the Environmental Defense Fund. It based its case on the charge that installation of the pipe would damage the permafrost, alter the ecological balance and greatly inconvenience many of the furry, finned and feathered residents of the region. It could offer no proof to back up its contention, but at this point in history, proof was not needed. All you had to do to stop progress was suggest that the wildlife *might* be harmed.

Between litigation and mounting pressure on the Department of the Interior and the Environmental Protection Agency, the opponents of the Alaska project were able to stall it month after month, year after year. From time to time, they would run an advertisement in newspapers to keep public opinion on their side. Such an ad appeared February 23, 1972, in *The New York Times*. It was signed by The Wilderness Society, the National Audubon Society, the Sierra Club and Trout Unlimited, and it featured a plaintive appeal on behalf of animals.

"One can only imagine," the copy said, "how many millions of caribou, mountain sheep, moose, ducks, geese, deer and salmon make Alaska their home. But how precious few are the wolves, polar bear, falcons and other threatened species that can thrive only in this, a last remaining habitat."

There was no mention in the advertisement of how many millions of human beings might expire without fuel to heat their homes or power their machines. Nor was there any reference to the fact that the overwhelming majority of the *people* living in Alaska were wholeheartedly in favor of both the pipeline and the oil wells.

In a letter to the authors, Robert B. Atwood, editor of the *Anchorage Daily Times*, addressed himself to that aspect.

"I would speculate," he wrote, "that 299,000 of the 300,000 residents of this big piece of real estate feel frustrated because the preservationists, conservationists, ecologists, environmentalists and various other so-called experts have thrown so many question marks around the trans-Alaska pipeline project. The other thousand Alaskans, I assume, are happy because they feel a kinship with all the kooks who want to lock up Alaska as some sort of permanent wilderness."

After doing what they could to cut down the supply of atomic energy and petroleum, the "preservationists, conservationists, ecologists, environmentalists and various other so-called experts" turned their attention to the last remaining primary source of power: coal. Their specific target was not coal itself but rather one of the methods used to extract it from the ground. The coal industry calls it surface mining. The Disaster Lobby employs the term strip mining. By any name, it is the procedure by which coal is scooped out of deposits relatively close to the surface by mechanical shovels, as opposed to the more expensive and slower "deep mining" method that involves the drilling of shafts and the removal of coal far below ground level.

Surface mining has become more and more popular in the wake of increasing demands by electric utilities for a low-cost energy material. The utilities, in turn, are under mounting pressure from government regulatory agencies to provide inexpensive power to consumers. By 1970, due to these factors, more than two-fifths of all the coal mined in the United States came from surface operations.

In lobbying and suing to close down surface mines, the environmentalists contended that the practice was doing irrevocable damage to the nation's landscape, particularly in the Appalachian Mountain areas of Kentucky and West Virginia. Their argument received a hefty amount of publicity when *The New York Times* devoted both the cover and lead-article positions in its December 12, 1971, Sunday magazine section to the subject. Author of the piece was James Branscome, a director of Save Our Kentucky, Inc., a coalition of ecology groups opposed to surface mining.

According to Branscome, in the year 1970, "strip mining led to the destruction of an estimated 17,300 acres in eastern Kentucky alone." If the practice is allowed to continue, he wrote, "the hills and mountains of Appalachia will be irreparably scarred."

Words like "destruction" and "irreparably" are favorites of

the Disaster Lobby, which believes, with considerable justification, that it can win the American public over to its
side by conveying the impression that anything done to
alter the natural environment is not only evil but irreversible.
A tree cut down can never be replaced by another tree. Grass
torn up by bulldozers can never be replanted. Dirt scooped
up by steamshovels can never be filled in.

All this is arrant nonsense, as Carl E. Bagge, president of
the National Coal Association, pointed out in a letter to the
Times in reply to the Branscome article. Bagge said the coal
industry had already restored much of the land used for
surface mining and was in the process of restoring the
remainder. As a result of this program, he reported, "58,000
acres were officially accepted by the states as satisfactorily
reclaimed in 1970."

In order to qualify as genuinely "reclaimed", he said, the
mine sites must undergo extensive repairs. "The laws vary,
but in most cases they require the land to be graded, revege-
tated and that a specified high percentage of the vegetation
survive for one or two growing seasons," wrote Bagge. "We
would be happy to show an impartial reporter thousands of
acres of land reclaimed so thoroughly that it is difficult to
tell it was once mined for coal."

He also noted the urgent need for surface mined coal.
"Electric utilities," he said, "used 198 million tons of surface
mined coal in 1970 to produce 28.2 percent of all electric
power generated in the United States. To replace that much
surface mine output with deep mine production would require three to four years, recruiting more workers in an
industry already short of skilled miners, and an investment
of $2.5 billion or more—not to mention abolishing the jobs
of men now employed in surface mining, junking the equipment and abandoning coal reserves which cannot be mined
except by surface methods."

There were two noteworthy sequels to the Branscome-
Bagge exchange. On January 30, 1972, the National Coal
Association, in response to demands by The Friends of the
Earth for a blanket injunction against all surface mining,

provided figures showing that "more ravaged land is being returned to use each year than is being stripped anew." The Friends of the Earth rejected the figures as irrelevant.

Then came what might be described as The Story of the Two Pictures, and a fascinating story it was. On the cover of the *Times* magazine section containing the Branscome article had been a large color photograph of a surface mine site in Appalachia. It showed several long, parallel furrows in a treeless landscape, and it bore the caption, "Strip Mining—Like Flaying the Back of a Man." It was clearly designed to put surface mining in the poorest possible light and to arouse public sentiment against it.

Several weeks later, the authors received a photograph from a friend who had been a real estate agent in Arizona. The photograph appeared, at first glance, to be identical to the one published on the cover of the *Times* magazine. It, too, showed parallel furrows minus vegetation of any kind. The only substantive difference was that this photograph was taken, not at the site of a surface mine in Appalachia, but in a desert area of Nevada. The furrows were gulleys chewed out of the desert floor by centuries of erosion. It is typical of the landscape in certain sections of the Southwest and Far West—sections, it should be mentioned, that are jealously guarded by the Sierra Club in a determined effort to prevent their alteration by land developers.

The import was clear. If nature makes furrows, they must be preserved in perpetuity. If man makes furrows, regardless of the need that drove him to it, they must be obliterated. Or better yet, they must not be made in the first place. Such was the philosophy of the Age of Unreason, and as an example of mind-boggling paradox, it would be almost impossible to top.

When exaggeration, distortion and false implication failed to produce the desired results, the Disaster Lobby was not averse to a soupcon of outright falsehood. In an attempt to shut down elements of the timber industry, it spread the word that the nation's trees were being chopped down faster than they were being replaced. The impression conveyed was that, in time, what used to be our forests primeval would be mile after mile of ragged stumps.

Preconditioned Americans accepted the charge as fact. The same people who were willing to believe that DDT was a threat to human life, that air pollution was getting worse and that the mercury in tuna fish came from careless and avaricious factory owners now went around complaining about the disappearance of the trees. *Time* magazine gave the matter added impetus by devoting a news item to our incipient defoliation, while the Sierra Club ran an advertisement in which it stated that "we must not sacrifice the forest environment . . . to build more suburban sprawl." The ad failed to mention just where the Sierra Club would like to have people live, but obviously it was not in the suburbs.

Many thousands of Americans heard and were convinced by the voices of ecological doom. Few Americans ever encountered the truth, which appeared in a single advertisement in the spring of 1971. The ad was prepared by the American Forest Institute in an attempt to offset the propaganda of the conservationists and stave off anticutting legislation by the government. The case against the Disaster Lobby was made neatly and eloquently in three simple sentences:

"In the last 15 years, we harvested 197 billion cubic feet of timber in the United States. Growth amounted to 246 billion cubic feet. We are growing about nine cubic feet for every eight cubic feet we harvest."

So there, in a short burst of facts, went the whole environmentalist argument. We weren't losing trees each year, we were *gaining* trees. The trouble with the Disaster Lobby was that it couldn't see the forest *or* the trees.

Nor did it, apparently, believe in evolution. To a dedicated Disaster Lobbyist, animals did not become extinct in Twentieth Century America; mankind exterminated them. Some of the most irrational prose turned out by the nature set had to do with its attempt to save the so-called "endangered species." To prevent these species from vanishing, the ecology buffs waged a furious campaign against the killing of everything from alligators to leopards. The nation's fur industry was especially hard hit. In some circles, the wearing of a fur coat of any description was greeted in the 1960's with the same kind of lip-curling revulsion that once had been reserved for those sporting the scarlet letter "A."

It was mostly in the United States that this fatuous animal worship flourished. An attempt was made by concerned Americans to have the tiger ruled off limits for hunters in India, but the Indians vetoed the proposal. They very sensibly pointed out that, since the tigers in India seemed to have their hearts set on exterminating people, there was no reason why the people shouldn't exterminate the tigers first. This attitude may help explain why today there are more people in India than there are tigers.

The image of mankind as the deciding factor in the life or death of animal species is preposterous to begin with. Since the first dawn on earth, there have existed roughly 100 million species of animals. Today there are approximately *one* million. In other words, 99 percent of all the species that ever lived—99 million of them—are now extinct. And virtually all of them entered that sorry state long before the appearance of homo sapiens.

According to the curator of New York City's Bronx Zoo, about seventy-five types of birds, mammals and reptiles have perished so far in the Twentieth Century. A total of eighty-four became extinct in the Nineteenth Century. And in the Eighteenth Century, before the advent of the Industrial Revolution, the figure was roughly the same. Wildlife has been vanishing at a fairly steady clip century after century, millenium after millenium, for millions of years. To blame man for this natural process or to suppose that man could materially alter it—or *should* alter it—is to do violence to simple logic.

A basic theme running through all of the environmental tommyrot was the belief that anything that occurs or exists in nature is safe and beneficial while anything produced by man is very likely to be dangerous and malevolent. This was the philosophy behind the big boom in organic foods. The theory was that organic fertilizers, such as manure, would inject more wholesome goodies into the vegetables and fruits being grown than would those insidious, man-made, chemical fertilizers.

Absolute poppycock, as the University of California's Thomas Jukes noted. Organic fertilizers, he said, are not absorbed by the plants. What is absorbed is the chemical derivative, and the synthetic chemical is always identical to the natural chemical.

"There is no such thing as organic plant nutrition," said Jukes. "Plants utilize only inorganic forms of plant food. Compost and manure are broken down by bacteria to components, such as nitrate, potassium ion and phosphate, before they are assimilated. Hydroponics, in which plants are grown inorganically without soil, leads to the production of vegetables and fruits with the same protein, carbohydrate, vitamin and mineral content as when the same strains of plants are grown in the ground with lots of manure."

But the organic food buffs refused to be swayed by the facts. They went on paying exorbitant prices for their precious organically grown foods, and, such is the power of suggestion, they felt immeasurably healthier.

Opposition to man-made chemicals led to several highly effective crusades by the Disaster Lobby in the late 1960's and early 1970's. Each was designed to halt the manufacture and sale of products containing a specific laboratory compound.

There was, for example, hexachlorophene. A crystalline, phenolic, bacteria-inhibiting agent, hexachlorophene was for many years a widely used ingredient in a broad range of consumer products, including hand lotions, soaps, deodorants, shoe liners and shower curtains. Because of its germ-killing properties, it was also used almost universally in the solutions with which newborn babies were bathed in hospitals.

Then came the charges. In Washington, the attention of the Food and Drug Administration was directed to several cursory studies showing that rats fed on hexachlorophene and monkeys washed in it had developed brain lesions and other physiological damage. The F.D.A. panicked on cue and, in December of 1971, issued a bulletin referring to the rat and monkey research.

"These studies," said the bulletin, "challenge the safety of hexachlorophene bathing of infants, a practice which has been widely advocated as effective prophylaxis against nursery epidemics of staphylococcal skin infections."

The F.D.A. then adopted the Disaster Lobby approach by suggesting that hexachlorophene not only might be dangerous but might not even be effective as a bacteria fighter.

"A critical review of the studies on which this claim is based," the agency stated, "indicates that whereas there is no doubt that hexachlorophene bathing decreases skin colonization of gram-positive organisms, there is a lack of substantial evidence that hexachlorophene washings by themselves prevent staphylococcal disease or show antibacterial activity against gram-negative organisms. Hospitals are known to operate nurseries safely without the use of this product."

Here was the DDT syndrome all over again. The product is dangerous and it isn't even too effective in the first place.

The Food and Drug Administration concluded its bulletin by announcing that "the use of hexachlorophene for total body bathing of infants in hospital nurseries or at home is not recommended." As a substitute, the F.D.A. suggested "washing with plain soap and water or tap water alone for skin care of the newborn infants." It also directed that the labels of hexachlorophene products with 3 percent concentration—3 percent was the concentration most frequently employed by hospitals—be amended "to advise against their use for total body bathing."

Then on January 6, 1972, the F.D.A. issued a news release admitting that it was "not aware of any harm to humans from the use of hexachlorophene under recommended or normal conditions of use" but added that animal studies had shown absorption of hexachlorophene into the blood stream. "More information is needed about the cumulative exposure of humans to hexachlorophene through drug and cosmetic use and about the health implication of such exposure," the agency said. "Until we have such information, the only prudent course is to reduce the total human exposure to hexachlorophene."

Here again was the Disaster Lobby philosophy. Nothing should be used until it was tested so exhaustively—on animals as well as human beings, on succeeding generations of animals and human beings to determine hereditary effects, in amounts far greater than any human being would ever require—that it could confidently be said there was zero risk. Under such circumstances, penicillin would still be in the testing stage, and the millions of lives saved by penicillin would have been irretrievably lost.

In the matter of hexachlorophene, the Disaster Lobby and its yes-men in Washington got the results they wanted. Immediately after the F.D.A. warning went out, many hospitals stopped washing babies with hexachlorophene cleansers. Sales of these cleansers dropped sharply. Some companies began eliminating hexachlorophene from their products. A jittery nation was embarked on "the only prudent course" referred to by the Food and Drug Administration.

But was it a prudent course? On April 18, 1972, *The New York Times* carried a report on the secondary results of the antihexachlorophene movement.

"Within a few months [of the bathing change]," the *Times* said, "two dozen hospitals said that this action had led to a flurry of staphylococcus outbreaks among the babies. Staph infections on the skin can sometimes lead to life-threatening complications, including pneumonia, blood poisoning, meningitis, bone infections and brain abcesses."

The *Times* went on to note that the American Medical Association regarded 3 percent hexachlorophene products as being safe enough to be sold without a prescription. And Dr. Naomi Kanof, a Washington, D.C., dermatologist was quoted as having praised the product for its "excellent safety and effectiveness record."

Having weighed the pros and cons, most hospitals have gone back to the practice of using 3 percent hexachlorophene solutions to wash newborn infants, and staph infections have become less prevalent. Once again, the Disaster Lobby was wrong, but this time, fortunately, the error was rectified before too many human beings got sick or died.

The brouhaha involving hexachlorophene came at about the same time as a similar one in which saccharin was the alleged culprit. Saccharin is a crystalline compound several hundred times sweeter than sugar, and it has been used as a substitute for sugar for more than eighty years by diabetics and by other persons who must or desire to cut down on their intake of sugar. During those eighty years plus, there has never been any evidence that saccharin was harmful to human beings in the amounts normally consumed.

In July of 1970, the Food Protection Committee of the National Academy of Sciences issued a detailed report defending the use of saccharin.

"Tests in several species of animals and observations in man have demonstrated that the acute toxicity of saccharin is of low order," the report stated. "It is unlikely that even gross misuse of saccharin over a short period of time would be hazardous. It was concluded that an intake of one gram or less per day should present no hazard."

One gram of saccharin is equivalent to sixty of the small saccharin tables used as beverage sweeteners. It is also equal to the amount of saccharin found in seven twelve-ounce bottles of a typical diet soft drink. Few users of saccharin even approach that level of intake. As the Food Protection Committee report noted, "the highest average daily intake is not likely to exceed .21 grams."

But this was the Age of Unreason, and saccharin came under heavy fire. After all, it did not originate in a cane field or on a beet farm or in any other fiefdom of Mother Nature. Saccharin was put together in laboratories by man, and it was therefore suspect.

The Disaster Lobby began circulating data about tests in which the ingestion of saccharin produced bladder tumors in rats. What the Disaster folks failed to mention was that the rats had been fed the human equivalent of 100 grams of saccharin a day—an amount equal to the contents of 6,000 tablets or 700 bottles of diet drinks.

But the harm had been done. With the Disaster Lobby heated up, the Food and Drug Administration quickly came to a boil. On January 28, 1972, the F.D.A. put out a news release announcing that saccharin had been removed from the GRAS (generally recognized as safe) list of food additives. It also issued an order freezing the use of saccharin at levels then in effect in various diet products, and requiring that the amounts of saccharin be disclosed on the labels of all beverages, foods and food mixes in which the compound's use was permitted.

Curiously, the F.D.A. announcement acknowledged that "saccharin has been widely used in the food supply for over 80 years without any evidence of human harm", that the tumors in the rats had been induced through amounts of saccharin hundreds of times greater than the amounts consumed by the most saccharin-happy human being and that even those tumors had not been diagnosed as malignant.

So saccharin joined the many other boons to mankind on the no-no roster. Persons on a sugar-free diet, especially children fond of sweets, found it more and more difficult to find substitutes for sugar-sweetened food products as the food industry began phasing out saccharin. No manufacturer wanted to market goods bearing on their labels an ingredient that had just been removed from the F.D.A. list of additives "generally recognized as safe." Even if it was—and is—safe.

Exacerbating the problem was the fact that, prior to its action on saccharin, the Food and Drug Administration had totally outlawed another artificial sweetener: the sodium and calcium salts of cyclohexanesulfamic acid, commonly known as cyclamates.

The cyclamate case closely paralleled those involving hexachlorophene and saccharin. It began with laboratory tests involving animals that developed tumors as a consequence of being the recipients of massive quantities of the product under study. The Disaster Lobby became alarmed, and in 1968, the National Academy of Sciences and National

Research Council conducted an investigation. Their conclusion was that "daily intakes of five grams or less of cyclamates by an adult should present no hazard."

Just to be on the safe side, the Food and Drug Administration, on April 3, 1969, issued a recommendation that the ingestion of cyclamates by adults be limited to three and a half grams a day while that of children be held to one and a fifth grams. It formulated new labeling rules that would enable consumers to keep under that ceiling.

But this wasn't the remedy favored by the Disaster Lobbyists. They wanted total abolition. And total abolition is what they got. On November 14, 1969, Robert Finch, then Secretary of Health, Education and Welfare, announced a phaseout of all marketable products containing cyclamates, with the exception of those regarded as drugs. On August 14, 1970, even the drug items were outlawed.

Again, there had been no evidence at all of damage to human beings, but again that cold, hard fact was considered irrelevant.

Throughout the period, examples of this kind of thinking and regulation-making were the rule rather than the exception. Wherever there was a conflict between man and the animals or between man and foliage, the rulings invariably went in favor of the animals and the foliage. Wherever a product came under the flimsiest cloud of suspicion, the product was made illegal—or at the very least regulated into obscurity.

In the 1960's, there were several fatal accidents and a number of near-misses at New York City's Kennedy International Airport. Exponents of safer air travel urged that the runways at Kennedy be extended into Jamaica Bay, but the proposal was shot down by the advocates of better living conditions for birds. One of these was Rene Dubos, a former teacher and researcher at Rockefeller University, who led the successful fight against the runway extension.

"If we extend the runway," explained Dr. Dubos in an article in the October 17, 1971, *New York Times Magazine*, "Kennedy will work a little better for a while—but, for sure, the bird sanctuary [in Jamaica Bay] will be destroyed. I happen to think it's more important to improve the bird sanctuary than to improve Kennedy."

Nothing could be clearer than that. Justice Douglas was on the side of the fish and against people and Dubos was on the side of the birds and against people. And then, in the summer of 1971, there emerged a man who was on the side of the mountains and against people.

His name was William K. Verner, and he was curator of the Adirondack Museum in upstate New York. In an article in the August 24, 1971, issue of *The New York Times*, Verner was quoted as having complained about the increasing number of people who visited the Adirondacks each summer. He said they were "threatening the mountains with overuse."

And then there were the ecologists who won their fight to have the use of rock salt on highways banned in the city of Concord, Massachusetts. They admitted that the salt kept automobiles and trucks from skidding out of control on icy and snowy streets, but they argued successfully that it killed vegetation. The obvious premise was that dead motorists are preferable to dead vegetation.

Perhaps the most revealing and most irrational example of anti-man, stop-progress activism was the uproar surrounding the development of a supersonic transport. The SST was on the drawing board in the winter of 1970-1971, and the United States Senate was considering a bill to finance the construction of two prototypes that would be used to test not only the aircraft itself but its effects on the environment.

Although costs and other issues played major roles in the defeat of the SST, the effect of the plane on the environment became the most important issue with some of the senators.

On the floor of the Senate, the debate over the legislation was spirited. On the one side were lawmakers who understood that mankind's progress in the area of aviation could not end with the Boeing 747, that bigger and better and faster methods of transportation would ultimately be adopted and that some day the airplanes of the present would be regarded as we now regard the horse and buggy. These lawmakers were in favor of building the prototypes.

On the other side of the debate, intractably opposed to the sst, were the frontmen for the Disaster Lobby. It was their contention that the supersonic transport should not even be tested because the whole concept of supersonic flight was an affront to nature.

Senator George McGovern said he could not see why such an airplane should be built just "so that some rich international traveler can reach his destination a couple of hours earlier."

This ploy was also used by Senator Edmund Muskie, who described the sst as "a plane for a few of the affluent"; by Senator William Proxmire, who labeled it a device "for the few people who travel overseas"; and by Senator Edward Kennedy, who dismissed it as "a flying toy for the jet set."

Their statements were reminiscent of the remarks of astronomer William Pickering, who, in 1920, ridiculed the idea of regular commercial transatlantic flights. "Even if a machine could get across with one or two passengers," said the myopic Pickering, "the expense would be prohibitive to any but the capitalist who could own his own yacht."

But Senator Kennedy had another reason for condemning the sst. He articulated it in an impassioned speech on the Senate floor.

"Perhaps the most frightening specter of commercial supersonic flight," said Senator Kennedy, "came in investigations conducted by James McDonald, senior physicist at the Institute of Atmospheric Physics at the University of Arizona. He concluded that the additional water vapor pumped into the stratosphere by a fleet of sst's would reduce the ozone which filters ultraviolet rays from the sun. McDonald testified the increase in this ultraviolet radiation could cause 5,000 to 10,000 more cases of skin cancer in the United States."

What Senator Kennedy failed to mention was that immediately after testifying before a Congressional committee on the relationship between the supersonic transport and skin cancer McDonald had a few words to say about "unidentified flying objects." In his opinion, as expressed at the committee hearing, these objects, familiarly known as "flying saucers," had come from outer space and were wreaking considerable havoc in the United States. Among other things, he said, they had caused the electrical power failures in New York City.

But, then, this was the Age of Unreason. And the spectacle of a United States Senator devoting a speech on the floor of Congress to the warnings of a man who believed in flying saucers raised nary an eyebrow. Indeed, it was Senator Kennedy's side that won the debate. The sst legislation was voted down. It was all just one more sign of the times.

SEVEN

Whooping Cranes Yes, People No

Back in the lean gray years of the 1930's, anything that might take an American's mind off the Great Depression was greeted with interest and appreciation. It was this hunger for good wholesome entertainment that gave rise to a series of Sunday supplement articles prophesying the end of the world as the result of any one of a colorful assortment of calamities.

Perhaps the most popular calamity of all was a hair-raiser that might be called the Harrowing Heat-up. The Sunday scribblers would begin by citing weather station reports of a steady, year-by-year increase in average annual temperatures. At the current rate of climb, it was stated, the polar ice caps would start to melt by the summer of 1963, the volume of water in our oceans would immediately double and huge steaming floods would inundate all of the United States east of Chagrin Falls, Ohio, and west of downtown Chicago.

Of course, aside from a few nail-chewing neurotics, nobody —least of all the authors—really believed this nonsense. The tongue-in-cheek aspect of the whole business was underscored by the fact that, on alternate Sundays, the very same supplements would carry articles about an impending Catastrophic Cool-down. *These* stories would lead off with the observation that the North American glacier was traveling southward at a rate of sixty-seven miles a year (or was it sixty-seven inches a month?), which meant that in hardly any time at all our home continent would be encased in a solid sheet of ice as far south as a trailer camp on the outskirts of Guadalajara, Mexico.

With this kind of the-world-is-coming-to-an-end goofiness getting newspaper space in the relatively sane 1930's, it could have been predicted with reliability that the Age of Unreason of the 1960's would produce a doomsday topper. And it did. It was known simply but expressively as The Population Explosion, and its high priest was a young California entomologist named Paul Ralph Ehrlich.

There was in Dr. Ehrlich's forecast of imminent disaster a dash of poetic justice. For it was his contention that the instrument for the destruction of mankind was to be *mankind itself*. In the not too distant future, we were all going to overpopulate ourselves out of existence.

Here is where the essence of Disaster Lobbyism becomes manifest. In the 1930's, the forecasts of melting ice caps and galloping glaciers were read and enjoyed and promptly forgotten. In the 1960's, the equally inane announcement that the world was about to suffocate under a blanket of humanity threw large numbers of Americans, many of them members of the intellectual and cultural "elite," into a king-size panic. The great population hoax was swallowed right down to the last far-fetched assumption.

Ehrlich triggered much of the hysteria in 1968 by writing a book entitled *The Population Bomb*. In it he stated that at the rate of expansion then in effect, the population of the earth would reach "sixty million billion people" in 900 years.

"This," he pointed out, "is about 100 persons for each square yard of the Earth's surface, land and sea."

Then, presumably to disabuse his readers of the notion that these 100 persons per square yard would have to stand on each other's shoulders, he explained that all 60 million billion Earthlings could be accommodated in a 2,000-story building covering the entire planet.

But he went on to say that he did not really believe we would ever arrive at that Dantean state. No indeed. Long before mankind ascended into the 2,000-story Inferno, it would outpace its food supply and everybody would starve to death.

"The world," wrote Ehrlich, "is rapidly running out of food. We will not be able to prevent large-scale famines."

When would the ultimate famine begin? Ehrlich was quite willing to go out on a limb. We could expect the beginning of the end in nine years, he said, and since his book was published in 1968, the date to encircle in black on your calendar is 1977.

In other periods of time, the utterances of Paul Ralph Ehrlich would have been received with an indulgent smile or a hearty laugh. But not in the 1960's. Instead of dismissing *The Population Bomb* for the nonsense it was, America went out and bought it—and in such prodigious quantities that the book went through twenty-eight printings and became a two-million-copy best seller. The pixilated followers of the Disaster Lobby had clasped Ehrlich to their bosoms, had embraced his zany notions and had begun riding off in all directions in a desperate search for something, *anything*, to stave off this frightful overpopulation specter.

Although most people watchers of the period regarded Ehrlich as the originator of the overpopulation theory, everything he wrote emitted a powderful odor of déjà vu. Almost two centuries ago, the identical concept was being promoted by an English pedant named Thomas Robert Malthus. In his 1798 *Essay on the Principles of Population*, Malthus noted that since populations increase by geometric progression while food supplies increase by arithmetic progression, it must follow that mankind was doomed to famines of mounting frequency and severity.

For many years, the disciples of Malthus kept an eye peeled for the kind of massive starvation foreseen by their mentor. When none materialized, many lost faith in him but there was enough of a hard core left over in 1880 to form what became known as the Malthusian League, which, shortly after World War I, was reorganized as the New Generation League.

It was during the 1920's that most birth control movements, including those associated with Margaret Sanger, got their start. But these population-inhibiting groups had little in common with Malthus or his followers. The primary concern of Mrs. Sanger was not for the ecological effect of overpopulation on the world but for the economic, social and health problems entailed in having large families. She saw a plethora of children as being a strain on the parents rather than as a threat to the continued existence of mankind.

Not so Paul Ehrlich, neo-Malthusian and guru-in-chief of the antipregnancy crusaders who stumped the nation in the late 1960's. A thirty-six-year-old professor of biology at Stanford University when his population book came out, Ehrlich had a much more ambitious goal than did Mrs. Sanger. She wanted to help families. He was going to save the world.

When you examine the men and women most active in the population explosion mania, a curious pattern emerges. With few exceptions, they were wildlife-oriented. Their study specialties tended to involve animals and insects and plants, rather than human beings.

Ehrlich fit the mold in every respect. His first love had been insects. During his undergraduate years at the University of Pennsylvania, he had spent two summers as a field officer for a major national insect survey. After receiving a master's degree and a doctorate from the University of Kansas, he joined the Kansas faculty as an instructor in entomology. In 1959, he moved to the Entomology Department at Stanford, where he focused on butterflies. In 1961, he co-authored a book called *How to Know the Butterflies*, and he devoted several years to a study of the reproductive biology of butterflies and selective changes involving butterflies.

It was during those years of exploring the California countryside with a butterfly net that Ehrlich began developing his theories about people. There were too many of them, he decided. Not enough butterflies perhaps, but definitely too many people.

At about the same time, other nature lovers were coming to the same conclusion. There were the Paddocks, William and Paul, who in 1967 wrote a book called *Famine—1975!*, which gave mankind two years less to live than Ehrlich did. And even before the Paddocks, there were the Days, Lincoln and Alice, with a book called *Too Many Americans*, and anyone who thinks you can't tell a book by its cover hasn't read *Too Many Americans*.

While none of the population fighters could muster the following of Ehrlich, they contributed to the general feeling of uneasiness that made *The Population Bomb* not only a best seller but a call to action as well.

In the winter of 1968, a group of Ehrlich fans met in New Haven, Connecticut, and together with Ehrlich himself, formed an organization whose chief purpose was to make it unnecessary for our descendants to live in a 2,000-story building with 60 million billion fellow tenants.

Among the founders of this curb-the-people wing of the Disaster Lobby were Lincoln Day, who was still in search of just the right number of Americans, and Richard Bowers, an Old Mystic, Connecticut, attorney. Ehrlich, to the surprise of hardly anyone, was named president.

For its name, the organization chose the phrase Zero Population Growth—an invention of Kingsley Davis, a University of California demographer who favored the concept.

From an initial membership of some 700—most of them residents of California—Zero Population Growth quickly grew to six-figure size as chapters sprang up on college campuses across the country.

Undoubtedly the biggest impetus to z.p.g. was Ehrlich's 1970 appearance on the Johnny Carson late-evening network television show. An attractive young man with just the right mixture of wry humor and hair-raising statistics, Ehrlich thoroughly captivated a large segment of the Carson audience. So popular was his performance that he was invited back several times.

This would be as good a place as any to pay tribute to television as a critical factor in Disaster Lobbying and as a primary moving force behind the Lobbyists. For to be effective, a prophet of doom requires big audiences and a widespread acceptance of his way-out notions. The key words here are "big" and "widespread." Throughout history, there have been legions of men and women who insisted that calamity was just around the corner or that butterflies were more desirable than human beings. There was no way, however, for them to get their ideas across to large enough groups of their fellow citizens. The best they could do was to put on white sheets and stand in the marketplace waving crudely lettered signs. But how many adherents can you turn on that way? Then along came television, and the problem was solved. Suddenly, the world-is-coming-to-an-end folks could reach tens of millions of people in a single evening.

The effects of Ehrlich's TV presentations were phenomenal. Sales of his book skyrocketed, and throughout America there sprang up clusters of earnest and eager converts who began advocating everything from the elimination of tax exemptions for parents to the sterilization of anyone fathering or mothering more than two offspring.

For obvious reasons, most antipregnancy activists became members of Zero Population Growth, giving that organization tremendous political clout in Washington and in many state capitals. Backed by financial contributions from its swelling membership roster, Z.P.G. set up an office several blocks from the United States Capitol and furnished it with four full-time paid lobbyists, which are three more than are maintained by the average multi-billion-dollar corporation. An additional staff of eighteen salaried workers was laid on and distributed through installations in other cities.

But the influence of Zero Population Growth should not be assessed solely on the basis of what twenty-two employes could accomplish. The real damage was being inflicted by thousands of hard-working, long-suffering, amateur fanatics who spent most of their spare time in the late 1960's and early 1970's preaching the gospel of childlessness. It was like some gigantic infertility rite, with the postulants flaunting such symbols of their cult as birth control pills, mechanical contraceptives, lapel buttons with the numeral 2 (for no more than two children per family) and bumper stickers carrying typical cutesy-pie bumper sticker legends, like "Stop Heir Pollution" and "Every Litter Hurts a Bit" and "Overpopulation Begins at Home."

Zero Population Growth also began publishing a monthly called *National Reporter* and distributing it wherever people gathered—in places like state fair grounds and ballparks. In the autumn of 1971, according to a report in *Saturday Review*, sunbathers at Miami Beach were startled to see flying overhead an airplane from which trailed a sign stating "People Pollution Is a Drag—Z.P.G."

A favorite pastime of some Disaster Lobbyists was the badgering of advertisers—especially those advertisers who, in the opinion of the pressure groups, had violated one or more of their sacred principles. Such a campaign was mounted early on by Z.P.G., and one of its first targets, said a report in the March 11, 1972, *Saturday Review*, was an apparel manufacturer named Spunlo-Eiderlon. The crime of Spunlo-Eiderlon was its publication in a women's magazine of an advertisement showing a mother and her six children, all tastefully attired in Eiderlon panties. Stanley F. Gross, president of the company, soon received 7,500 letters, most of them containing the same words and phrases and all of them informing Gross that six children in one family were four children too many.

The manufacturer got the message. "Next year," he told an interviewer, "we are going to run an ad with just one kid."

Tenacity like this rarely goes unrewarded, and the anti-population movement has been spectacularly successful in attracting both broad-based public support and an impressive covey of prominent torchbearers. At last count, thirty-seven United States Senators were listed as sponsors of a Z.P.G.-endorsed resolution advocating a stabilized population in this country.

Meanwhile, still other organizations with similar goals

have sprung up to add their two-children's worth to the general babble. There is the Coalition for a National Population Policy, fronted by Milton Eisenhower, brother of the late President and former president of Johns Hopkins, in partnership with Joseph Tydings, former United States Senator from Maryland. And there are the Association for Voluntary Sterilization, the Commission on Population Growth and the American Future, the Population Crisis Committee, Planned Parenthood-World Population and so many others that the movement would appear to have its own overpopulation crisis.

And these groups established specifically to cope with overpopulation are only the tip of the organizational iceberg. Below the surface are literally hundreds of associations with other specific irons in the fire but with a willingness to lend a hand to any cause with a high enough publicity quotient.

Most outspoken on behalf of the ban-the-people movement have been the Sierra Club, Friends of the Earth, the Wilderness Society, the National Audubon Society, the National Wildlife Federation and the Izaak Walton League of America. Each is dedicated to the preservation and enhancement of some aspect of nature: trees, flowers, fish, birds, wild animals. This is not a happenstance. At the very heart of the population bomb crusade is the belief, rooted deep in the souls of so many nature-lovers, that trees and flowers and animals are more desirable than people and that one thing wrong with the world is an overabundance of homo sapiens and a paucity of flora and fauna.

If they had their druthers, the population of the United States might well consist of forty-seven human beings and two hundred million whooping cranes, instead of the other way around.

Also firmly allied with the population cutback lobby are large chunks of the academic community. Most Z.P.G. chapters were founded on college campuses and it is in the Groves of Academe where the movement attains its lushest growth. At the Massachusetts Institute of Technology, for example. In 1970, a team of seventeen scientists and graduate students from six nations convened at M.I.T. to analyze the effects of a runaway population. They met there under a grant from the Club of Rome, an international think tank operation financed by the Volkswagen Foundation.

After feeding some irrelevant statistics into a computer and harvesting some even less relevant output data, the conferees at M.I.T. went into an eighteen-month huddle and then brought forth one of the most highly publicized mice in history: a mournful tome entitled *The Limits to Growth*, which, in brief, takes the by now familiar position that, unless mankind stops reproducing himself with such abandon, he is doomeddoomeddoomed.

The book was brought out with a great deal of the Madison Avenue hoopla that M.I.T. deep-thinkers customarily deplore. Centerpiece for the book's debut was a lavish ceremony in Washington's Smithsonian Institution. Guests of honor included then Secretary of Health, Education and Welfare Elliot L. Richardson, whose title required him to be present, and several other dignitaries who had no such excuse. Among them were former Chief Justice Earl Warren, former Associate Justice Arthur Goldberg and former Interior Secretary Stewart Udall.

It can be assumed that all of the chatter about 60 million billion people and 100 persons per square yard and 2,000-story apartment buildings and massive famines and corroboration by M.I.T. computers tended to cause a certain amount of anxiety among the millions of Americans who, while not Disaster Lobbyists themselves, happen to be unusually receptive to the rhetoric of Disaster Lobbyists. Such an American was Lee Loevinger, a former member of the Federal Communications Commission. At a 1970 meeting of the American Association of Advertising Agencies, Loevinger took part in a panel discussion on the long-range outlook for mankind and devoted his remarks to a lengthy recitation of ills and woes. High on the roster of impending catastrophes, intoned Loevinger, was the threat of runaway overpopulation. "At present rates of increase," he said, "world population will be seven billion by the year 2000."

A few alert members of his audience were somewhat taken aback when, in almost the very next breath, he made this statement: "Responsible scientific opinion holds that, unless present trends are not merely halted but reversed, there will be not more than 35 to 100 more years to the end of all human life on earth."

In other words, Loevinger was predicting a doubling of world population and the extinction of mankind, both to occur roughly at the same time.

And so it went among the savants of the Age of Unreason.

Which brings us to a brace of pertinent questions. With so many prominent Americans spending so much of their time and effort alerting their fellow citizens to the dangers of excessive procreation, shouldn't we all be as worried as they seem to be? Isn't there a very real threat of overpopulation? After all, those statistics they toss out seem to be genuine and, if they are, so does the peril.

But therein lies the rub. Those statistics. And, more than the statistics, the interpretations engendered by them.

Take our worried friend, Thomas Malthus. His statistics were immaculate. He had positive proof that the world's population was increasing at a much faster rate than the world's food supply. And it is axiomatic that when populations grow faster than food supplies, people starve.

So many people believed Malthus, and they couldn't understand it when the famines failed to show up on schedule. Why didn't they show up? Because Malthus had fallen into one of the oldest traps in the prognostication game. *He had failed to allow for change.* It was that simple. He had assumed that because food output in the past had increased at a rate of, let us say, 2 percent per year it would always continue to do so.

And then, a few short years after his essay was written, along came the Industrial Revolution. And with it and in its wake came the reaper. And the thresher. And the combine. And the motorized tractor. And new strains of wheat. And hybrid corn. And powerful pesticides. And chemical fertilizers. And suddenly food supplies were growing at a rate of 3 percent a year. And 4 percent. And 5 percent. And food became so plentiful that farmers in the United States were being paid *not* to grow crops, and millions of bushels of unwanted grain were rotting in silos across the land.

Indeed, so vast is mankind's technological potential for producing food that, in a 1971 article in *Saturday Review,* Harrison Brown, a professor of geochemistry at Caltech, estimated that "there should be little difficulty in feeding a world population of a hundred billion persons"— or roughly thirty times as many as there now are.

The failure of overpopulation theorists to make allowances for trend shifts or future advances in science and technology drew a well-aimed barb from Norman Macrae, Deputy Editor of *The Economist.* In a scathing review of *The Limits to Growth,* Macrae observed that "by extrapolating present trends and yet assuming no change in technology it would have been possible in every human lifetime to prophesy some such ineluctable disaster." He cited as a hypothetical case in point the ability of an Englishman in the horse-and-carriage 1880's to prove beyond any reasonable doubt that the cities of the 1970's would be buried under mountains of horse manure.

And it was the horse manure syndrome that so transparently motivated the m.i.t. study group. It inserted reams of 1970-type nuclear waste statistics into a computer and came up with the prediction that by the year 2000 nuclear wastes would exceed 1,000 billion curies—a staggeringly lethal amount by any standards. What these latter-day Cassandras neglected to do was entertain the very excellent probability that new methods will soon be discovered for disposing of nuclear wastes, that nuclear energy itself will ultimately be superseded by something else and that by the year 2000 nuclear wastes will in all likelihood be as scarce an item as horse manure in 1970.

In another critique of the m.i.t. group's efforts, Yale University economist Henry Wallich declared: "I get some solace from the fact that these scares have happened many times before. This is Malthus again."

Of course, it *was* Malthus again, the only difference being that Malthus had no Johnny Carson show or three-ring circus at the Smithsonian to give his views overnight notoriety.

But failure to anticipate progress was only one of the fundamental errors committed by Malthus and by the neo-Malthusians of the Disaster Lobby. They also were guilty of extending past growth curves to make future growth projections.

Thus, in *The Population Bomb*, Ehrlich writes: "It has been estimated that the human population of 6000 B.C. was about five million people, taking perhaps one million years to get there from two and a half million. The population did not reach 500 million until almost 8000 years later—about 1650 A.D. This means it doubled roughly once every thousand years or so. It reached a billion people around 1850, doubling in some 200 years. It took only eighty years or so for the next doubling, as the population reached two billion around 1930. We have not yet completed the next doubling to four billion, but we now have well over three billion people. The doubling time at present seems to be about thirty-seven years. Quite a reduction in doubling times: 1,000,000 years, 1,000 years, 200 years, 80 years, 37 years."

Well, it doesn't take much of an inference—at least not for someone as inference-prone as Ehrlich—to assume from all of this that populations will continue to double at even shorter intervals until suddenly, about 900 years from now, our descendants are going to wake up some morning and find themselves signing leases for that 2,000-story apartment building.

Absurd? Of course. Yet thousands of otherwise rational Americans went for it. They bought the Ehrlich premise that because populations increased at such and such a rate in the past, they will obviously increase at the same rate in the future. That's like the not too bright mother who after observing that her infant son had doubled his weight in his first six months assumed that he would keep on doubling his weight every six months thereafter and would, at the age of ten, weigh seven million, eight hundred and sixty-four thousand, three hundred and twenty pounds, give or take a couple of ounces.

It is also similar to the kind of kindergarten calculation that promoted the Sunday supplement writers of the 1930's to warn about melting ice caps and gallivanting glaciers. They conveniently ignored the fact that average annual temperatures can stop rising and start falling (which is precisely what happened) and that glaciers do not necessarily go on forever.

In the area of population growth, the truth is—and it is a truth so obvious as to make the mind boggle at the naivete of the Disaster Lobby and its disciples—that the various factors causing populations to double so rapidly in the recent past are no longer operative. And conversely, all of today's pressure thrusts—every last one of them, from economic conditions to health considerations to moral values —are militating toward less and less population growth.

In the past, for example, vast sections of the world were peopled by men and women who knew nothing about birth control, who had no access to contraceptives and who therefore had large families out of sheer ignorance and poverty. This is no longer the case. Birth control information and devices are spreading rapidly into the most remote regions, as is a growing acceptance of abortion.

Also in the past, large numbers of children were regarded as family assets because most societies were agrarian and while food and living space were plentiful labor was not. The more kids you had in those days, the more land you could farm and the wealthier you became. Today, with the shift to urbanization, children have become liabilities. The more children you have in a big city, the more money you spend—for food, for housing, for clothes. And child labor is a virtually unsaleable commodity.

So the pressures for population increase have dissipated.

Furthermore, the planet Earth is not nearly so crowded as the population bogeymen would have their audiences believe. Actually, it is so sparsely settled that you could put

every last Earthling—all three and a half billion of them—
into the tiny state of Rhode Island. And each person would
have ten square feet of land to stand on.

In the United States itself, there are roughly thirty-seven
acres of land for every American family.

Admittedly, our distribution of people is not ideal. Americans have a tendency to clump together in certain places,
thus precipitating what might be called elective over-
crowding. But all one has to do is fly over sections of the
American West—or even the pine barrens of New Jersey,
a scant eighty miles from the heart of New York City and
even less from Philadelphia—to find the kind of *lebensraum*
that might have appeased even an Adolf Hitler.

Another preposterous notion of the antipeople people is
that world population will go on increasing year after year,
century after century, until one day there will be too many
people. It should be apparent to the meanest intellect that
long before that happened steps would have been taken to
abort the trend. With typical Disaster Lobby logic, the Ehrlichites demand that such steps be taken immediately, even
though there is not yet any need for them, which is like
asking someone to amputate a perfectly healthy finger on
the ground it might someday become infected.

Yale's Henry Wallich put it this way in his review of the
M.I.T. book: "To stop growing now, generations before the
real problems of growth arise, if ever, would be to commit
suicide for fear of remote death."

But the most cogent argument that can be mustered
against the dire predictions of the population bomb theorists
is that the world already *has* stopped growing—at least at
the old clip. According to figures supplied by the World
Health Organization, the birthrate in every major country
on earth is substantially lower today than it was fifty years
ago.

In the United States, the current birthrate of about
seventeen per thousand population is the lowest in history
and is only one-third of what it was before the Civil War.

And while our birthrate keeps dropping, our death rate has leveled off. It was 9.5 per thousand in 1950 and it is 9.5 today.

Obviously, with the United States birthrate falling and the death rate holding fast, the inevitable result must be a slackening of growth. It is, in fact, difficult to resist pulling off an Ehrlich-type projection in which you extend the latest birthrate and death rate curves far into the future. What you would arrive at is a point at which there will be absolutely nobody left in the entire country. Not zero population *growth*. Zero *population,* period.

Throughout much of Continental Europe, officials have watched the United States population scare with limitless astonishment. The reason? European birthrates have fallen even more precipitously than ours, generating acute fears of *under*population.

In March of 1971, for example, Stefan Cardinal Wyszynski, the Polish primate, announced from Warsaw that Poland's birthrate was dropping so rapidly that "our very existence as a nation is in danger."

According to official estimates, the population of Poland will remain fairly stable until 1977, at which point it will begin to decline at an average of 200,000 to 250,000 a year. (It will be remembered that 1977 is also the year in which Paul Ehrlich's overpopulation famines are scheduled to get under way.)

During the past several years, similar reports of dwindling birthrates and net losses in population started filtering out of other European capitals. An Associated Press dispatch from Paris in December of 1971 alluded to worries about underpopulation in France and added that "births are not keeping up with deaths in West Germany, Sweden, Denmark, Finland, Portugal, Czechoslovakia and Hungary."

At the same time, French Labor Minister Joseph Fontanent issued an urgent appeal to his fellow citizens to start having more children. He noted that the number of economically active people in France had remained at about 20.5 million *since 1900* and that without an increase of 600,000 in the number of foreigners in France since the turn of the century the active population would actually have declined.

The birth slump phenomenon is not confined to the United States and Europe by any means. In 1971, Japanese officials voiced concern about the drop in birthrates there. If the rate now in effect remains constant and does not decrease any further, the population of Japan—now 103 million—will climb to only 136 million by 2027. That's a gain of just 35 percent in fifty-five years, and small as it is, it is predicated on a reversal of the long-term trend toward fewer and fewer Japanese pregnancies.

While the news media as a whole ignored the telltale signs of an onrushing population bust throughout the 1960's, preferring to devote their space and time to the hellfire warnings of the Ehrlichites, the facts ultimately became too numerous and too obvious to bury.

On April 4, 1971, *The New York Times* exploded the rumor about runaway procreation in mainland China. (The population explosion people had started to concede that perhaps the situation *was* under control in Europe and North America, but they insisted that nothing had changed in such backward nations as India and China.) In a dispatch from China, the *Times* correspondent noted the widespread use there of all methods of contraception, including birth control pills and vasectomies. As a result, he said, "the birthrate and population growth rate are dropping appreciably."

Then in the summer and fall of 1971, the headlines began cropping up. The following were gleaned from the *Times* over a period of less than six months:

"Birth Rate Declines Here"

"Falling Birth Rate"

"Population Growth Rate in U.S. Found Sharply Off"

"Population Increase Second Smallest in Nation's History"

"New Census Study Projects Decline in Rate of Births"

"Fertility Rate Plummets"

"Birth Rates Found in a Sharp Decline Among Poor Women"

Other publications awoke at about the same time.

"Census Bureau Startled by Dip in '71 Birth Rate," said the *New York Post*.

"Large Families Lose Favor in Sharp Decline from '67," said the *Baltimore Sun*.

"Fewer Children for U.S. Women," said *U.S. News & World Report*.

"Prepare for Slower Growth," *Marketing/Communications*, an advertising trade paper, advised its business community readers.

A fairly complete summary of these developments appeared in a front-page article in *The New York Times* of February 16, 1972. Datelined Washington, D.C., it began with the statement that due to a major decrease in the number of anticipated pregnancies, "the nation is fast approaching zero population growth among younger women."

The *Times* continued:

"The average number of children expected by wives aged 18 to 24 dropped from 2.9 to 2.4 in that period [1967 to 1971], a Census Bureau report said. Applied to all women in that age group, married or not, this might well mean a fertility rate of 2.2 children."

The newspaper noted that 2.1 was generally regarded as the replacement rate—the level at which births balanced deaths and therefore the level of zero growth. In other words, the new fertility rate was just a razor's edge above the point where our population would begin to decline, as it has in parts of Europe.

The *Times* story went on to say that if the fertility rate remained at the level reported by the Census Bureau "that will mean 25 million fewer Americans by the year 2000 than there would otherwise be. The total population then would be about 280 million."

This would be from 20 to 25 million fewer Americans than had been predicted by responsible demographers—and 50 million fewer than the alarmist estimates circulated by Zero Population Growth.

But even the 280 million estimate was soon revealed to

be on the high side. On September 24, 1972, the *Times* published another front-page story on population, this one reporting a Census Bureau announcement that the nation's fertility rate had already declined to the replacement figure of 2.1 children per women of child-bearing age. Said the *Times*: "For the first time, fertility in the United States has dropped to the replacement level—the threshold of zero population growth."

Then on December 5, 1972, the *Times*, citing Federal statistics, added the clincher. "Nation's Births Show Drop Below Zero-Growth Level," said the newspaper's front-page headline. The story revealed that the fertility rate was now down to 2.08, or .02 below the point at which replacement occurs.

A fertility rate that low would indicate a United States population for the year 2000 of from 250 million to 260 million. The lower figure was cited in a major 1971 study commissioned by *Family Circle* magazine at the suggestion of the National Association of Food Chains, whose members have an understandable interest in knowing how many people will be around in the years ahead. Conducting the study was Ben J. Wattenberg, a prominent demographer and co-author of two books on American population trends. In commenting on the findings, he said, "It would be wise to start considering that the [U.S. population] figure [for the year 2000] may be as low as 250 million."

The Wattenberg report, titled *The Demography of the 1970's: The Birth Dearth and What It Means*, begins with this noteworthy statement:

"With no fanfare, in late August of 1971, a highly significant set of government statistics was routinely made public. The data concerned the U.S. birth rate for the first six months of the year, and although the numbers were still officially categorized as 'provisional', it was odd that they attracted such scant attention. For the statistics showed something quite remarkable. The birth rate had dropped, during the first half of the year, to the lowest level in all

American history—to a level 10 per cent lower than the years of the depression."

He went on to observe that the fertility rate was now "just barely" above the replacement rate of 2.11 children per family (the Census Bureau had not yet reported the 2.08 rate) . . . that "there are indications there will be still fewer babies in the years to come" . . . that "we may very soon see fertility rates in America at levels well below replacement" . . . that "in the judgment of this author the gloom-and-doom rhetoric about population that is dispensed by the ecological crisis-mongers is exaggerated and sometimes hysterical" . . . and finally, and unequivocally, that "there will not be as many more people as we've been led to believe."

Wattenberg is to be commended for his painstaking research and his perceptive—and refreshingly rational—conclusions. However, he exhibited a trace of naivete when he described as "odd" the fact that the low birthrate figures attracted little attention. He should have realized that we were still in the Age of Unreason, and what is odd in normal times is perfectly normal in odd times.

EIGHT **The Pot Stirrers**

On the afternoon of July 5, 1972, William McMahon, the Prime Minister of Australia, did something he had never done before. He issued a public statement denouncing a visitor from the United States. The target of the Prime Minister's wrath was the American consumer advocate Ralph Nader, who had arrived in Australia the previous day and who, shortly after checking out his luggage at the airport, lodged a formal complaint about the Australian automobile safety laws, which he said were outdated, and its libel laws, which he attacked as being inhibitive of criticism.

Considering the provocation, Prime Minister McMahon's comments were quite mild. He described Ralph Nader as "a professional and paid pot stirrer," the term "pot stirrer" being Down Underese for troublemaker, and he went on to inventory some of Nader's more outstanding defects.

"He," said the Prime Minister, "has been in Australia 24 hours and set himself up as a judge of Australia without a proper knowledge of the country and its people. Nader will be paid normal courtesies as a visitor but an Australian who went to America and made the same criticisms would not be well received."

There, the Prime Minister was incorrect. During the 1960's and early 1970's extremist Americans would—and frequently did—welcome with open arms, public adulation and huge monetary offerings from anyone who cast aspersions on the United States, and the more bitter the aspersions the warmer the welcome. If in the early 1970's a kangaroo had arrived in Los Angeles from Brisbane carrying in its pouch an indictment of the American free enterprise system, it might well have been acclaimed by the Disaster Lobbyists as a fresh new voice in consumer advocacy. For this was the time of the pot stirrers, and it didn't matter who—or what—stirred the pot as long as the ingredients got a fearful shaking up.

As national pot-stirrer-in-chief, Ralph Nader had made a career, and a reputed annual income of close to a quarter of a million dollars, out of condemning most of the major public and private institutions in the United States. His charges were often based on even flimsier evidence than the scraps he had picked up in Australia, but, unlike Prime Minister McMahon, many Americans were too beguiled, too intimidated or too prejudiced in his favor to object to what he was doing.

Indeed, the entire consumerism movement in America, which could be said to have begun with the publication in 1965 of Nader's philippic against the automobile industry, *Unsafe at Any Speed,* was predicated on the willingness of many of America's thought leaders and communications media to accept and pass along to the public the most outrageous, the most preposterous and the most baseless charges against industry in general and specific companies in particular.

It was all part of the Disaster Lobby philosophy that permeated the period. America's free enterprise system had to a great degree tamed nature, had converted a wilderness into a land of comfort and luxury and had given mankind the highest standard of living the world had ever known, so the free enterprise system was obviously evil and had to be replaced.

Thus the stage was set and the critics all waiting to applaud when, in 1965, a tall, lean, dark, stern-jawed and piercing-eyed young man strode into the limelight with a book that, on the surface, appeared to be an accusation aimed at the manufacturers of motorcars but in fact was a denigration of the entire free enterprise system and of Twentieth Century man himself.

Ralph Nader, the apotheosis of consumerism in the United States, was born February 27, 1934, in Winsted, Connecticut, a small town about twenty miles northwest of Hartford. He was the son of Lebanese immigrants who had a deep regard for the value of an education, and from his first days in school, Ralph Nader was a brilliant student. In 1955, he was graduated magna cum laude from Princeton University, where he had easily made Phi Beta Kappa, and three years later he received a law degree from Harvard. Admitted to the Connecticut bar in 1958, he practiced law in Hartford for several years and moonlighted occasionally as an instructor in history at the University of Hartford.

It was during these years that he became interested in the subject of automobile safety—a subject that was to launch him into a brand-new career and the Disaster Lobbyists into still another manifestation of rampant illogic.

In the preface to *Unsafe at Any Speed*, Ralph Nader made two points eminently clear. He had little fondness for the makers of automobiles and he had no fondness at all for the kind of careful research and balanced reporting that are the *sine qua non* of a worthwhile exposé.

"For over half a century," begins the preface, "the automobile has brought death, injury, and the most inestimable sorrow and deprivation to millions of people. With Medea-like intensity, this mass trauma began rising sharply four years ago, reflecting new and unexpected ravages by the motor vehicle."

Nader ended the preface with these words: "The time has not come to discipline the automobile for safety; that time came over four decades ago. But that is not cause to delay any longer what should have been accomplished in the nineteen twenties."

What the author obviously wanted his readers to believe was that the automobile, and particularly the American-made automobile, was not only "unsafe at any speed" but was becoming less and less safe all the time. The text of the book carried out this implication by citing highway accident reports involving equipment failure. Singled out for special condemnation was the Chevrolet Corvair, a compact model that had been introduced in 1959. According to Nader, these cars had an extraordinary tendency to roll over when put into a sharp turn.

The fact that none of this was true did nothing to keep *Unsafe at Any Speed* from becoming a runaway best seller and its author from becoming one of the most beloved individuals in the nation's history. The extent of his popularity was revealed in 1971, when the Louis Harris organization conducted a nationwide poll to get a fix on his public image. Of those questioned, 53 percent said Ralph Nader was doing more good than harm, while a minuscule 9 percent said he was doing more harm than good. That is a favorable rating of about six to one, and you would have to go back to George Washington to find an American to equal it.

So substantial was Nader's following by 1972 that Gore Vidal, the ultraliberal author and sometime straight man for William F. Buckley, Jr., wrote a magazine article suggesting that Nader be nominated for the presidency of the United States. The article, for some reason, infuriated Nader, as he later told a magazine interviewer. Perhaps he realized that the only thing that could topple him from his pedestal would be an endorsement from Gore Vidal.

Another admirer of Ralph Nader was Dr. George Wald, the Harvard professor who knew so much about biology that he won a Nobel Prize and so little about politics that he embraced much of the anti-Establishment philosophy espoused by the likes of Abbie Hoffman and Jerry Rubin. In his introduction of Nader when the young consumerist won the Max Berg Award "for a major achievement in prolonging or improving the quality of human life," Wald stated, with more emotional involvement than scientific detachment, that "by the time Ralph Nader is through he will have prolonged more lives and improved the quality of life more than all the other award winners put together."

While *Unsafe at Any Speed* had a great deal going for it to begin with—much of the reading public of the United States was unable in 1965 to resist anything that simultaneously condemned big business and the easy, motorized life —it got added sales impetus from two events that occurred shortly after its publication.

One of these was the series of United States Senate hearings on automobile safety, held in 1966 and chaired by Senator Abraham Ribicoff of Nader's home state of Connecticut. Senator Ribicoff, astute enough to recognize headline material when he saw it and himself an outspoken critic of big business, invited Nader to testify. And Nader testified.

The news media covering the hearings provided the publicity Nader and Senator Ribicoff had desired. As *Saturday Review* was to note years later, "he [Nader] was perceived by reporters to be what in fact he is: the enemy of their enemies."

At about the same time, Nader created his own publicity by filing a multidigit invasion of privacy suit against General Motors. Actually, General Motors had been asking for it. Ever since Nader began nosing around its Detroit headquarters in the early 1960's to get material for his book, General Motors had been trying to dig up something damaging about Nader that it could use to discredit him when his book ultimately appeared. It hired private detectives to do the digging, and they were about as discreet as Attila the Hun. They were also unsuccessful. There simply wasn't anything damaging to be found about a man who works eighty hours a week, avoids the company of women, eschews alcoholic beverages, doesn't gamble and, while earning hundreds of thousands of dollars a year from speaking engagements, keeps only $5,000 of it for living expenses and uses the rest to finance what he and the general public regard as worthwhile, humanitarian projects.

The private eyes would have had an easier time getting the goods on Albert Schweitzer or the Tooth Fairy.

Unable to pin anything on Nader and caught with its own hand in the cookie jar, General Motors eventually settled the suit out of court by giving the young crusader $280,000, which he promptly and with understandable relish used to continue his investigation into what was wrong with General Motors.

But there was nothing small or parochial about Ralph Nader. General Motors was his first adversary—it was, after all, the biggest company in the nation's biggest industry—but he had no intention of stopping there. His goal was to expose everything he regarded as evil about the productive system in the United States, and he quickly branched out.

In the late 1960's, he fired off heavy barrages against America's coal mine operators, foreign car importers, airlines, tobacco companies and railroads. And whatever he said was reported in the press, along with glowing tributes to the dedication and selflessness of this latter-day St. George.

When anyone dared to criticize Nader for his many obvious shortcomings, the news media either played the story down or omitted it entirely. The consensus was expressed by John D. Morris of *The New York Times,* who said, "I don't want to be associated with any negative stuff about Ralph Nader." And an editor of a major news magazine, who requested anonymity, had a word of caution for his subordinates after one of them wrote an item questioning a piece of Nader research. "We have to watch that kind of stuff," the editor said. "It sets back the cause."

As the Nader snowball grew—favorable publicity in the media produced more and more public support that, in turn, generated more publicity—he began to expand what had begun as a one-man operation. He took on as helpers some of the thousands of eager young men and women who, having picked up in college the anti-Establishment virus, saw in the service of Ralph Nader an opportunity to slay the wicked dragon once and for all.

By the early 1970's, there were 300 of these acolytes almost literally slaving away at the feet of the master, each of them willing to live on an annual salary of not much more than $5,000 for the privilege of being able to advance the cause of consumerism.

The media fell for them too, bestowing on them the catchy title of "Nader's Raiders" and imputing to them all of the virtues of the number one consumerist himself.

Nader welcomed the converts as enthusiastically as would any Messiah. He realized that no one man, not even an eighty-hour-a-week, nongambling, teetotaler, could accomplish by himself all that had to be accomplished to expose the drawbacks of unfettered capitalism. "There's no reason," he said, surveying his small but growing army, "why, in five years' time, I shouldn't have four or five thousand professionals all over the country."

To hasten the day, he organized a covey of Public Interest Research Groups and Public Interest Action Groups on college campuses. To do this, he took advantage of the small-print rules at many colleges that make it possible for a dedicated minority of students to have their pet projects financed by the entire student body. All they have to do is circulate a petition and obtain the signatures of more than 50 percent of the registered students.

The standard procedure was outlined in a flyer bearing an introduction by Ralph Nader and distributed in the spring of 1971 at Indiana University.

"A majority of students on a campus can petition the student senate or the Board of Regents or Trustees to increase activity or incidental fees by a few dollars a year," the flyer pointed out. "This money can then be used to hire a staff of lawyers, scientists and engineers to work full time on behalf of students."

By employing this method, the Oregon Student Public Interest Research Group was able to collect close to $200,000

from fourteen state and private schools in the fall of 1971—
money that could be used to assist Nader's Raiders.

Meanwhile, similar fund-raising campaigns were under
way in Minnesota, West Virginia, Wisconsin, Illinois and
New Jersey. It isn't difficult to see that if this program became nationwide in scope and a trifle deeper in intensity,
it could channel tens of millions of dollars annually into
just the Nader branch of antibusiness activism. And it
could enlist scores of thousands of college students, paid
lawyers and paid scientists in the movement to undermine
the Establishment.

The prospect becomes even more alarming in the light
of an assessment of Nader by Charles McCarry, who spent
a great deal of time studying him in preparation for his
generally sympathetic biography, *Citizen Nader*. In the
book, McCarry says of Nader: "He is a revolutionary in
despair over what he regards as a society on the brink of
shipwreck, animated by a burning sense of righteousness,
endowed with personal magnetism and gripped by the
ruthless love of an idea."

Take that charisma and that drive and add to it an
adoring cadre of followers and a hefty infusion of funds
and you have provided all of the ingredients necessary for
a cataclysmic socioeconomic upheaval, perhaps even a political one.

Nader kept stirring the pot in the early Seventies as he
and his Raiders investigated—and, in due course, blew the
whistle on—some of the largest and most respected companies in America, including E. I. Du Pont de Nemours
and the First National City Bank of New York.

On the surface, all of this activity would appear to be
in the public interest. Here were hundreds of young, earnest
and indisputably honest young men and women devoting
their lives, with no thought of personal gain, to the task
of finding out what was wrong with the methods and
products of American industry and unselfishly passing on
their discoveries to the nation's consumers. Their activities

would appear worthy of a special medal, except for two pertinent facts.

Fact one: Neither Ralph Nader nor any of his Raiders had more than a superficial acquaintance with the highly complex businesses into which they delved. As a result, the information they collected and passed on was frequently wrong.

Fact two: Almost without exception, Nader and his followers entered into each investigation with as rigid a set of preconceived notions and outright biases as anyone has displayed since W. C. Fields looked into the merits of the temperance movement. The Naderites did not trust businessmen, did not understand businessmen and did not believe businessmen should be permitted to conduct their activities without stringent government controls.

Lack of knowledge and lack of objectivity. It would be hard to conceive of two more crippling handicaps for an investigator.

Curiously, even Nader's most ardent admirers inadvertently kept calling attention to his naivete and to the wide and numerous gaps in his mental image of the real world. In *Citizen Nader*, Charles McCarry notes that when making a speech in Cleveland about pollution of Ohio's Cuyahoga River, Nader kept referring to the body of water under discussion as the Kēē-a-hoe-ga. McCarry thought it amusing that Nader had never bothered to find out that the accepted pronunciation was Kī-oh-guh. It apparently never occurred to the biographer that if Nader had done the kind of research such a speech demanded he would have inevitably discovered the correct pronunciation. Obviously, he had not conducted that kind of research. He had not talked to anyone familiar enough with the river to call it by its right name. Yet there he was condemning company after company for polluting it. And there he was demanding the most sweeping reforms.

Elsewhere in the book, McCarry notes that Nader is disenchanted with his fellow Americans because he envisions them as frittering away their time on such useless pursuits as the playing of Mah-Jongg. "Nader," writes McCarry, "may be the last American who believes that Mah-Jongg is a national fad."

Again, there is no astonishment, or even moderate surprise, that the nation's number one consumer advocate knows so little about the nation's consumers that he pictures a substantial number of them playing a game that went out of style at least a quarter of a century ago.

Actually, the tipoff about Nader came—or it should have come—in the book that catapulted him to fame. For in *Unsafe at Any Speed*, Ralph Nader revealed the shallowness of research, the dearth of technical training and the unwillingness to tell both sides of a story that were to characterize virtually all of his efforts in later years and that were to be the hallmarks of much of the consumerism movement.

Unsafe at Any Speed was, at best, an outlandish exaggeration. Its message, as interpreted by reviewers and readers alike, was that the American automobile was a menace to public safety when it first went on the market and that it had become more and more of a menace as the years went by.

The truth lies 180 degrees in the other direction. Actually, the very first American automobiles were remarkably safer than the horse-drawn vehicles they replaced, and the automobiles of the early 1960's, when Nader prepared his book, were about five times as safe, in terms of highway fatalities, as the earliest models.

In other words, contrary to the Nader indictment, the manufacturers of American cars had been making their products safer and safer and safer, year after year after year.

According to the National Safety Council, the most dangerous vehicle ever driven in the United States was that device so beloved by the conservation lobbyists: the horse-and-carriage. It accounted for about ten times as many fatalities per hundred million miles of travel as does the modern automobile.

But it was the Safety Council's comparison between fatality figures for the earliest cars and data for the cars of 1960 that spotlighted the errors in the Nader book. In 1913, when the Council began compiling its figures, the highway death rate per 10,000 registered motor vehicles was 23.8. The rate dropped year by year until 1960, when it reached an all-time low of 5.1.

In 1923, the Safety Council also began recording highway deaths per 100 million travel miles, which is acknowledged by experts to be the most meaningful method of determining trends in safety. During the period of 1923 to 1927, the average number of highway deaths for every 100 million miles traveled was 18.2. From 1928 to 1932, it was 15.6. By 1940, it had dropped to 11.4. It was 7.6 in 1950 and 5.3 in 1960.

Almost incredibly, in view of the fact that there were three times as many vehicles on United States roads in 1960 as there were in 1939 and that they were racking up three times the mileage at much higher speeds, there were actually fewer total highway deaths in 1960 than there were in 1939. Of course, other factors were involved—there had been improvements in road design, traffic signals and driver education—but nevertheless anyone looking at the figures with an open mind could have come to only one conclusion: the automobile manufacturers of the United States had been making their products safer through the years.

Of course, Ralph Nader came to no such conclusion and many beguiled Americans, already conditioned to think the worst of industry and industrialists, did no checking on their own. They took his and the media's word for it and they began hammering at Washington for tougher safety legislation. It was in the wake of this Nader-induced frenzy that automobile seat belts became mandatory, that shoulder harnesses became mandatory, that other so-called "safety innovations" became mandatory and that the motorist, forced to buy these devices even if he had no intention of using them, found his car-purchase sticker prices climbing rapidly.

It has been estimated that the safety features mandated in the 1960's increased the price of the average car by well over $200, and this was in addition to the more than $700 tacked on by the introduction of equipment designed to reduce exhaust emissions.

The National Motor Vehicle Safety Act of 1966 also required automobile manufacturers to recall cars for dealer servicing whenever a possible defect was uncovered. As a result of this legislation, more than 14 million automobiles —14 *million*—were recalled in one year alone: June 1971 to June 1972. The cost, all of which was ultimately borne by car buyers, amounted to hundreds of millions of dollars and in many cases mechanics working on recalled cars could find nothing in need of repair. The manufacturers, however, were powerless to buck the law or the public pressure whipped up by the Naderites.

If all of this monumentally expensive and time-consuming activity produced any material benefits, they might be construed as worthwhile. As the Disaster Lobby people loved to say, if only one life is saved, it's worth all the trouble and expense.

(This, incidentally, was one of the more moronic sayings of the period. Obviously, the saving of one life was not then and never had been worth an infinite amount of time or money. Human beings have always subconsciously put a price tag on their own lives, concluding that some risks are worth taking. And it is fortunate they do, for without such a rationale, there could be no progress. If people regarded the saving of a single life as being more important than the saving of trillions of hours of travel time for billions of people, man would still be walking instead of riding, and the richness of Twentieth Century life, with its fabulous mobility, would be merely a wistful dream. For it must be transparently clear that you could eliminate *all* traffic fatalities by the simple expedient of eliminating all traffic. Indeed, you could do away with accidental deaths of every type by locking people up in padded rooms and feeding them through pneumatic tubes. It may be that the Nader folks favored such an extreme measure—much of what they did leaned in that direction—but something must have told them that the public would not cotton to being penned up, even to avoid the possibility of being run over by some Detroit-made juggernaut. The American public had its eccentricities, but they did not include the acceptance of that hogwash about one life being worth *any* expense or *any* inconvenience.)

Actually, with regard to Ralph Nader and his automobile book, the entire matter is more or less academic. It is academic because the Nader program—with its seat belts, its shoulder harnesses, its massive callbacks—had no apparent effect on highway fatalities. In fact, it seemed to have a negative effect. To the astonishment of the consumerists, the 1960's became the first decade in automobile history in which there was no decrease in the number of highway deaths per 100 million miles traveled. And it was the first decade in which there was an actual increase in fatalities per 10,000 registered vehicles.

The travel-mile figure was 5.3 in 1960 and it was still 5.3 in 1969. The rate per 10,000 vehicles was 5.1 in 1960 and 5.3 in 1969. The number of actual deaths soared from 38,000 in 1960 to 56,000 in 1969.

Between 1969 and 1971, the death toll did drop slightly— fatalities were down from 56,000 to 54,700—and some Nader fans attributed the decrease to the effects of government-mandated safety devices. What they overlooked was the fact that such declines had been commonplace long before the onset of Naderism. In the twenty-three years between 1937 and 1960, there were ten years in which the number of highway fatalities dropped. And in five of those years, the decrease was larger than the one registered between 1969 and 1971. From 1957 to 1958, for example, the number of highway deaths fell by more than 1,800.

In any case, the credit claiming was short-lived. By 1972, the highway death toll had climbed to an all-time high of 57,000.

Since the authors of this book know fully as little about

automobile safety as Ralph Nader apparently did when he wrote his book, they would not presume to offer their own opinion as to why the traffic fatality picture failed to improve after the introduction of all of those Nader-inspired reforms. There has, however, been speculation among some automotive experts. As they see it, the pattern was changed after Nader arrived on the scene. Prior to that time, trained engineers had been in charge of developing safety devices for automobiles. And the automobiles became safer. With the advent of Nader, there was tremendous public and governmental pressure to adopt his home remedies, and the professionals were sidetracked. Instead of building solid safety into their cars, they began tacking on all of the frills and flourishes suggested by the amateurs. Result: a bottoming out in the highway fatality curve after almost fifty years of substantial declines.

This was essentially the view of L. B. Bornhauser, described by the trade publication *Automotive News* as "Chrysler Corporation's top quality expert." In December of 1972, Bornhauser, a Chrysler vice president, told a meeting of the American Society for Quality Control that government pressures for impractical product changes and deadlines were inhibiting the industry's efforts to improve the quality of cars.

Unfortunately, Nader refused to reconcile himself to the fact that the design of automobiles should be left in the hands of those who know how to design automobiles. In mid-1972, he was hard at work pushing his campaign for the mandatory installation in all passenger cars of inflatable air bags.

Nader interested himself in air bags when it became obvious that the seat belts and shoulder harnesses were a billion-dollar flop, a billion dollars being a conservative estimate of the amount of money spent on belts and harnesses since they became standard equipment. The idea is to install the bag, deflated, between the driver and the dashboard. When the car hits something, the bag is supposed to inflate rapidly, thus providing a cushion that would keep the driver from hurtling forward into the dashboard, the steering wheel or the windshield.

The key word in the above paragraph is "supposed." In tests, air bags have inflated prematurely, with the impact on the driver of a medicine ball thrown in anger and the sound of a shotgun blast in an echo chamber. The thought of what this kind of mishap would do to the unwary motorist tooling along some turnpike at seventy miles an hour is enough to make a nervous driver turn in his car keys.

In other tests, the bags have inflated on schedule but with sufficient force to rip the head off the dummy used (providentially) in place of a human driver.

Even *The New York Times*, a Nader fan of long standing, admitted that the air bags were, in the summer of 1972, still a long way from being ready for the assembly line.

"Some problems remain to be ironed out," the *Times* said. "The explosive rush of air into the bag makes a loud noise that could damage a passenger's eardrum or so startle a driver as to cause an accident. Some are worried, too, about the effects of an abrupt increase in air pressure in a closed car."

But neither Ralph Nader nor the United States Department of Transportation was concerned about these lethal booby traps referred to euphemistically by the *Times* as "some problems." In March of 1970, the department ordered their installation in all cars produced for the 1974 model year. When the automobile manufacturers pleaded for more time so that they could try to get rid of those "problems" before the problems got rid of the motoring public, the transportation agency agreed to a brief delay.

Nader was reportedly furious. Describing the air bags as "the most important life-saving system in recent automotive history," he demanded that the Department of Transportation rescind its delay edict and restore the 1974 deadline. In view of the weight Nader carries in Washington and since it was he who had pushed the air bags in the first place, there is a good chance he will get what he wants.

Which means there is an equally good chance that motorists in 1974 will be paying an estimated $100 extra for a piece of equipment that could cause as many injuries as it prevents.

It is significant that one of the most outspoken advocates of a delay in installing the bags was Ben Kelley, a vice president of the Insurance Institute for Highway Safety. Referring to the very same devices that received a clean bill of safety from Ralph Nader, the insurance executive stated: "We haven't had nearly enough field tests to determine possible hazardous by-products and take steps to avoid them."

Nader saw nothing wrong in pressing for immediate adoption of a partly-tested, potentially dangerous device because, like many laymen, he lacked the scientist's patience and attention to detail. The case of the Chevrolet Corvair points up this shortcoming, along with the flaws in his research methods and the tremendous amount of harm a man like Nader can do by presenting personal opinion as verified facts.

The Corvair was the primary automotive whipping boy in *Unsafe at Any Speed.* Nader singled it out for special censure, calling attention to what he regarded as its instability and its tendency to roll over when other cars would remain upright. Largely as a result of the Nader charges, Corvair sales began to plummet and the model was discontinued in 1969.

But that did not satisfy Nader. He demanded a government investigation, and in 1970 Washington began what was to be a two-year study of the Corvair. The findings, certified by a panel of three independent engineers, two of them university professors, were released on July 21, 1972. They showed that the 1960-1963 Chevrolet Corvairs, the models specifically criticized by Nader, were as safe as comparable models of other cars sold in the same period.

"The limited accident data available indicate that the rollover rate of the 1960-1963 Corvair is comparable to other light domestic cars," the report stated. "The handling and stability performance of the 1960-1963 Corvair is at least as good as the performance of some contemporary vehicles, both foreign and domestic."

In covering the story, *The New York Times* said, "Extensive tests of a 1963 Corvair and five other compact cars of various makes showed that the Corvair's handling in a sharp turn was no more dangerous than that of the other cars, and did not result in abnormal potential for loss of control."

Although it was Nader who had insisted on the study originally, he now rejected the findings as "a shoddy, internally contradictory whitewash."

General Motors issued a statement declaring that the study "confirms our position on the handling and stability characteristics of these cars."

So General Motors was officially vindicated, but not before it had lost an incalculable amount of money as a direct result of Ralph Nader's broadside. Those who find it impossible to muster any sympathy for an automobile company might instead contemplate the collective suffering of all those workers who lost their jobs when the Corvair was taken off the market.

But while Nader had been able to collect $280,000 from General Motors for having his privacy invaded, the company was in no position to return the favor, even though its losses were far more tangible and infinitely more substantial. You just don't sue the nation's number one consumer advocate, not in the Age of Unreason, you don't.

The attitude at General Motors was one of resigned wistfulness. Its former chairman, James Roche, had expressed the feeling somewhat earlier when, after noting the effects of one of Ralph Nader's more outlandish escapades, he said, "You wonder sometimes if Mr. Nader had come along about 60 or 70 years ago, where the automobile business, or where the United States, might be today."

Indeed, you do wonder. And sometimes, if you have a vivid imagination, you shudder.

But although Ralph Nader had not been born soon enough to block the introduction of the automobile or keep the first airliner from taking off, he did come along in time to create a sizeable portion of latter-day havoc. Among his achievements was the temporary crippling of Hawaii's tourist industry.

At the start of 1971, the State of Hawaii was happily living up to its alliterative designation as "the prosperous paradise of the Pacific." A key factor in that prosperity was the tourist industry, second only to national defense in terms of dollar income. More than 1.5 million persons had visited Hawaii the previous year, and that is double the state's population. On any given day, there were in Hawaii over 38,000 sun-bathing, camera-carrying, money-spending tourists.

Then, in February of 1971, there arrived in Hawaii a twenty-six-year-old member of Nader's Raiders named J. Davitt McAteer. After a whirlwind tour of the islands and a few conversations with some students at the University of Hawaii, McAteer issued a four-page brochure entitled "Facts You Should Know to Appreciate Fully the Aloha State!"

The "facts" that McAteer thought everybody should know about the Aloha State were that the air was polluted, the beaches were overcrowded, the ocean was contaminated with raw sewage and the fields were inundated with pesticides in concentrations ten times greater than on the mainland.

These were the McAteer "facts." The non-quotation-marked facts were that the air over Hawaii is purer than it is almost anywhere else on earth—Honolulu consistently ranks lowest among all major cities in air pollutants as measured by the National Air Pollution Control Administration. The beaches are overcrowded only by comparison with, let us say, Little America. Although some sewage is dumped into the ocean by cities in Hawaii (and, it should be noted, by cities everywhere), the waters in which people bathe are scrupulously monitored. And we have already examined the negligible effects of pesticides.

To make sure that his brochure exerted a maximum

effect, McAteer mailed it out, with Nader funds, to thousands of tourist agencies and airline and steamship offices throughout the United States. He did not destroy Hawaii's tourist industry, but there were enough cancellations of tourist bookings to elicit an outraged blast at McAteer from local civic, business and government leaders, including several Congressmen.

Then, in the fall of 1971, the Nader organization released the results of what, in terms of the paper consumed, must be regarded as one of the most ambitious consumerism projects ever launched. It was a study of the Du Pont company and its relationship to its home state of Delaware. The final Nader report, entitled "The Company State," ran to 850 pages and bore a price tag of $25.

(It is somewhat interesting, if not necessarily productive, to contemplate the reactions of Ralph Nader if some private, profit-making enterpreneur had offered for sale at the price of $25 as shoddy a piece of merchandise as the Nader report on "The Company State.")

According to a series of articles in 1971 issues of *Chemical Week*, Nader's investigation of the giant chemical processing and manufacturing concern began in the summer of 1970, when the consumer advocate dispatched seven of his young Raiders to the company headquarters in Wilmington, Delaware. They ranged in age from twenty-three to twenty-five. Four were graduate students at universities, three of them at Yale and one at the University of Pennsylvania. One was a lawyer. One was an anthropologist. And the seventh was a political scientist.

Not one of the group was old enough to have had any substantial training in corporate business affairs, let alone practical experience. But what they lacked in qualifications, they amply made up in basic attitude. They apparently shared with Ralph Nader the conviction that Du Pont could never have become as big and rich as it was without having done something despicable.

When Du Pont was advised of the imminent arrival of what came to be known as the "Delaware Study Group", it assigned one of its vice presidents, Irving Shapiro, to the job of assisting the seven and acting as liaison between the Naderites and the company. Shapiro was immediately impressed by one salient attribute of the young investigators. They were almost totally devoid of knowledge about the subject they were investigating.

"I don't believe they had any idea of what Du Pont is," he later told a magazine reporter. "I couldn't see any fundamental understanding of how our company, or any large corporation, operates."

The Delaware Study Group lost little time in displaying its naivete. It demanded authorization to examine Du Pont's private records.

"They had the notion," said an astonished Shapiro, "that they could have free access to all of our files, our people and our buildings. We advised them that neither the Attorney General of the United States nor newspaper reporters nor our stockholders were ever treated like that and neither would this group."

Shapiro spent considerable time with the Nader people during the year that followed, and although he came to admire their courteous manners and their obvious dedication, he felt that their sense of clinical detachment left something to be desired.

"The company was presumed guilty until proven innocent," he remarked, "and Nader's group played the role of prosecutor, judge and jury. As the defendant, we never had the chance to see or dispute any of the 'evidence' before it was presented in the report."

In light of the two most outstanding characteristics of the study team—it knew nothing about big business and it had decided in advance that Du Pont was wrong—the final report was pretty much what might be expected. In brief, it concluded that the giant corporation had not been fulfilling its responsibilities as a member of society, and it offered several suggestions for possible remedies, including one that cropped up again and again in Nader analyses of American industry. It recommended that at least three public-interest directors be appointed to the Du Pont board as representatives of all those Americans who are not Du Pont stockholders.

A careful examination of the report reveals the lengths to which the Nader group went to put Du Pont in a bad light. For example, at one point the study team is sharply critical of a member of the Du Pont family for having avoided the payment of inheritance taxes by leaving the bulk of his estate to a charitable foundation. Later on in the study, the company is denounced for its failure to contribute to charity the full 5 percent of net income it is permitted to deduct for tax purposes. "In other words," noted a Du Pont executive, "we were damned if we did and we were damned equally if we didn't."

Shapiro, perhaps repaying the courtesy extended to him by the Nader people, used a good deal of restraint in his critique of their findings. He contented himself with the euphemistic declaration that the report was "loose with the facts." Just how loose it was can be seen in a comparison between the Nader version of certain actions and situations and the actuality, as revealed to newsmen by Du Pont with corroborative evidence.

Nader: Du Pont spends a minuscule amount of money on pollution control. Du Pont: The company spent $207 million on pollution control from 1966 to 1970—far more than any other chemical producer—and will spend $600 million between 1970 and 1975. In 1971, Du Pont devoted to pollution control activities the equivalent of 1,300 employes working full time.

Nader: Du Pont influence has resulted in a tax structure in Delaware favoring the wealthy. Du Pont: Delaware has the highest rate of personal income tax of any state in the nation. Also, Delaware's corporate income tax of 7.2 percent is higher than that of other states, where it averages about 6 percent.

Nader: Du Pont selected a private local organization, the Wilmington Business Opportunity and Economic Development Corporation, as an aid to minority business rather than an organization affiliated with the government. Du Pont: The company did not select the organization. It was chosen by the black community.

Nader: The Du Pont company and family were instrumental in having Highway I-95 routed through the center of Wilmington so as to serve corporate offices. Du Pont: The company did not take part in any discussion of the highway location. There were no corporate contacts in the matter. Furthermore, Highway I-95 had been planned from the outset as following the route it ultimately took; there had never been an alternate route.

While the country's various pot stirrers, including Nader and his Raiders, were scurrying around hurling charges of unethical and irresponsible behavior at businessmen with all of the fervor and accuracy of a Little League pitcher in his first season, their own ethics and responsibility cried out for attention.

There was an advertisement that appeared in the October 31, 1971, issue of *The New York Times* soliciting funds for an organization called Public Citizen, Inc. The full-page ad, signed by Ralph Nader and headlined "Ralph Nader urges you to become a Public Citizen," contained the following copy block:

"Imagine that 25 or 30 years ago citizens concerned about the future quality of life in America had gotten together to do something about it. Suppose they had begun an effective citizen's campaign to make government agencies and industry management sensitive and responsive to the needs of the people . . . Think how much that was already wrong would have been corrected by now. Think how much that has gone wrong since would never have been allowed to happen . . . The air would not be as filled with vile and violent contaminants and the land not ravaged by insensitive corporate and government forces wasting our resources faster than they are replenished . . ."

So here was Ralph Nader saying that our resources were being used up "faster than they are replenished." Yet two days earlier, on October 29, 1971, at a press conference in

Houston, Texas, the same Ralph Nader had told newsmen that the nation's much publicized energy crisis was only a figment of the venal imagination of the gas, oil and coal companies—the purpose being to push prices up—and that "they are finding it [fuel] faster than the public can consume it."

Nader's assessment of our natural resources is curiously elastic. One day, they are so plentiful that we can't keep up with the output. Two days later, to encourage public contributions to his environmental crusade, these same resources are so scarce that we are in grave danger of running out. Will the real Ralph Nader please stand up?

Throughout his career as the self-appointed conscience of American businessmen, Nader has displayed a dual standard: one for businessmen, the other for himself and his fellow pot stirrers. The businessmen must adhere to rigid rules of behavior; the consumerists may wander hither and yon.

There is the example of Nader's membership on the Motor Vehicle Safety Advisory Council. The 22-member Council was established as a branch of the United States Department of Transportation in the National Traffic and Motor Vehicle Safety Act of 1966, its purpose being to advise the Secretary of Transportation in the development of new automobile safety regulations. Because of his avowed interest in highway safety—*Unsafe at Any Speed* had come out the year before the safety law was passed—Nader was appointed to the Council. As a member, he could have made a genuine contribution toward reducing accidents, but he didn't. In fact, he rarely attended any of the Council meetings. Early in 1972, because of his "frequent absences," Ralph Nader was dropped from membership in the government body whose formation he had endorsed and whose existence was due in part to his book. Nader felt it was the duty of *other* citizens to serve on the Safety Advisory Council, but he apparently could not find the time. Any businessman on the Council with Nader's absentee record most certainly would have felt the lash of the consumer advocate's tongue for having failed to measure up to his civic responsibilities.

Another pot stirrer with two sets of standards was Esther

Peterson. When in the 1960's she was serving as a special assistant for consumer affairs in the United States Department of Labor and later when she occupied the position of chairman of President Johnson's Committee on Consumer Interests, Mrs. Peterson was a stern, almost Rhadamanthine arbiter of fairness in advertising. The most innocuous sales message was apt to bring from her office a ringing denunciation of the advertiser in question, his agency and the moral values of marketers who would stretch a point in pursuit of the almighty dollar.

Then in 1972, Mrs. Peterson was hired as an expert on consumer affairs by the Giant supermarket chain. One of her first acts was to prepare an advertisement for Giant carrying her photograph, her signature and the headline, "You have a right to be informed about meat prices," in which Giant stated that it had to raise its retail meat prices because the farm price of meat had "skyrocketed." The ad urged shoppers to buy poultry and fish as substitutes for meat.

When a group of Congressmen from farm states saw the ad in Washington, D.C., newspapers, they applied half a dozen pejorative adjectives to it, ranging from "deceptive" and "untrue" to "fraudulent" and "libelous." At a hearing of the House Agriculture Subcommittee on Livestock and Grains, testimony was introduced to the effect that wholesale meat prices had been declining for eighteen days before publication of the Giant ad, that a major reason for high meat prices was an increased markup by supermarkets and that meat prices were no higher in relation to what they had been ten years earlier than were the prices of other food products.

Mrs. Peterson's answer to the charges leveled by the Congressmen was that she was indeed sorry for any misunderstanding caused by the ad. It was an answer she herself would have sternly rejected during her years as chairman of the Committee on Consumer Interest.

Perhaps the most famous consumerist of them all was Betty Furness, a highly photogenic lady who first became known to the public as a motion picture actress and who subsequently achieved even greater fame by starring in a series of television commercials in which she, among other things, opened and closed the doors on Westinghouse refrigerators. In 1967, President Johnson named her his special assistant for consumer affairs—she was, in effect, a successor to Esther Peterson—and when the President's term expired, Miss Furness was appointed to the post of chairman of the New York State Consumer Protection Board by Governor Nelson Rockefeller.

It was while serving in the latter capacity that she established a new high-water mark for consumerist gobbledegook. She had been speaking at a meeting of the Springfield, Massachusetts, Bank for Cooperatives when, according to the trade publication *Advertising Age*, she announced that manufacturers in their advertisements "must tell not only all they know about a product but also what they don't know." What Miss Furness apparently had failed to take into account was the fact that, aside from consumer advocates, very few people have the ability to talk about what they don't know.

Then there was Bess Myerson, a consumerist who, as a former Miss America, was at least as photogenic as Betty Furness.

As New York City Consumer Affairs Commissioner under Mayor John Lindsay, Miss Myerson spent a good deal of her time appearing on local radio and television programs and telling her audience about the wickedness rampant in the business community. Among her accomplishments was the filing of charges against several New York City banks on the ground that in ads offering free gifts to persons opening new accounts they had put the details of the offer in a type size that Miss Myerson regarded as too small. The banks, not unreasonably, felt a bit miffed because Miss Myerson had never informed them about the size of type she considered to be adequate.

Miss Myerson was also instrumental in the enactment of New York City's Consumer Protection Law that set the rules for the advertising of sales, bargains and discounts. Explained the Commissioner: "The advertising of sales has long been a nether world of recondite terminology with chimerical bargains and illusory discounts." (When it comes to terminology, the Commissioner thus demonstrated that she can be as recondite as the best of them.) Under the new city law, a merchant who advertises a "sale, bargain or discount" must offer a "meaningful" reduction from his usual price. What would be meaningful to Miss Myerson? A saving of at least 5 percent, she told *The New York Times*. Apparently, a discount of 4.9 per cent would be meaning*less*, but *why* it would be meaningless was never explained.

It wasn't often during the Age of Unreason's consumerism outbreak that one of the targets of the outrageous slings and arrows had an opportunity to fire back. The rare chance did come for the president of the Miller-Morton Company of Richmond, Virginia, and it was Bess Myerson's office that set it up.

It began with the publication of an ad for Chap Stick, a product of the Miller-Morton Company. Miss Myerson's staff saw the ad, became suspicious and sent the following letter to Miller-Morton:

"Your advertisement for Chap Stick, which appeared in the February 1971 issue of *Playboy*, stated that 'Nothing soothes and helps heal dry, chapped lips better than Chap Stick Lip Balm.' Would you please send me a copy of the documentation supporting this claim, including the methodology and results of any tests that were employed."

In his prompt and courteous reply, the president of Miller-Morton said he would be delighted to furnish the information requested if the City of New York would send him documentation supporting its own advertising claim that New York is "Fun City." He said he would also like to have from the Federal government some scientific substantiation for its statement, "In God We Trust."

But despite the disarming antics of the Petersons, the Furnesses and the Myersons, there was in the consumerism movement of the 1960's and 1970's a much more serious threat to the nation than at first met the eye. For the chief purpose of the protagonists was not merely to annoy, harass and make life as difficult as possible for American business-men. Apparently their aim was to foster a gradual increase in the number and scope of government regulations affecting private industry until, ultimately, control of industry would shift to government bureaus.

It is indeed ironic that at the very moment Ralph Nader was being praised by many prominent industrialists for, as one put it, "his efforts to help businessmen improve their service to the consumer," Nader was actually hard at work trying to strip them of their managerial prerogatives.

His true feelings emerged one evening in January of 1971 when he addressed an audience of 500 eager would-be consumerists at Rhode Island College in Providence. The Associated Press reported that at the meeting "consumer advocate Ralph Nader . . . proposed that corporations that abuse the public interest should be transferred to public trusteeship and their officers sent to jail."

Since Nader had already accused scores of the country's largest companies of having abused the public interest, there was little doubt about what he wanted. He apparently wanted public trusteeship for American industry. He wanted the government to run the nation's businesses.

While still chairman of General Motors, James Roche delivered a speech in which he identified the major con-sumerism leaders as being part of an "adversary culture" that was misleading the young, the courts and the government.

"They thrive on the sensational accusation and the publicity it gains," said Roche. "They crusade for radical changes in our system of corporate ownership, changes so drastic that they would all but destroy free enterprise as we know it."

Citing specifically one of Ralph Nader's pet projects, that of installing public-interest directors at General Motors, Roche said the Nader philosophy "is antagonistic to our American ideas of private property and individual responsi-bility."

The General Motors executive said the persecution of private industry by Nader and others had "added significantly to the cost of doing business," creating unnecessary expenses that must be passed on to the consumer. "This unjustified harassment—and much of it is unjustified—is a covert danger that we can no longer ignore," he declared.

Roche concluded his remarks with a somber appraisal of the effects of the antibusiness movement. "The cloud of pessimism and distrust which some have cast over free enterprise is impairing the ability of business to meet its basic economic responsibilities, not to mention its capacity to take on new ones," he said.

What Roche neglected to mention—and it's a fascinating element in the case, especially in view of the enthusiastic support Ralph Nader and his followers got from left-wing organizations and pseudointellectuals—is the fact that what the top consumerists were advocating was nothing more or less than plain, old-fashioned, Mussolini-type fascism.

In an article in *The Wall Street Journal* of May 21, 1971, columnist Jeffrey St. John noted that none of the consumerists appeared to be advocating the type of government takeover of industry associated with socialism or communism. What they favored was an industrial system featuring private ownership and government *control*.

"Fascism, unlike socialism, leaves the industrial system in private hands while the state regulates and tightly controls what will be produced and how," wrote St. John. "Mr. Nader's insistence that government's regulatory powers be made stronger and more severe is a further step in that direction."

Nader's plan to force acceptance by General Motors of "constituent" board members who would represent consumers, workers and dealers prompted Henry G. Manne, a law professor at Rochester University, to draw a parallel recalling recent events.

"Only one instance in modern political history is suggested by the constituent director proposal," said Manne. "That was Mussolini's fascist state, in which various social and economic interests in society were represented in the higher echelons of government. I have never heard that scheme called democratic."

The greatest anomaly in the consumerism movement was not, however, the fact that a fascistic scheme was being endorsed by left-wing idealists. It was the fact that the most severely damaged victim of the movement was the consumer himself.

This becomes clearly evident in an examination of the effects of the various Nader campaigns involving the American automobile.

One of his first efforts in this area triggered the introduction of compulsory seat belts and shoulder harnesses in all cars. Since two-thirds of all motorists refuse to wear either belts or harnesses—which is their prerogative since only their own safety is involved—some six million car buyers each year have been spending a total of a quarter of a billion dollars for automotive equipment they never use.

And because most motorists won't buckle up, the Nader people, among others, talked the government into requiring car makers to install warning buzzers, lights and other devices to encourage more use of belts and harnesses. These devices will tack additional tens of millions of dollars onto the consumers' car-purchase outlays.

Meanwhile, antipollution gadgets endorsed by the Nader team have cost motorists billions of dollars for the gadgets themselves, for the additional gasoline they eat up and for increased maintenance. The proposed new antipollution system mandated for 1975 cars will cost even more and will waste an estimated three *billion* dollars' worth of gasoline annually—with each dollar coming from the consumers' pockets.

And then there is the experimental air bag, which Nader is fighting for and which will tack about one billion dollars to the nation's aggregate annual car-purchase expenditure. Again, it is the consumer who will pay.

Nader is also very much interested in requiring manufacturers to make car bumpers heavier and sturdier. If he succeeds in having this equipment made mandatory, American consumers will say good-bye to another billion dollars a year. (Some of this money may, but not all of it, be recouped in lower repair bills.)

On top of all of this, Ralph Nader has petitioned government agencies to outlaw annual model changes for automobiles, thus depriving the consumer of his option to buy an American car with changes or a foreign car without changes. If Nader has his way, the United States motorist will be driving the same basic car, year after year, whether he wants to or not.

So this is what Ralph Nader has done to "help" the American consumer in the automotive market. He has inspired, introduced or endorsed design changes that have cost car buyers billions of dollars for unused equipment and wasted fuel. He has been responsible for the compulsory installation in automobiles of devices that most motorists regard as unnecessary and annoying. He has proposed the abolition of the consumer's right to determine the kind of car he would like to own and drive. And he has done all this without making our highways any safer, according to figures of the National Safety Council.

That this man has been almost universally acclaimed as the champion of the American consumer is an aberration worthy of note even in a period when aberrations were a dime a dozen. Nothing explains better how the Age of Unreason got its name.

NINE **Cleats for the Little Old Lady**

On a triangular plot of land at the confluence of Pennsylvania and Constitution Avenues in downtown Washington, D.C., within four long brassie shots of the Capitol, stands a triangular building that is smallish by Washington standards and that houses the offices and staff of the Federal Trade Commission.

The Commission was established under provisions of the Federal Trade Commission Act of 1914. Its purpose, as provided in the law and as set forth in the *United States Government Manual of 1971/1972,* is "the maintenance of free competitive enterprise as the keystone of the American economic system." It is the responsibility of the FTC, says the *Manual,* "to prevent the free enterprise system from being stifled or fettered by monopoly or corrupted by unfair or deceptive trade practices."

For more than half a century, the Federal Trade Commission quietly but efficiently went about its job of guarding the free enterprise system. It slapped down monopolies whenever they surfaced, and it dealt similarly with unfair or deceptive trade practices.

Then came the Age of Unreason and, swept up by the general hysteria, the Federal Trade Commission abandoned its statutory role as guardian of free enterprise and adopted a brand new posture as censor of advertisements, controller of industrial output and arbiter of the nation's tastes in consumer goods. In the process, it very nearly destroyed the free enterprise system it had been created to protect.

The abrupt about-face was signaled in September of 1970, when Miles W. Kirkpatrick took over as Commission chairman. For years, the nation's Disaster Lobby had been complaining that the FTC wasn't doing enough to control businessmen, and Kirkpatrick decided to accommodate them. He immediately began issuing statements about a new militancy in the Commission's attitude toward errant entrepreneurs. One subordinate quoted him as saying, "The Little Old Lady of Pennsylvania Avenue [the FTC] has taken off her tennis shoes and has put on cleats."

And indeed she had. Unfortunately, the Federal Trade Commission used its cleats to trample not only the rights of businessmen to manufacture and sell their goods but the rights of consumers to buy and enjoy them. Within the brief space of two years, the industrial community was to be reduced to a state of mind-boggling confusion while more and more consumers were to find it impossible to purchase their favorite products in the sizes and shapes and colors that appealed to them.

A concise look at America's free enterprise system is in order at this point. As handed down from Colonial times, the system is predicated on the simple premise that the best way to ensure an optimum distribution of goods and services is to allow businessmen to make and sell whatever the public wants to buy and use, limited by rules outlawing fraud and the sale of anything that could cause injury or death, *but limited only by those rules.*

At the very heart of the system is the belief that it is the prerogative of a free man to do whatever he wishes just so long as what he does interferes in no way with the rights and pursuits of others.

One obvious advantage of free enterprise is that it puts the real power into the hands of the consumer. Whatever he wants, he gets. Whenever he stops wanting it, it goes off the market. It is consumer demand, and consumer demand alone, that determines what is made and sold.

Of course, in some cases, what the consumer wants is not the most efficient or the most nutritious or the most artistically perfect product of its kind. Very often some consumers have a yen for—and businessmen obediently supply—items that are regarded by the leading consumer advocates as wasteful or ugly or out-and-out ridiculous. These would include large automobiles with chrome trim, crunchy breakfast cereals without Vitamin A, cap pistols for children and television shows like *The Beverly Hillbillies*. They are all guaranteed to set a consumerist's teeth on edge, but if there is a consumer market for them, there is a free-enterprise businessman who will produce them.

This is how the system works, and it does work. It has given the people of the United States by far the highest standard of living, with the greatest freedom of choice, of any people anywhere.

As Mortimer Adler pointed out in *The Time of Our Lives: The Ethics of Common Sense:* "... from the point of view of providing the external conditions of a good human life for a larger percentage of its citizens, the United States is, on balance, as good as, if not better than, any other country in the world today, and vastly better than any state that ever existed in the past."

And in a *Saturday Review* article on the Adler book, critic J. H. Plumb added his own encomium. "In America," wrote Plumb, "more people are living well than have done so in any other time or place in human history."

This, then, was the halcyon state when, borne on Disaster Lobby wings, the plague of consumerists descended on America. Consumerism, it should be noted and underscored, is often at cross-purposes with free enterprise. For the concept of consumerism—radical consumerism, that is—is rooted deeply in the principle that the selling of goods and services should *not* be conducted on a basis of free choice but should instead be regulated rigidly by government. It is the conviction of just about every prominent consumer advocate, from Ralph Nader to Bess Myerson, that there is a right type of merchandise and wrong type of merchandise and that the consumer should be forced, through government control of the marketplace, into buying the right type, *whether he wants to or not*. Such consumerists would therefore abrogate one of the most precious of all freedoms: a human being's right to make a fool of himself if he so desires.

Basically, the Nader type of consumer advocate is a consummate snob. He believes that he knows what is best for other people. He believes he knows what kind of car other people should drive, what kind of cereal other people should eat, what kind of house other people should occupy. And he goes one critical step further. He believes the government should make his preference mandatory by outlawing, or severely penalizing the sellers of, those products and services he deems inferior.

Thus, despite the fact that by their purchases millions of consumers have shown their approval of annual changes in automobile models, Ralph Nader, supported by thirty-nine consumerist members of the *Yale Law Journal*, petitioned the government to outlaw annual changes in cars.

And although tens of millions of shoppers with small families have demonstrated their need for food products packaged in small containers, groups of consumer advocates have demanded that these relatively expensive containers be taken off the market in the interest of cutting prices.

In his book on Nader, Charles McCarry takes note of the consumerist's elitist attitude, which can properly be described as anticonsumer. "He [Nader] is a puritan who is repelled by America's gluttonous society," McCarry wrote. And he quoted a friend of Nader's as having said, "Ralph is not a consumer champion; he is just plain against consumption."

Another self-styled friend of the consumer who fought vigorously against the consumer's right to buy what he wants is Robert Choate, a Washington, D.C., promoter who, in July of 1970, launched the Great Breakfast Cereal Caper.

The uproar, helped along by detailed reports in the news media, began when Choate told a Senate consumer subcommittee that two out of every three breakfast cereals then on the market contained so little nutritional value that they represented little more than "empty calories." He accused the cereal industry of promoting "nutritional illiteracy" by featuring some of its least nutritious products on Saturday morning television commercials aimed at children. It was his view that these commercials should be replaced, by government edict, with sales messages for the kind of breakfast food he regarded as nutritious.

"Among the 6,000 different items on your grocer's shelves are 60 different breakfast cereals," Choate announced. "The consumer is entitled to know which are the best."

And therein lay the rub. Which *are* the best? To Choate, the only yardstick by which breakfast cereals should be measured was vitamin and protein content. To children, the key criterion was taste. And to millions of housewives faced daily with the task of inserting some kind of food into the digestive systems of their recalcitrant offspring, the test for breakfast cereals was, "Will the kids eat it?"

Unfortunately, nutritional value and palatability do not co-exist in breakfast cereals. Food processors admit that they have been unable so far to combine the two to any significant extent. What Choate, a typical consumerism elitist, wanted the government to do was institute rules making it impossible or, at best, difficult for manufacturers to supply the American consumer with breakfast cereals that appeal to the taste buds of the kindergarten set. If Choate had got what he wanted, breakfast would have become a nightmare in households across the country.

Furthermore, Choate's idea of what constitutes a nutritious breakfast was at variance with the opinions of numerous persons whose credentials are considerably more impressive than his own. Among them are Dr. Frederick Stare, the Harvard nutritionist, and Dr. W. H. Sebrell, Jr., of Columbia University, both of whom testified in opposition to Choate at the Senate hearing.

According to Stare, the popular cereal brands condemned by Choate are responsible for highly nutritious meals because they are almost never eaten alone. They are invariably accompanied by milk or cream and frequently by fruit, and many children will consume milk and fruit in no other context.

"A breakfast of cereal and milk along with some fruit, toast, margarine and jelly or jam is just as nutritious as a breakfast of bacon and eggs, with fruit, toast, margarine and jam," Stare told the Senators. Actually, the cereal breakfast is superior, said the Harvard expert, "because the cereal breakast has less saturated fat and cholesterol."

The snobbish elitism of the Disaster Lobby consumerist was evident in a statement issued May 14, 1971, by New York State Attorney General Louis Lefkowitz. The Attorney General had just conducted an investigation of retail outlets, and he had discovered that "a wide variety of products, from food to children's toys, from razors to vitamin pills, all come wrapped in glossy, many-colored and totally unnecessary packaging." Elimination of these gaudy frills would enable manufacturers to cut their prices, said Lefkowitz, and inasmuch as he was the state's number one lawman, what he said carried the implied threat of government injunction. At the very least, it was high-level arm twisting.

The obvious flaw in the Lefkowitz reasoning is that if the packaging were "totally unnecessary" it would not exist. No rational businessman would waste his money by spending it on nonessential frippery. The purpose of the packaging is to attract customers, who apparently prefer "glossy, many-colored" wrappings to dull, monochromatic ones. A package's appearance can make a big difference in the viewer's mood, as any recipient of a gift can testify. And who, after all, is Louis Lefkowitz to tell the American public what it should and should not respond to in packaging?

At about the same time, Ralph Nader was launching an attack on men's toiletries. He had decided that men do not need toiletries and, decrying sales messages for these products as "tom cat advertising," he urged at a press conference that such ads be banned by law. The next step would probably be a ban on toiletries themselves, since neither men nor women really "need" them.

During the consumerism infestation, there was a widespread but erroneous belief that the typical shopper had been tainted by the virus and had suddenly acquired a whole new set of values. Some businessmen swallowed the canard, much to their eventual regret.

In the February 1, 1971, issue of the trade paper *Advertising Age*, columnist E. B. Weiss contributed to this fantasy by assuring his readers that "a new kind of consumer is emerging whose wants are less materialistic and whose first concerns include preserving the environment."

This was unadulterated claptrap. But quite a few otherwise level-headed industrialists fell for it. Several major oil companies began marketing low-lead, low-octane gasolines with the announcement that, while these gasolines were not as powerful as high-test brands and while they would sell for the same price as high-test brands, they would inject fewer pollutants into the air. The appeal, therefore, was to the Weiss kind of consumer "whose first concerns include preserving the environment."

So few of these consumers existed outside of Weiss' vivid imagination, however, that hardly anybody bought the new gasolines and, one by one, they began to disappear. The ones that remain are the poorest sellers on the market.

Then there was the school of consumerism that embraced the theory of prices-*über-alles*. It was the contention of these misguided souls that price was the overriding consideration in the purchase of goods and services and that the only reason everybody didn't buy the cheapest brand available was the inability of most people to decipher all of those odd-quantity, fractionated-price hieroglyphics printed on product packages for the express purpose of confusing everybody.

Bess Myerson was so beguiled by this illusion that she got the City of New York to adopt an ordinance requiring the larger supermarkets to post two sets of prices for each item on sale: the actual price of the item and the unit price of the contents. For example, a two-pound package of sugar selling for 42 cents would have to carry tags reading "42 cents" and "21 cents per pound."

This unit pricing plan aimed at helping the relatively few grammar-school dropouts who are incapable of dividing one number into another had one effect Bess Myerson never anticipated. It caused supermarkets to raise their prices. The explanation is simple. It costs money to hire clerks to stamp prices on food containers. And when you have twice as many prices to stamp, you have to hire additional clerks. And when you hire additional clerks, you raise your prices.

Unit pricing hurt consumers in still another way. It discouraged supermarkets from having sales, since each sale would involve the posting of *two* sets of new prices instead of one.

So once again, the consumerists proved to be the consumer's worst enemy.

But what really disturbed the Bess Myersons the most was the fact that very few shoppers took any note of unit pricing, which is what the food processors and supermarket managers had predicted all along. Experience had showed them that most shoppers are much more brand conscious than they are price conscious. They buy a particular item because they, or a family member, prefer the taste or because they trust the manufacturer or because it comes in a desired size or shape or color or texture. The knowledge that another brand sells for a penny less per pound is of relatively little interest.

The failure of this scheme of the consumerism crowd was noted in a *New York Times* article in the issue of January 31, 1972. Headlined "Unit Pricing Called Something of a Dud," the report told of a survey by the Consumer Research Institute in which supermarket shoppers were asked whether they had been helped by unit pricing. Fewer than 10 percent answered in the affirmative. Unfortunately, 100 percent of the shoppers had to pay the higher checkout counter tabs that unit pricing made necessary.

The off-the-record comments of consumer advocates who urged the adoption of unit pricing reflected the movement's elitist motivation. Again and again, you would hear statements similar to the one made by a Metuchen, New Jersey, women's club president who spearheaded a number of consumer advocacy drives. "You and I may be able to do the arithmetic on those odd package sizes," she told her fellow officers at an executive meeting of the club, "but most women can't. We need unit pricing to help the average consumer."

And in one of her unusual speeches, Betty Furness said she had never forgiven her old employer, Westinghouse, because the company neglected to say in its advertisements that it takes more electricity to operate a self-defrosting refrigerator than it takes to operate a non-self-defrosting refrigerator. It was her assumption that nobody could figure that out for himself. She might also have indicted General Motors for failing to notify the public that it takes more gasoline to operate a Cadillac limousine than it does to propel a motor scooter.

Of all the Disaster Lobby factions operating in the Age of Unreason, none had a lower regard for the intelligence of the consumer than did the consumerists. And as usual, the consumerists were dead wrong. When it came to smart, heads-up, knee-in-the-groin shopping, the American housewife made Ralph Nader look like a country bumpkin in a shell game. Her favorite pastime was not, as Nader thought, the playing of Mah-Jongg. It was the giving of ulcers to thousands upon thousands of businessmen who had to keep coming up with new ways to win her patronage and retain it without losing their shirts in the process.

A 1970 *Wall Street Journal* editorial put the subject into accurate perspective. "Far from being gullible," said the *Journal,* "Americans by and large are probably the most sophisticated and demanding consumers in the world, well prepared by good education and long exposure to competitive claims to cope with a free market."

Something else American consumers are is pretty much satisfied with the free enterprise system and the products it turns out. A study by the magazine *Progressive Grocer* revealed that the average supermarket shopper selects thirty-two items from among about 6,000 in the store in fifteen minutes of actual shopping time. Would she be able to make her purchases so rapidly if she lacked confidence in the store management or in the integrity of the food processers? *Progressive Grocer* thought not. The behavior of shoppers, said the magazine, is cogent evidence of their faith and confidence.

A similar conclusion was arrived at by the Gallup research organization when, in the early 1960's, it conducted a study of the problems worrying Americans. Its interviews turned up a list of thirty-nine concerns, ranging from family finances and family health to the fear of atomic annihilation, but nothing about the plight of the consumer. Hardly anyone at that time felt he was being victimized as a shopper by entrepreneurial fraud, misrepresentation, deception, overcharging or any other of the long list of sins included in the latter-day consumerism litany.

As Woodrow Wirsig, president of the Better Business Bureau of Metropolitan New York, pointed out in a 1970 speech, it wasn't until the consumer advocates began raking their muck that the public became aware of the existence of such a thing as a consumer problem. Then having created the problem, the consumerists carefully nurtured it. They kept telling the nation's shoppers they were being cheated and they kept urging them to do something about it.

According to Wirsig, both Esther Peterson and Betty Furness, as consumer advisers to Presidents Kennedy and Johnson, often lamented privately that consumers were too complacent, that they weren't complaining enough. To discourage this tendency toward contentment, both officials organized gripe sessions at which shoppers were exhorted to find something, *anything*, wrong with the business establishment and to register an indignant beef.

The plan worked. Where in 1960 there were so few consumer complaints that the opinion polls didn't even take notice of them, by 1967 an Opinion Research Corporation study revealed that 55 percent of all adult Americans felt the need for new consumer protection laws. By 1969, the figure had increased to 68 percent, and by 1971, it had topped 70 percent.

From the evidence, it would appear that the consumers

of America had been talked into feeling persecuted. They now wanted legislation to shield them from the Robber Barons, and legislation they got. In 1971, there were 512 different consumer protection bills pending in Congress, with 400 consumer programs already under way by reason of Federal funding. And for every piece of legislation taken up in Congress, there were at least a score dumped into committee hoppers in state houses and city halls from coast to coast. In November of 1971, Lee H. Bloom, administrative vice president and general counsel of Lever Brothers, said so much consumer protection legislation was being enacted on local levels, most of it vague and mutually contradictory, that many manufacturers simply did not know what products they could sell and what products had been, or were about to be, proscribed.

He announced that statutes affecting phosphate levels in soaps and detergents had been enacted in seven states, eight counties and fifty-six cities and had been proposed in another thirty-five states and sixty municipalities. Since the various laws rarely contained the same provisions, a detergent acceptable for sale in St. Louis might be forbidden in Chicago. This lack of consistency, said Bloom, not only created chaos in industry but reflected the amateurishness of the lawmakers. Nobody really knew how much phosphate was too much phosphate, but a lot of people seemed determined to slap on some kind of phosphate ceiling.

But the phosphate laws were only a slender sapling in what was rapidly becoming a dense forest of consumer legislation. According to Bloom, lawmakers in twenty-four states had introduced a total of sixty-seven bills in 1970 regulating the use of games and contests in the sale of merchandise. There had been another fifty-seven bills in nineteen states that zeroed in on false advertising claims. The use of trading stamps was the target of thirty-nine bills in fifteen states. Packaging and labeling of consumer goods were to be affected under forty-six bills in seventeen states. Unit pricing was proposed under legislation in eighteen states, while the open dating of perishable foods was recommended in twenty states. There were 113 bills in twenty-three states that called for the establishment of new consumer protection agencies that presumably would inaugurate their own set of rules to supplement those contained in the huge agglomeration of statutes.

And all of this, as overwhelming as it appears, does not begin to cover the full scope of consumerism frenzy in just that single year of 1970.

What makes this activity all the more astonishing is the fact that it was piled on top of a consumer-protection base that was already more than adequate. As long ago as 1961, years before Ralph Nader had started to convert the American consumer into a paranoiac with delusions of supermarket persecution, the Federal government alone was spending almost $1 billion a year on consumer protection. There were back in 1961 a total of 65,000 Federal workers in thirty-three departments and agencies whose only duty was the safeguarding of the health and pocketbooks of consumers.

By 1970, the annual outlay for consumer protection had climbed to a staggering $10 billion. And because nobody had bothered to analyze with objectivity the need for such programs or even to coordinate them, we were spending that $10 billion—in the words of the Better Business Bureau's Woodrow Wirsig—"without knowing whether it is too much or too little, without knowing whether it is useful or wasteful."

Much of the evidence would indicate that the expenditure was both too much *and* wasteful and that, under the influence of the Disaster Lobby, the United States was experiencing a paroxysm of largely meaningless law-passing, some of it self-defeating, most of it at cross-purposes and virtually all of it harmful to the consumer.

For one thing, it was the consumer who had to pay for that $10 billion worth of government help. His payment took the form of higher taxes—an average of $200 in taxes per family per year. And for another thing, he paid at the retailer's cash register, since the consumerism movement added to the cost of doing business and business costs are always passed on to the customer.

As Ralph K. Winters, Jr., a law professor at Yale, noted in his highly perceptive treatise, *The Consumer Advocate vs. the Consumer*: "Too often [the consumer] is left with the view that increasing product testing by 1,000 percent, making cars 'safe,' keeping all drugs off the market until they are absolutely 'safe,' forcing companies to spend large sums litigating and clearing things with a government bureaucracy and paying for the bureaucracy itself will cost nothing in out-of-pocket cash, increased taxes or foregone profits. It is hard to think of a claim of commercial advertising more misleading than that proposition."

Winters put his finger on another aspect of consumerism that was damaging to the consumer: its tendency to limit the shopper's options in the marketplace. He pointed out that it was the goal of many consumer advocates to inhibit the manufacturer's use of advertising and to dictate the suppression of advertising and the standardization of prod- terms under which his products can be offered for sale. "The ucts," said Winters, "tend to dampen competition between companies and are frequently anti-innovative and restrictive influences."

The annals of consumerism are filled with case histories of the kind of anticonsumer pressures referred to by Win- ters. For while the American consumer kept demonstrating through his selective patronage that he was fond of such offshoots of atomic-age capitalism as trading stamps, high- powered sports cars, low-vitamin snacks and avocado green refrigerators, the elitists in the consumer movement were working overtime in an effort to outlaw trading stamps, high-powered sports cars, low-vitamin foods and expensively colored appliances. They were doing this, of course, for the consumer's own good.

Typical of this philosophy was the campaign launched in the late 1960's against odd sizes in food packages. It was the contention of the self-anointed experts that the food companies were putting out their wares in fractional weights and volumes for the sole purpose of making it impossible for the shopper to figure out which package was the biggest bargain. Was a four-and-a-half-ounce jar of pickles at 43 cents a better buy than a seven-and-a-quarter-ounce jar at 67 cents?

The impression conveyed by the consumerists was that the nation's food processors stayed awake nights trying to figure out which weights at which prices would pose the biggest puzzle for the harried housewife. The truth was at the opposite pole. For starters, it is impossible to fool the American housewife. The few companies that have tried to are no longer in existence. And for finishers, there is a perfectly legitimate reason for the odd sizes in the supermarket.

In some cases, foods are packaged in odd amounts because the same size containers are used, in the interest of economy, for different products with different specific gravities. A box that would accommodate an even pound of pretzels might contain, let us say, only fourteen-and-a-half ounces of potato chips, since potato chips weigh less than pretzels on a cubic-inch basis. If processors had to market everything in even amounts, the cost of packaging would increase and it would be the consumer who would have to pay for it.

There are other valid reasons for those odd weights, as Charles Mortimer, former chairman of the board of General Foods, once pointed out. He observed that his company put out a vanilla pudding mix in a three-and-a-quarter-ounce package. This was done because the contents of the package, when mixed with an even two cups of milk, would produce four half-cup servings of pudding. If General Foods had switched to a three-ounce package, the contents would have to be mixed with one-and-eleven-thirteenths cups of milk and the housewife would have an interesting time trying to figure that one out in her measuring cup.

Yet this is the kind of nonsense the consumer advocates sought to inflict on the nation's consumers, again, ostensibly, for their own good.

A pet goal of the consumerism crowd was enactment of a Federal statute that would permit any consumer to file damage suits against businessmen on behalf of all other consumers. If, for example, the purchaser of a Chevrolet felt that he had been cheated, he could sue General Motors not merely for the $3,000 he spent but for $3 billion, the amount spent by a million Chevrolet buyers. In the event the verdict went in his favor, the $3 billion would be distributed among the various Chevrolet owners.

It is not difficult to imagine the kind of chaos such a law would induce. The amount of litigation that would descend on every Federal court in the country boggles the mind. Lawyers who are reluctant to waste their time suing General Motors for a picayune $3,000 would have no such hesitation about entering a complaint for $3 billion. Any consumer with a grudge against virtually any company would have no trouble enlisting counsel, and court calendars would come apart at the seams.

On industry's side, the problems would be even more crippling. Fighting law suits would become the chief occupation of thousands of corporations. The quality of their products would probably deteriorate, they would have to raise their prices to cover litigation costs and, as usual, the consumer would ultimately suffer the most as a result of steps taken on his behalf.

Yet as preposterous as class action suits would be—"class action" was the name given to the scheme by its proponents —so powerful were the consumer advocates of the Disaster Lobby that legislation providing for such suits was actually introduced in Congress. The Consumer Redress Bill, as it was known, came up before the United States Senate in 1970, was reported out of the Senate Commerce Committee but was never voted on by the full chamber. Additional hearings on the bill were held in 1971, but again no final action was taken. If the consumerists run true to form, pressure to get the bill enacted will continue and, if Congress runs true to form, the bill, or one similar to it, will eventually be passed.

Mention has already been made of another piece of "consumer help" legislation that had consumers climbing the walls: the law requiring seat belts and shoulder harnesses in all highway vehicles. From the outset, only one-third of all car owners with mandated belts in their vehicles ever used them. Fewer than 5 percent used the harnesses. Yet every car owner had to pay for the belts and the harnesses and many car owners devised ways to get the equipment out of the way to avoid ruining their clothes or raising welts on their persons.

The failure of the motoring public to cotton to belts and harnesses was no fault of the do-gooders. They exerted every effort and pulled every string to make buckling up popular. So insistent were they that the nation's media donated almost $200 million worth of radio and television time and newspaper and magazine space for commercials and advertisements urging Americans to use their seat belts. It was by far the largest amount of advertising time and space ever devoted to the selling of a single product or idea, and the fact that it failed—and it did fail, since the use of belts never climbed above the 33 percent mark—is positive proof that, contrary to the claims of the consumerists, advertising can never make people do what they don't want to do.

And most people did not, and do not, want to use seat belts in automobiles. In 1968 and 1969, more than $60 million in television time alone was allocated to a special "buckle-up" campaign, and studies made just before and just after the commercials ran showed belt usage clinging tenaciously to the one-third level. In 1971, according to the Insurance Institute for Highway Safety, a nine-month "saturation" program that employed all methods of communication was conducted in a "medium-sized American city" in an attempt to increase the use of belts there, and it too was a flop.

Faced with this evidence of a certain lack of cooperation on the part of the public, the consumer advocates went into Phase Two. (When a consumerist makes up his mind to help consumers, he doesn't give up easily. A woman scorned hath no fury like a Ralph Nader spurned.)

After it became apparent that American motorists had no intention of using those belts and harnesses foisted on them, car makers were ordered by the Federal government —under consumerist goading—to install devices that would encourage the occupants of cars to buckle up. These devices took the form of warning lights and buzzers that would blink on and sound off unless seat belts were fastened.

But the public was too clever for that one. Many drivers simply hooked up their belts and sat on them or shoved them under the seats.

Enter Phase Three. By now, the consumer advocates were really angry. They decided that, come hell or open rebellion, the American motorist was going to use seat belts. After all, they knew what was best for the average man, didn't they? So they talked the Federal authorities into drafting a new rule that would make it mandatory to *use* both seat belts and shoulder harnesses. The regulation was drawn up in 1972 by the Department of Transportation and, if it wins final approval after hearings, it would provide fines and possibly jail terms for any motorist who failed to fasten his safety equipment. States refusing to enforce the directive would face a loss of all Department of Transportation grants-in-aid and 10 percent of all Federal road-building money.

In getting involved in the seat-belt-and-shoulder-harness affair, the Federal government was, of course, overstepping its Constitutional perimeters by a substantial margin. Under the Constitution, no branch of government—Federal, state or local—has the right to make an American citizen do anything that is designed for his own good alone. Governmental bodies are authorized only to establish rules aimed at protecting one citizen from another. They can therefore set automobile speed limits, prohibit the operation of a motor vehicle by an inebriate, issue or withhold drivers' licenses and prescribe standards for such critically important equipment as brakes, tires and headlights. All of these regulations are manifestly for the purpose of preventing one motorist from injuring other motorists or pedestrians. The use of seat belts and shoulder harnesses, however, protects only the user. For that reason, the Federal government has no legal —or moral—right to make it mandatory or even to require the purchase of the devices themselves.

It is easy to see where such Big Brother meddling could lead. If Federal officials can require motorists to buckle up their seat belts to keep themselves from being hurt, why not a law prohibiting all persons from venturing out of doors when it snows or when the temperature rises above 100 degrees Fahrenheit? Or a law compelling everyone to do limbering-up exercises each morning? Or one banning the consumption of rich desserts? Each of these statutes would save more lives than a seat-belt law, and none is any more outrageous in a free society.

If there was anything that infuriated consumerists more than unbelted drivers, it was advertising. With some justification, the Ralph Naders of the Age of Unreason saw in advertising the keystone of the private enterprise system, so they made advertising their number one target. In statement after statement, in lawsuit after lawsuit, they sought laws and court rulings that would eliminate advertising as we know it.

In late 1970, Ralph Nader demanded a Federal regulation prohibiting advertisers from making assertions that were not "fully and completely substantiated by scientific tests" or from promoting products that had not been proved totally safe and nonpolluting beyond any doubt. Such a rule could obviously be used to ban all advertising since there are precious few assertions made anywhere, including courts of law and the halls of Congress, that could be "fully and completely substantiated by scientific tests" and since every commercial product made in this country might, under certain circumstances, be harmful to man or to the environment.

Several months later, the Nader people published a 1,150-page study of American business operations entitled *The Closed Enterprise System*, in which Nader proposed a statutory ceiling on the ratio of advertising to sales in specified industries.

Other consumerist groups kept up the anti-advertising tattoo. A gaggle of George Washington University law students banded together under the acronym SOUP (for Students Opposed to Unfair Practices) and urged the government to require that all chemically identical products be labeled as such in advertisements. The goal was clear and the tactics Machiavellian. For the truth is that most products in a given classification are chemically identical. One firm's canned chicken soup has the same ingredients as another's. Aspirin is aspirin. And all automobiles are constructed primarily of steel and glass. Since the average company would be reluctant to spend money on ads stating that its products were chemically identical to competitive products, the salient effect of the SOUP law would be a drastic reduction in the amount of advertising prepared and placed by businessmen.

But the ultimate attack on advertising came from United States Representative Benjamin Rosenthal, a New Yorker with a penchant for consumerism who could accurately be described as the Man of the Hour of the 1960's; if there was anyone ideally suited by temperament and ideology to sit in the Congress of the United States during the time of the Disaster Lobby, it was Benjamin Rosenthal. In a statement that should go down in history alongside such other gems as "Let them eat cake" and "Peace for our time," Rosenthal told a press conference that "Advertising is the greatest enemy of the consumer today."

It is interesting and perhaps significant to note that, on the same day he made his fatuous remark about advertising, Representative Rosenthal accused the Food and Drug Administration and the nation's food manufacturers of "working together to reduce the nutritional value of food."

In addition to denouncing advertising as a general concept, America's consumerists often directed their barbs at specific advertisers and specific ads. For example, there was a television commercial for Hershey's Krackel candy bars that evoked an angry official complaint to the National Advertising Review Board. What was Hershey's crime? Well, according to the filer of the complaint, in the TV commercial, the crackling sound of the candy bar being broken was somewhat louder than the crackling sound made by the breaking of an actual Krackel bar. Horrors!

Another consumerist group was unhappy about a commercial for Luden's 5th Avenue candy bar in which a football player announces that "I eat a case of 5th Avenue candy bars before every game." Such a remark, said the petitioner, presumably with a straight face, would lead viewers to believe that football players customarily eat cases of 5th Avenue candy bars before trotting out onto the gridiron.

And there was a frightful amount of indignation about the American Dairy Association commercial in which a female cartoon character drinks a single glass of milk and immediately undergoes a miraculous transformation for the better, acquiring a new hair-do, longer lashes and a fashionable gown, along with other improvements. The consumerists who lodged a complaint about the A.D.A. message were apparently afraid that the public would expect similar miracles from a glass of milk. Here was still another outcropping of intellectual snobbery. The elitists who gave the consumerism movement its thrust regarded the average consumer as a moron who would take literally the broadest and most obvious strokes of satire, parody and slapstick burlesque. If an announcer on TV were to say, "Everybody's talking about Mother Macrae's Pretzels," the audience would naturally assume, in the opinion of the consumerists, that at that moment all 210 million residents of the United States were talking about Mother Macrae's Pretzels. So the announcer shouldn't say things like that.

It is apparent from much of what they wrote and did that the consumerism people viewed advertising men as latter-day Svengalis who could, at the drop of a two-page color spread, hypnotize huge segments of the populace into buying the most worthless kinds of claptrap. Nothing could be less true. There isn't a major manufacturing company in America that doesn't have in its files at least one story of an excellent product that failed, despite vast sums spent on advertising, simply because the public didn't cotton to it. Ford's Edsel is the most publicized case in point, but there are literally thousands of others. As mentioned previously, the seat-belt advertising campaign proved conclusively that no amount of advertising can get even a small number of people to do what they don't want to do. And then came the ban on cigaret commercials, which proved that an *absence* of advertising can't make people stop doing what they *do* want to do. When hundreds of millions of dollars in cigaret commercials were sliced from the airwaves by Federal law, the sale of cigarets did not decline, as the consumerists had predicted, but rose. As a matter of fact, in the six months following the discontinuation of commercials, cigaret sales scored their biggest increase in history.

For despite the viewers-with-alarm, there is nothing magical or mysterious about advertising. Its purpose is simply to inform the consuming public about the existence of an available product and to put that product in the best possible light, competitively. That is all advertising is meant to do, and that is all advertising can do. And to a businessman, it's enough. By telling millions of people about a new product and then by reminding them of the product again and again, advertising can in a single month push sales up to a level it would take individual salesmen many years to achieve. It can do this providing the product is a good one and the public is in a receptive mood. If the product is without merit or the public is, for some reason, indifferent, all the advertising in the world won't make the cash register jingle.

In time, complaints against advertising became so numerous and so unreasonable that advertisers found themselves in the untenable position of the courtroom witness who is asked when he stopped beating his wife. Whatever they said and however they said it, the consumerists could be counted on to denounce them.

Consider the Mobil case as typical. In the late 1960's, in

response to consumerist demands for more emphasis on environmental problems and less on purely materialistic values, the Mobil Oil Corporation began stressing in its television commercials the detergent properties of its gasoline. It noted that Mobil gasoline contained elements designed to clean automobile engines and it stated that "A cleaner engine can mean cleaner air."

Were the consumerists delighted with this evidence of corporate response to the ecology crusade? Of course not. They were furious. In Washington, a spokesman for the Nader organization berated Mobil for having announced that "a cleaner engine can mean cleaner air."

"Why did they use the word 'can'?" asked the suspicious Naderite. "Does a cleaner engine mean cleaner air or not? One thing we know is the most dangerous pollutants that come from cars are invisible. So that the fact that your engine is cleaner does not mean that there are less dangerous pollutants in the air, necessarily."

This exercise in nit-picking non sequitur was duly reported in the press and prompted the Mobil company to issue a reply, which received considerably less publicity. According to Dayton Clewell, a Mobil senior vice president, the word "can" was used in the commercials because the word "will" might have been misleading.

"A cleaner engine *can* mean cleaner air if the right parts are cleaned," explained Clewell. "It will not mean cleaner air if, say, only a bearing is cleaned. Mobil researchers have proved conclusively that the company's detergent gasolines clean dirty carburetors and dirty crankcase ventilating valves and keep them clean. When these parts are dirty, combined emissions of unburned hydrocarbons and carbon monoxide will increase by as much as 50 percent."

But the consumerists had not yet finished with Mobil. The Consumer Federation of America lodged a formal complaint with the Council of Better Business Bureaus charging that Mobil had no right to advertise the detergent properties of its gasoline since other brands of gasoline also had detergent properties.

Now this is a fascinating concept indeed. What the Federation was saying in effect was that no company should be permitted to advertise its wares unless they are totally different from products put out by other companies. Such a rule would allow advertising only by those manufacturers who happen to own the exclusive rights to an item of merchandise. It would discourage other companies from developing competitive products because once a similar product was developed it could not be advertised. In other words, here was a consumerism group advocating a process that, in the end, would foster monopolies and inhibit the kind of competition that keeps prices down and quality up.

Even more astonishing is the fact that an identical stance —a position opposed to the advertising of products lacking exclusive properties—was adopted by the Federal Trade Commission, which, it may be recalled, was established in 1914 for the purpose of defending "free competitive enterprise as the keystone of the American economic system" and preventing that system "from being stifled or fettered by monopoly." In the celebrated Wonder bread case of 1971-1972, the FTC assumed precisely the same attitude as the Consumer Federation of America did with relation to Mobil.

Actually, the FTC began behaving somewhat irrationally several years earlier when, apparently stung by consumerist charges that it was pro-business, it directed the Colgate Palmolive Company to stop airing its "sandpaper" commercial on TV. The commercial showed what seemed to be a sheet of sandpaper to which was applied a coating of Colgate shave cream. A razor then whisked off the "sand," while the announcer talked about how effective Colgate shave cream was in the handling of "sandpaper beards."

Well, the sleuths of the FTC soon discovered that Colgate wasn't using real sandpaper in those commercials. What it was using was a sheet of glass on which sand had been sprinkled, so when the razor came along all it had to do was strip the sand from the glass.

This, the FTC contended, was blatantly deceptive. Television viewers, it said, had been led to believe that Colgate shave cream could actually soften the surface abrasives on sandpaper to such an extent that it could be removed from the paper. Obviously, the FTC shared Ralph Nader's conviction that the average American consumer was a mental defective.

Not long after the Colgate farce came the Campbell Soup silliness. In photographing a cup of its vegetable soup for showing on TV commercials, Campbell had found that the vegetables had a tendency to sink to the bottom. The cup thus appeared to contain nothing but liquid. To show off the vegetables, the company inserted a few glass marbles in the cup, a procedure that forced the vegetables to the surface.

Deception, cried the FTC, which envisioned millions of housewives rushing out to their supermarkets to buy Campbell's vegetable soup under the erroneous impression that each can contained three more peas and one more carrot chunk than it did.

But it wasn't until the Wonder bread case that the Federal Trade Commission finally emerged into the open as being four-square behind total irrationality.

The affair became public early in 1971. For several years before that, the Continental Baking Company had been marketing its Wonder bread under the advertising slogan, "Wonder helps build strong bodies 12 ways." It was this slogan that prompted the Federal Trade Commission to crack down on Continental. It wasn't that the FTC disputed the company's claim. The Commission was quite willing to concede that Wonder bread did indeed help build strong bodies twelve ways. What motivated the FTC to enjoin Continental from using the line was the argument that "Wonder is a standardized enriched bread" and that "the amount and kind of nutrients contained in said Wonder bread is the same as that contained in most other enriched breads." Since "most" other enriched breads also help build strong bodies twelve ways, said the FTC, Wonder should not be allowed to state in its ads that Wonder helps build strong bodies twelve ways.

Here, then, was the forerunner of the Mobil complaint. The FTC posture was typical of the period. It was anti-business, it was anti-advertising and it was thoroughly irrational. The FTC was, in effect, telling advertisers that they could not discuss the merits of their products if other brands happened to have similar merits. Thus, an automobile company could not state that its cars provided a quiet ride if a rival company's cars also provided a quiet ride. A soft drink bottler could not advertise its product as a thirst quencher if some other soft drink also quenched thirsts. Presumably, a retailer could not advertise a half-price sale if the store down the street was also marking its merchandise down by 50 percent.

The absurdity of the FTC position was brought out at a Commission hearing on the Wonder bread case. Hearing Examiner Raymond J. Lynch asked Lynne McCoy, the FTC attorney, whether, under the new FTC rules, a bakery advertising fresh bread "would have to say in its ads that Mr. Jones also has fresh bread."

"There's a difference," replied Miss McCoy.

"What is it?" Lynch asked. "I've been waiting for a month to hear."

There was no answer from Miss McCoy.

Later in the hearing, Randall W. Hackett, Vice President for Marketing of Continental, testified that his company had recently adopted a freshness approach in its advertising. Wonder bread was now being promoted under a "fresh guys" theme, he said. Miss McCoy immediately sprang to the attack.

"Are you saying that Wonder bread is fresher than other breads?" she inquired.

"No," said Hackett. "Just as fresh."

"Do you say that in your advertising—that other breads are just as fresh?" Miss McCoy asked.

"No."

"Why not?"

"Because," Hackett replied, with impeccable logic, "we're only interested in selling Wonder bread."

What the FTC was interested in, it appeared, was forcing as many companies as possible to stop advertising. Toward this end, it began filing charges against all kinds of advertisers on all kinds of grounds, most of them flimsy and many of them imaginary. In its eagerness to reconstruct the nation's marketing procedures, the Commission frequently filed complaints when it had nothing to complain about. It cited as "false, misleading and deceptive" Du Pont's TV commercials for Zerex anti-freeze—the ones in which a can of Zerex is punctured and promptly reseals itself—but dropped the charge when Du Pont proved conclusively that its commercials were scientifically valid and absolutely truthful. The FTC condemned as "unsupported" Pfizer's ads for Unburn suntan lotion and then retracted its indictment when Pfizer provided cogent support in the form of test evidence.

Of course, the ultimate winner in each case lost by the FTC was, paradoxically, the FTC. By holding press conferences to announce its charges against Du Pont, Pfizer and other companies, the Federal Trade Commission succeeded in making the public suspicious of the defendants and their advertising claims. Substantial losses in sales often followed. By the time the advertisers were vindicated, it was too late. The damage had been done. Millions of consumers had become doubtful about the sales messages of the specific companies and about advertising in general.

So prolific was the FTC as it fired away at the business community with all the restraint and accuracy of a hung-over hunter on the first day of the duck season that by the early 1970's the marketing trade journals were devoting more front-page space to the Commission than to sales conventions. The lead page of the March 22, 1971, issue of *Advertising Age* was typical of the period. It contained no fewer than five major news stories about the FTC: one about the Wonder bread case; one on another FTC complaint against Continental Baking, this one involving Profile bread; one on an FTC order aimed at getting the Firestone Tire and Rubber Company to run ads correcting what the Commission said was past advertising errors; one on a consumerist demand that the FTC force advertisers to devote 40 percent of their ads to corrections of former errors and that the FTC further prohibit "particularly successful cigaret brands" from doing any advertising at all; and one on a bill before Congress that would give the FTC additional powers to control the production and marketing operations of major business enterprises. And those were only the front-page stories. Inside pages of that same *Advertising Age* issue contained an additional two dozen articles relating directly or indirectly to actions taken or contemplated by the Federal Trade Commission.

This kind of publicity was sought rather than avoided by the Commission. Throughout the period, it made no bones of the fact that its new mission was to mold American business into a social pattern favored by the consumerism activists. No longer was the FTC merely going to concern itself with deceptive practices among businessmen. It was now going to see to it that businessmen responded to what FTC Commissioner Mary Gardiner Jones referred to as "the changing mores of consumers."

Gerald J. Thain, Assistant Director of the FTC's Bureau of Consumer Protection, was even more explicit when he addressed the 11th Annual Washington Conference on Business-Government Relations in the spring of 1971. Henceforth, said an obviously stirred-up Thain, the FTC would not limit itself to issuing cease and desist orders whenever some errant company lied or cheated. The Commission, he said, would now invoke "the unfairness doctrine" and would seek severe penalties when that doctrine was violated.

Just what was the unfairness doctrine? Thain made it crystal clear. The unfairness doctrine was a brand new rule under which the FTC would prosecute any businessman who did something the FTC considered to be unfair. The businessman might be telling the truth. He might be perfectly honest. But if the Federal Trade Commission believed that he was being unfair in any way, it would do its damnedest to throw him into jail.

It was the unfairness doctrine the Continental Baking Company had apparently desecrated when it advertised that Wonder bread helped build strong bodies twelve ways without mentioning in its ads that certain other brands of bread were also nutritious.

"Unfair," observed Thain, "goes beyond deceptive."

And in invoking the unfairness doctrine, the Federal Trade Commission went beyond logic, beyond reason and way beyond its statutory instructions. At times, it went all the way into the never-never Wonderland of Alice. There was something in Thain's explanation of the unfairness doctrine that was strongly reminiscent of the ramblings of Humpty Dumpty. "When I use a word," Humpty Dumpty said, "it means just what *I* choose it to mean—neither more nor less." In the Age of Unreason, the word "fairness" meant just what the Federal Trade Commission chose it to mean. That's one reason it's called the Age of Unreason.

TEN "The Galbraith Plan" and Other Absurdities

On Sunday morning, August 22, 1971, the more than one million men and women who receive *The New York Times Magazine* as lagniappe with their copies of *The New York Times* were exposed to an article that epitomized the foolishness of the period. The article was entitled "The Galbraith Plan to Promote the Minorities" and it was jointly written by John Kenneth Galbraith, a professor of economics at Harvard University and a leading exponent of Unreason, and by Edwin Kuh and Lester C. Thurow, economics professors at the Massachusetts Institute of Technology.

The Galbraith Plan was simple and straightforward. After noting that 96 percent of the nation's over-$15,000-a-year jobs are held by white males, the three professors suggested that a law be passed requiring corporations to stop hiring white males as executives and to start hiring women, blacks, American Indians and Spanish-speaking people.

In essence, the proposal merely provided a label and legal machinery for what many in the intellectual community had been recommending for several years. For it was the conviction among prominent eggheads of the day that the proper way to eliminate inequities under which people were not hired or admitted to colleges because their skin was black, red, brown or yellow was to set up a system whereby people would not be hired or admitted to colleges because their skin was white.

And this, of course, is precisely what the Galbraith Plan would have done. It would have forced companies to turn down job applications by qualified white males in favor of applications by females, Negroes, Indians and Spanish-Americans, regardless of their qualifications.

"We propose," said Galbraith et al in their *Times Magazine* piece, "that the Congress now enact legislation declaring it to be national policy that employment of women, blacks, American Indians and Spanish-speaking minorities be in accord, throughout the various salary brackets in industry and government, with the numbers in the working force. To enforce this we propose that there be created a competently staffed body . . . called the Minorities Advancement Commission. The law would empower the commission to require any firm that has employed more than 5,000 people during the previous five years to submit a plan for bringing the distribution of women, blacks and Spanish-speaking workers in its salary hierarchy into conformity with the representation of these groups in the working force of the community or communities in which it operates. The time allowed for full compliance would be 10 years."

Firms with 2,000 to 5,000 employes would, under the Galbraith Plan, be permitted a bit more time to get rid of their white male executives, while firms with fewer than 2,000 employes would be exempt. Also exempt, although encouraged to participate, would be educational institutions.

By exempting colleges and universities, the authors were protecting their own jobs and those of their colleagues, since you would have had to search very long and very hard to find a $15,000-a-year American Indian on the faculties of such institutions of higher learning as Harvard and M.I.T. Without that exemption, the Messrs. Galbraith, Kuh and Thurow might have found themselves dispossessed by a trio of Wampanoags from Somerville.

Even more puzzling than the free ride for colleges was the authors' selection of minorities to be ungraded. Why

only women, blacks, Indians and persons with Spanish sur-
names? Why not Polish-Americans? Why not Hungarian-
Americans? Why not underprivileged white residents of
Appalachia? Certainly all of these minorities, along with
scores of others, are under-represented in the top executive
echelons of American industry.

But the most baffling aspect of the Galbraith Plan had
nothing to do with self-serving exemptions or racist exclu-
sions. What astonished clear-thinking Americans most about
the Galbraith Plan was why, after the country's liberals had
fought so passionately and so successfully for so many years
to eliminate the infamous quota system from our society and
to replace it with a color-blind merit system, these three
"liberal" professors were now demanding that the quota
system be revived.

And the Galbraith Plan *was* the quota system in its purest
form, as the proponents freely admitted. "Not merit but sex,
color and ethnic origins would become the overriding considerations [in hiring]," the article stated.

Sex, color and ethnic origins were, of course, the overriding considerations in hiring a generation ago, when most
companies and all of the better colleges had a carefully
worked out table of percentages for the admission of women,
Jews, Catholics and other segments of the populace. Then,
as enlightenment came to America, the quota system waned.
Gradually, most of us trained ourselves to consider only a
person's ability in screening him or her for a job or a place
in a student body. We dropped the lines about race and
religion from application blanks. We began to admit women
to previously all-male universities. We outlawed different
sets of schools for different races.

And through it all, the liberals—the true liberals—were in
the vanguard for progress. It was they who insisted on sub-
stituting merit for sex, color and ethnic origins in hiring
and academic enrollment. It was they who implored their
fellow Americans to be color-blind in their assessment of
others.

As recently as the late 1950's, the ultra-liberal American

Civil Liberties Union was petitioning the Federal government to have the question of race deleted from the 1960
census schedule. A person's race is irrelevant in census-
taking, the ACLU declared.

So successful was this movement to obliterate discrimination that by 1971 French author Jean-Francois Revel was
proclaiming that "the United States is one of the least racist
countries in the world today."

America was plainly on the right track until the Disaster
Lobby came along and, warning of a possible revolution if
blacks didn't get better jobs, shunted the entire nation onto
a manic spur line headed toward a topsy-turvy junction
where the very same intellectuals who had once condemned
the quota system would soon be clamoring for it.

The handwriting went on the wall at the Democratic
National Convention of 1968. At that convention, the party's
left-wing fringe was thwarted in its attempt to nominate the
candidate of its choice and to insinuate its extremist views
into the official party platform. One thing it did manage to
do was convince a majority at the convention that steps
should be taken to alter the machinery by which delegates
were chosen. Another thing it did was to load its own people
onto the commission appointed for the purpose of altering
the machinery.

The result was predictable. On November 19, 1969, the
Democratic Party Reform Commission, under Chairman
George McGovern, adopted a series of resolutions declaring
that at the 1972 convention each state delegation should
contain a racial, ethnic, age and sex mixture roughly comparable to the percentages of these groups within that state.
In other words, the good old quota system.

But the McGovern Commission, its eyes glued firmly on
the main chance, was just as selective in 1969 as John Kenneth Galbraith was to be in 1971. The statements issued by
the Commission made it clear that the only race it was concerned about was the black race and the only age group was
the eighteen-to-thirty group—these being regarded as safe
for McGovern—and, sure enough, at the 1972 convention

these were the minorities that got all the attention. Orientals were grossly under-represented at the convention, as were Malayo-Polynesians, but nobody appeared to care.

And compared with the aged, the young were grossly *over*-represented. This disparity attracted the attention of freelance Walter Goodman, who asked in *The New York Times Magazine*, "If we are assuring representation of the young, why not of the old, a substantial part of the population with substantial and special needs?" To Goodman, the 1972 Democratic Convention, with its accent on racial and religious and age and sex quotas, was "rather like a return of vaudeville."

Unfortunately, it was far more ominous than that. It was more like a return of slavery, or at the very least, of segregation. What made it all the more tragic was the fact that the protagonists knew exactly what they were doing. Shortly after the Democratic Reform Commission adopted its delegate resolutions, Chairman McGovern told an interviewer: "The way we got the quota thing through was by not using the word 'quota'."

There is something in that statement that is pure Orwell.

By the time the 1972 primary elections rolled around, the Democratic candidates for the presidential nomination were promising to make cabinet appointments solely on the bases of pigmentation and ethnic background. Senator Hubert Humphrey said that if he were elected President he would name a Chicano to his cabinet, while Senator McGovern was quoted by a black Congressman as having said that under a McGovern presidency 10 percent of *all* Federal patronage jobs would be given to blacks.

At the Democratic Convention that nominated George McGovern, the quota system was enforced rigidly and, to some observers, illegally. The Chicago delegation, duly elected by the people of Illinois under the laws of Illinois, was rejected on the ground that it did not contain enough blacks or young people.

Curiously, there were almost no objections to delegations that contained more black and young people than there should have been if the ratios were to be reflective of the population as a whole. When the Ohio delegation elected two whites and two blacks to serve on the Democratic National Committee, the chairman of the delegation, Ohio AFL-CIO President Frank W. King and an opponent of quota systems, tried to point out the danger of such systems by replacing one of the blacks with a white. He noted that a unit of two blacks and two whites would have over-represented the blacks in the Ohio citizenry.

"I don't like quotas," said King, "but that's what the rules are now. You can't have it both ways. You can't have your cake and eat it too."

He was wrong. They *could* have their cake and eat it too. The left-wing powerhouse in control of the convention ignored King and seated on the National Committee the two blacks and two whites originally designated.

Although Richard Nixon personally had no use for quota systems, so many influential voices were raised in their behalf that again, as in the case of environmental "reforms", he acted against his better judgment. At the mid-point in his first Administration, he inaugurated what came to be known as the Philadelphia Plan. Supervised by the Department of Labor and suggested by civil rights legislation enacted in the Johnson Administration, the Philadelphia Plan required all contractors bidding on Federal projects to have in their work forces a racial blend similar to that in the population as a whole. It got its name from the City of Brotherly Love, where blacks comprise one-third of the population but only a tiny fraction of the personnel in the building trades.

Eventually, some form of the Philadelphia Plan was put into effect in fifty-five cities across the nation. And in every one of those cities, it aroused the ire of white men who found themselves turned down for construction jobs because of the color of their skin. The Galbraiths of America regarded this as a matter of poetic justice—the whites were at last learning what it was like to be discriminated against—but old-time liberals recognized the menace. They knew that discrimination was evil, regardless of the intent. And they knew something more. They knew that it was one thing to discriminate against a small minority—there was a limit to what that minority could do—but it was quite another thing to make second-class citizens out of the majority. Sooner or later that majority would lose its patience and, as a majority, would make its displeasure known in a very forthright and very effective manner.

This is precisely what did happen in the elections of 1972. The astounding popularity of George Wallace in the primaries and the resounding defeat of George McGovern in the main event were due in large measure to a white middle-class rebellion—a rebellion of the majority—against the trend toward favoritism for various selected minorities. Many middle-class whites—Catholics, Jews and so-called "ethnics" —were the children and grandchildren of the persecuted minorities of the past. Nobody had shown their forebears any favoritism, they announced. Quite the contrary. Rightly or wrongly, they saw no reason to subsidize, through the loss of hard-won jobs and promotions, a program of favoritism for some new crop of minorities. "Let them hack it the way our people did," said one construction worker, a third-generation American of Lithuanian ancestry, in what could be regarded as the "Remember the Alamo" of the 1970's.

In was this hard-nosed, self-righteous, fed-up-to-here Middle America that saw an ally in George Wallace and an enemy in George McGovern and that turned the nation sharply rightward in 1972, as the vintage liberals had both predicted and feared.

But the swing of the pendulum came as the Age of Unreason was drawing to a close. Indeed, it hastened the end of that fascinating, if illogical, period. Just before the change of direction, the pendulum had been traveling the opposite way at an eye-blurring clip. The neo-racists had all but succeeded in convincing the country's leaders that while government-sanctioned discrimination against blacks had been despicable, government-initiated discrimination against whites would be a fine and noble experiment. And nowhere did they achieve as much success as in the field of education.

It had started sanely and rationally enough. In 1954, the Supreme Court struck down the concept of "separate-but-equal" school facilities, a device used in most sections of the South as a means of segregating the races. The Court ruled that the races must be desegregated in all school systems throughout the country.

Gradually, boards of education in the South began to comply with the Court order, many of them with reluctance. By the late 1960's, *de jure*—or statutory—segregation had been abolished in virtually every school district. What remained in many places in the United States, including the progressive Northeast, was *de facto* segregation: a black-white division caused not by local ordinances but by residential concentrations of each race. Many schools in New York City's Harlem, for example, continued to have a heavily black enrollment while schools in high-income neighborhoods of nearby Riverdale remained almost entirely white.

It was at this point that the voices of the Disaster Lobby piped up loud and clear. The races *must* be mixed in schoolrooms, they insisted. Such a blending, they said with more good will than evidence, would raise the standard of education and would prepare the children for a racially mixed world. It was their recommendation that buses be used to transport children from black neighborhoods to schools in white neighborhoods and vice versa. Thus was born the concept of busing.

What the proponents of busing failed to comprehend was that, while *de jure* segregation was wrong because it singled out certain people for special treatment on the basis of their race, the use of busing to eradicate *de facto* segregation was wrong for the same reason. It singled out certain people for special treatment on the basis of their race. If it was immoral to bus children to special schools in the name of segregation, so was it immoral to bus children to special schools in the name of integration.

It had taken mankind several millenia to become color-blind with regard to human beings, and now, just as the light was beginning to shine through, some of the most prominent intellectuals of the United States had reached out to switch it off.

Busing was not only racist and therefore immoral, but preposterous as well. After all, what was a desirable mixture of the races? Was it the same as the national ratio: 12 percent black, 86.5 percent white and 1.5 percent other? Was this the proper blend for every school? If so, how would you handle the situation in rural schools in the West, some of them hundreds of miles from the nearest black families? Busing would be out of the question. You would have to resort to flying, setting up an airlift so weird in its motivation that Kafka might have rejected it as far-fetched.

Or would you stipulate that the ideal mixture of the races was the one existing in the community in which the school was situated? This would mean that Negro enrollment would be 33 percent of the total in each school in Philadelphia, 71 percent in Washington, D.C., 1 percent in Salt Lake City, 20 percent in Pittsburgh and .6 percent in Independence, Missouri. But that arrangement makes even less sense than the airlift. How could the correct blend be 71 percent black, 29 percent other, in one city and .6 percent black, 99.4 percent other, in another city?

And we haven't even considered the races that are neither black nor white. How many Orientals should be sprinkled in? How many American Indians? How many Asiatic Indians? And after the decision was made, where would you find them?

Although the subject is far too absurd to have warranted scholarly analysis, scholarly analysis is what it got plenty of during the early 1970's. One of the few scholars who made any sense at all was Nathan Glazer, professor of education and social structure at Harvard. Said Glazer: "What's so ideal about a mathematically precise distribution of human beings? What's so inherently evil about a block in which all the homeowners (or a classroom in which all the pupils) happen to be black? Or white? The ideal is a situation in which race is irrelevant to assignment."

Fortunately, busing to achieve a racial mix never became

prevalent. For one thing, it was vehemently opposed by the general public, black and white alike. A Gallup study conducted in 1972 revealed that 76 percent of all adult Americans were against the practice.

In communities where busing was made optional, few families elected to use it. New York City's experience was typical, declared columnist Joseph Alsop. "New York's primary, elementary and junior high schools have long had open enrollment, permitting children to leave their neighborhood schools and providing for their transportation to their schools of choice," he said. "In 1971, New York had a school population of 1,143,853 boys and girls. Of these, 392,714 were black and 260,040 were Puerto Rican. But of this black and Puerto Rican total of 652,754 children, just 11,687 chose open enrollment."

One reason for the lack of enthusiasm was a mountain of evidence that the changing of a school's racial blend did little or nothing to improve the quality of education, which was supposedly the chief goal. On May 21, 1972, *The Washington Post*, an early advocate of busing, carried a story that must have made its editorial writers just a trifle less sure of themselves. The article made its point in the lead paragraph:

"A major study of school desegregation by busing in five Northern cities concludes that achievement test scores of black students have not been raised. Moreover, the busing experiments, in several cases, have led to a worsening of race relations."

The story added that "the grades of Negro students generally fell when they were transferred to predominantly white schools because grading standards were higher."

The sixty-four-page study report had been written by David J. Armor, an associate professor of sociology at Harvard and a former researcher for the United States Civil Rights Commission. It covered research conducted in Boston, Ann Arbor, Hartford, Riverside, California, and White Plains, New York.

While most school busing was counter-productive and served only to heighten people's awareness of racial distinctions, it was perhaps the least reprehensible of all the educational experiments advanced during this era. There were other programs abroad at the time that were far more evil and considerably more dangerous.

There was, for example, the infamous "affirmative action" campaign of the United States Department of Health, Education and Welfare. This abomination, based on a twisted diagnosis of the Civil Rights Act of 1964, made it compulsory for universities to provide the government with detailed breakdowns of their employes by race, sex and national origin and to take steps—or "affirmative action"—to increase the numbers of those groups under-represented on campus. Institutions that failed to comply faced the loss of Federal grants and contracts.

As might be expected, the program elicited howls of protest from the academic community, whose members were predominantly male and predominantly white. Their own jobs were in jeopardy, and the same professors who previously had demanded the hiring of more women and more blacks by industrial corporations now had nothing but contempt for quota systems. Suddenly, it was their ox that was being gored.

Joining the faculty spokesmen in opposition to a helping hand for campus minorities were many of the great liberal newspapers. In an editorial on March 2, 1972, *The New York Times* noted that Columbia University might lose $13 million in Federal contracts unless it gave in to HEW and added some women and blacks to its faculty.

"Resort to quotas, which is the unmistakable suggestion in HEW's approach, will inevitably discriminate against qualified candidates," said the *Times*, which had never raised its editorial voice against quotas for private industry. "It can constitute a direct threat to institutional quality."

The *Times* thus went on record in favor of a double standard. It apparently could see nothing wrong with quotas and discrimination against qualified candidates in private industry, but it recoiled in horror from the same quotas and discrimination as applied to universities.

But Columbia wasn't the only institution of higher learning to receive a race-quota ultimatum from HEW. By the spring of 1972, ten other universities had been told to replace some white males with some blacks and females or say good-bye to those lucrative government contracts. As more and more pressure was exerted on more and more universities, the voice of the professor was heard in the land, and it was a piteous sound indeed. Racial "reform" had caught up with the authors of racial "reform", and they hated it.

A covey of indignant academicians at San Francisco State College made public an official SFSC notice to the effect that the institution had adopted HEW's affirmative action plan and would seek "an employe balance which in ethnic and male-female groups approximates that of the general population of the Bay Area from which we recruit." The professors who complained were especially unhappy, as well they might have been, about the following sentence in the college notice: "What [the new hiring plan] means is that we have shifted from the idea of equal opportunity in employment to a deliberate effort to seek out qualified and qualifiable people among ethnic minority groups and women to fill all jobs in our area."

That word "qualifiable" is of critical significance. Since in the opinion of the reformers almost every human being on earth was capable of mastering just about any academic subject under the proper environmental conditions, it followed that almost every human being was "qualifiable." In other words, San Francisco State College could now replace its white male faculty members with virtually any persons it wished, provided they met the ethnic and sex guidelines. Conceivably, it could make an illiterate the head of its English Department simply by pronouncing him or her "qualifiable."

This point was brought up by several Cornell University faculty members who wrote a letter to *The New York Times* stating that Cornell, too, had gone along with the HEW plan. It was now Cornell's policy, said the letter, to hire "additional minority persons and females even if 'in many instances it may be necessary to hire unqualified or marginally qualified persons'."

Still another academician to register a protest was Professor Sidney Hook of New York University. Unlike many of his colleagues, Hook, a political moderate, had never advocated a quota system in the first place, not even for those nasty old industrial corporations. In an article printed in the April 15, 1972, issue of *Human Events*, he denounced the HEW program as one that "threatens to destroy [the universities'] integrity as scholarly institutions." He noted that "HEW regional directors have instructed presidents of universities, in making faculty appointments, to give weight to other than professional qualifications, to establish numerical goals and a timetable to realize them. HEW has also advised specific changes in graduate school curriculum in order to ease the way for hiring of persons presently unqualified by professional experience."

That last sentence was a terrifying one, even by Disaster Lobby standards. It advanced the possibility that, in the not too distant future, there might be unleashed on the public of the United States an army of physicians and dentists and architects and engineers who had received their education from unqualified instructors.

In the course of condemning the HEW project, Hook had a few words of scorn for the rationale that led to the project. It had been the government's contention that radical measures were called for because the dearth of women and blacks on college faculties indicated widespread discrimination. Such logic, said the professor, "would prove that members of the Republican party are victims of crass discrimination in higher education because their numbers on university faculties, in comparison to the ratio of Republican party members to the general population, is so extraordinarily small."

In some cities, education officials decided to apply the affirmative action principle to their own operations. This was the case in March of 1971 when the San Francisco School Board voted to eliminate certain administrative positions in the interest of economy. Notices of "deselection"—the board's euphemism for "demotion"—were to be sent to 125 administrators. But which ones? Ordinarily, the board would have demoted those persons with the least seniority or the least talent. Not this time, however. This time was Disaster Lobby time, so the heads of the San Francisco school system very carefully went through the dossiers of all administrators in the department and placed each person into one of nine classifications: "Negro/Black, Chinese, Japanese, Korean, American Indian, Filipino, Other Non-White, Spanish Speaking/Spanish Surname and Other White." According to one of the officials in charge of the program, "strict seniority would be followed in deselecting administrators who have been classified as Other White, and all those administrators in the other eight designated minority groups would be exempted from such deselection process." The language was pure bureaucratese, but the intent and the effect were quite clear. What he meant was that the only persons who would be demoted were Other Whites. And that is how the City of San Francisco carried out its "deselection" campaign. All of the 125 administrators put on notice for demotion were "Other Whites."

In eliminating Jews from the school systems of Germany in the mid-1930's, Adolf Hitler had employed the same technique. Of course, the analogy would have infuriated the members of the San Francisco School Board. They would have hastened to remind whoever made the comparison that *they*, unlike Hitler, were discriminating against a certain race for the good of the nation as a whole. But then, come to think of it, that was Hitler's excuse too.

Although it was by no means unique, the San Francisco school purge drew a great deal of criticism from many prominent liberals, who by now were beginning to realize that something had gone haywire. So much fire was directed at the school board in San Francisco itself that the members decided not to demote anyone, which was a neat, if not very conclusive, way out of the dilemma.

Perhaps the most incisive commentary on the affair came

from Earl Raab, Executive Director of the Jewish Community Relations Council of San Francisco. In a *Commentary* magazine piece, Raab pointed out that "A subtle but critical line was crossed . . . in the case of the deselected administrators. For here it was no longer a matter of giving members of a disadvantaged group an edge in the process of competition; here it became a matter of eliminating the concept of competition altogether. It was not a matter of affirmative action toward equal opportunity, but a matter of eliminating equal opportunity altogether."

Raab also underscored the insanity of singling out certain minorities for perferential treatment while ignoring others. He cited an exchange at a hearing in San Francisco between an attorney for the deselected administrators and the representative of the school board. The questions were asked by the attorney.

"Q: Do you know that Armenians, as well as being a minority ethnic group, have had a history of persecution and disadvantage?"

"A: No, I never studied that."

"Q: Did you ever hear of the persecution of the Armenians by the Turks?"

"A: Not as I recall."

"Q: Did you ever hear of the disadvantage which Armenians in California suffered?"

"A: I am not aware of it."

"Q: If the [demoted Armenian administrator] respondent in this case says, 'I am an Armenian and I want to be treated as a separate minority,' what would you do with his case?"

"A: For the purpose of this, I would judge him to be white and put him in white because there is no specific Armenian classification."

"Q: Would you consider that the Jewish people were an ethnic group?"

"A: Yes."

"Q: Do you believe that there is a history of persecution and disadvantage which the Jewish people have had?"

"A: I have some remote knowledge of this."

"Q: Now suppose one of the respondents in this case came to you and said, 'I am a member of an ethnic minority, one of the Jewish people, and I believe that by reason of our historical disadvantage that we would like to be treated as a separate ethnic group,' what would your reply be?"

"A: That we have no category for you as a Jew."

According to Raab, the decision to allow the 125 administrators to keep their jobs did not signal an end to the quota system in San Francisco. The virus seems to be a stubborn one. "The Superintendent of Schools in San Francisco," said Raab, "has recently proposed a plan whereby no more than 20 percent of Other Whites will be hired or promoted to administrative positions in the first year, no more than 10 percent in the second year and no Other Whites at all in the ensuing years until ethnic and racial proportions among administrators equal the respective proportions in the school population. Here we have a good example of the use of quotas . . . as a way of replacing achievement with ascription by political fiat and without any reference to competitive performance."

But while the field of education was the most fertile one for the germination of quota-system lunacy, it was by no means the only one. In 1972, a New York City examination for the purpose of choosing Police and Fire Department aides was struck down as unconstitutional by the New York State Supreme Court because the applicants had been limited to persons residing in predominantly black and Puerto Rican neighborhoods. Undaunted, the New York State Civil Service Department went right ahead and announced that only blacks and Spanish Americans could apply for nineteen openings as state prison counselors.

On December 29, 1971, the United States Department of Labor made another contribution to the general nuttiness by notifying private companies with government contracts that they would henceforth have to maintain lists of their employes by religion and ethnic background. These lists would be subject to government inspection whenever a specific company was suspected of discriminating against minorities. Since there are some 250,000 companies that do business with the Federal government and since these companies employ 30 million persons, or more than one-third of the total civilian labor force, the Department of Labor order carried more than token weight.

The courts surprisingly did little to inhibit the trend toward a quota system society. Very often, it was a member of the Federal judiciary or some local jurist who set the quota system wheels in motion. In February 1972, a Federal judge in Alabama ordered that state's Department of Public Safety to hire Negroes and whites on a fifty-fifty basis until Negroes made up 25 percent of the Department's personnel. United States District Judge Frank M. Johnson, Jr's., ruling was in response to a suit filed by the National Association for the Advancement of Colored People.

In New York City, the agency that did the most to establish a quota system was the city's Commission on Human Rights. Among its achievements was an ethnic census carried out among New York's 400,000 municipal employes, a census that was widely interpreted as the first step in the establishment of preferential treatment for certain minority groups.

When the Human Rights Commission came under fire for having initiated the census, the Commission chairman, Eleanor Holmes Norton, had this explanation:

"Invariably these affirmative action orders are attacked as being violative of the rights of non-minorities by establishing perferential treatment of the previously excluded class. The short answer to this claim is that the majority has for too long enjoyed an advantage of its own, based on the discriminatory exclusion of another group."

Translation: the white folks used to take advantage of the black folks, so now the black folks are going to take advantage of the white folks. It's the kind of tit-for-tat mental process you would expect from a street gang of ten-year-old delinquents.

Encouraged by all of this "preferential treatment" in official circles, private citizens soon launched preferential treatment programs of their own. The board of directors of

Union Theological Seminary voted to establish a quota system whereby blacks would make up one-third and women
one-half of the Seminary's students, faculty, staff and
directors. "It is unrealistic," said Mrs. Horace Havemeyer,
chairman of the board, "to educate people for work in a
pluralistic society in an environment that is overwhelmingly
white and male-oriented."

At the time of the vote, blacks comprised 6 percent of the
Seminary's student body and women, 20 percent. It is therefore obvious that during the next few years white persons,
Oriental persons, American Indians and men will be discriminated against by Union Theological Seminary—in the
interest, of course, of nondiscrimination.

The hysteria quickly spread. In mid-1972, two black politicians, United States Representative Louis Stokes of Ohio
and Mayor Richard Hatcher of Gary, Indiana, declined to
appear on the American Broadcasting Company's Issues and
Answers program because the network had refused to accede
to their demand that the interviewing be conducted by a
person of their own race.

Occasionally, although far from frequently, a voice of logic
and reason and common sense could be discerned above the
manic babel. In May of 1972, the American Jewish Congress,
meeting in Cleveland, adopted a resolution stating that it was
"deeply troubled" by a growing acceptance of the idea that
jobs, promotions and college admissions should be determined by mathematical formulas based on the proportion of
various groups within a community. The AJC charged that
government agencies, in enforcing antidiscrimination laws,
have "sometimes taken the position that race is an indispensable occupational qualification. The American Jewish
Congress," said the resolution, "opposes this philosophy in
principle and in practice. We regard quotas as inconsistent
with the principle of equity and non-discrimination."

Throughout most of the battle over racial quotas, President
Nixon remained on the sidelines, waiting to see which faction attracted public support. (Richard Nixon's enemies
regard this wet-finger-in-the-air attitude of his as being

despicable, but there is nothing wrong in a President's desire to gauge his countrymen's sentiments before acting. A President is, after all, a representative of his people as well as a leader of his people.) In the primary elections of 1972, President Nixon got his message. George Wallace's victories indicated that most of the people of the United States were opposed to the quota system and were especially opposed to that manifestation of the quota system known as school busing. The President proposed a moratorium on all new and additional busing and asked Congress to set uniform national standards for school desegregation, in which busing would be a remedy of last resort.

On August 24, 1972, President Nixon issued a statement that showed where he stood on the issue. "Busing forced by a court to achieve an arbitrary racial balance is wrong," he said.

But characteristically, it was Vice President Spiro T. Agnew who more clearly, more rationally and more devastatingly than anyone else on the national scene placed a finger squarely on the fundamental weakness of school busing. Unlike the President, the Vice President had never waffled on busing or any of the other quota aberrations. He had been against such lunacy from the start, and he had no compunction about saying so.

"Years ago," Vice President Agnew told a Westfield, New Jersey, audience on April 22, 1972, "the quota system was a method used to assign certain minorities to certain schools on a basis of arbitrary ratios. It was an abomination then and it was opposed by all clear-thinking Americans, including most Congressmen from both sides of the aisle. Today, however, some of these Congressmen—including Senators McGovern, Muskie and Kennedy—are on record as *favoring* the quota system. They *want* to assign certain minorities to certain schools on a basis of arbitrary ratios. Only now . . . they don't call it the quota system. They call it busing. Well, allocating people on the basis of their religion or the color of their skin was dead wrong in 1920 and it was dead wrong in 1954 when the Brown decision put a stop to dual school systems and it is dead wrong today."

Although by this time most Americans had made up their minds about quota systems—the consensus, as reported in public opinion polls, was heavily against it—*The New York Times* kept hopping from one side of the fence to the other. The *Times* favored the quota system in hirings by private companies under the Philadelphia Plan, opposed the quota system in faculty appointments by universities and favored the quota system in the case of school busing. In an editorial in its issue of August 29, 1972, the *Times* referred to opponents of school busing as "demagogic", "segregationist" and "deceptive." It was symptomatic of the period that people—and newspapers—were continually applying to others those adjectives that were best applied to themselves.

ELEVEN

Two ... Four ... Six ... Eight ...

When some day the historians gather to discuss the 1960's
and 1970's, there may be a spirited debate over whether the
goofiness of this epoch was the result of the various protest
movements or whether the protests grew out of the goofiness. Whatever the chroniclers decide about the cause-and-
effect relationship, they will surely agree that never before
had the outbreaks of dissidence in the United States been
so numerous or so fatuous.

In earlier times, protests had served a purpose. In the
1960's, most of them served only the protesters. The scream-
ers and the placard wavers seemed to want nothing more
than a minute or two on a television newscast. And frequently the message they conveyed was diametrically opposed to the point they ostensibly were trying to make.
Bands of sloppy, smelly, slovenly kids, almost grotesque in
their ugliness, roamed the streets complaining about ugliness. Amateur ecologists carried garish signs demanding that
garish signs be outlawed. Dreamy-eyed pacifists, festooned
with "LOVE" buttons, went around the country planting
bombs and hurling bricks and maiming policemen, all in the
name of nonviolence.

Whenever the activists appeared, the paradoxes hammered away at you without a letup. Elderly humanitarians
who once quoted John Donne about no man being an island
and who, throughout the 1930's, had inveighed against iso-

lationism now organized massive rallies at which they insisted that we get out of Southeast Asia and mind our own business. Men and women who called themselves defenders of the oppressed mounted podium after podium to denounce South Vietnam, a nation that had been invaded, and to praise North Vietnam, the nation that had done the invading. College students clamored for a bigger role in shaping university policies on the ground that they had the moral and intellectual capacity to handle that role. To show how levelheaded they really were, they kidnaped college officials, burned down buildings, destroyed priceless books and records and chanted such edifying slogans as "One . . . two . . . three . . . four . . . we don't want your f . . . ing war" and "Two . . . four . . . six . . . eight . . . we refuse to negotiate."

But you couldn't really blame the youngsters. They were simply passing along, in the form of riots, some of the drivel they had heard in their lecture halls. For in the middle and late 1960's, many members of this nation's academic community were spouting the most arrant nonsense ever to assail the ears of the impressionable young.

There was, for example, a speech by the president of Yale University, Dr. Kingman Brewster, Jr., who, on the eve of the trial of members of a militant Negro organization, said he doubted whether a black revolutionary could get a fair trial anywhere in the United States. Several years later, after the acquittal of just about every black revolutionary taken into custody in the 1960's, Brewster admitted that he had been mistaken. He said he now believed that it *was* possible for a black revolutionary to get a fair trial in the United States. Of course, by then the Yale students had already rioted in support of black revolutionaries. By then the heads had already been broken. The buildings had already been demolished. By then it was too late.

Also at Yale, Professor Charles Reich contributed to the general unrest by declaring, "America is at the brink of a police state." And at Harvard, Professor Allan Dershowitz loudly lamented "the contraction of our civil liberties," which was a puzzling charge since his own freedom to make the statement contradicted it.

But the Ivy League had no monopoly on irresponsible or befuddled faculty members. At Stanford University, an associate professor of English named H. Bruce Franklin devoted much of his time to an unusual extracurricular activity. At a trustees' hearing to determine whether he should be dismissed from his job, it was charged that on January 11, 1971, Franklin had dropped in on a scheduled speech by Henry Cabot Lodge, former United States Ambassador to South Vietnam, and by various methods, prevented Lodge from speaking. It was further charged that on February 10, 1971, Franklin had incited Stanford students to disrupt university functions by occupying and shutting down the Computation Center. It was further charged that on a number of other occasions Franklin had encouraged Stanford students to engage in conduct that threatened injury to individuals and property.

The nature of that "conduct" was spelled out in detail by Henry L. Packer, Professor of Law at Stanford, in an article in the April 1972 issue of *Commentary*. According to Packer, "The years between 1967 and the present were a very bad time for Stanford . . . The period can be characterized as something like a reign of terror. 'Trashing' or window-breaking cost the university about a quarter of a million dollars. There were at least five sit-ins during the period, which disrupted the lives of the community. There were numerous incidents of arson, including destructive fires in which scholars lost irreplaceable papers. A staff member had his house fire-bombed. Another was shot at through the front window of his living room. The president's office was destroyed by arson. On occasion, faculty, staff and students stood round-the-clock fire watches. Throughout the period, Franklin was in the forefront, accelerating the coercion and violence through his charisma as a tenured professor, and urging young people on to ever more activity."

After listening to the charges against him at the dismissal

hearing, Franklin was thoroughly unruffled. "They ain't proved nothing," said the associate professor of English.

Whether they proved anything or not, Franklin was ultimately ousted. In his wake, one question lingered. If Franklin had done all the things he was accused of doing, why did Stanford officials wait so long—from 1967 to 1971, according to Packer's article—to institute dismissal proceedings? Why hadn't they fired him immediately? The probable answer: back in 1967, so many professors were fomenting so many riots at so many colleges with so much media support that public opinion would have been on Franklin's side. The university *couldn't* have fired him without making him a martyr.

At the height of the madness, campus troublemakers often went outside Academe to find guest lecturers and speakers who shared their curious predilections. Such a speaker was John V. Lindsay, Mayor of the City of New York. On April 29, 1970, Mayor Lindsay addressed a student convocation at the University of Pennsylvania. During the week in which he spoke, scores of American soldiers were killed or wounded in the rice paddies and on the mountain slopes of South Vietnam. The mayor had nothing to say about them. "The ones I have unending admiration for," he told the students, "are the guys who say 'I simply will not serve in the Army of the United States in Vietnam . . .' These are the guys who are heroic."

Lindsay also had an opinion about the trial in Chicago of seven men accused of complicity in the 1968 Democratic National Convention riots. Lindsay didn't think much of the trial. Like Kingman Brewster, he had a low opinion of American justice. The trial of the Chicago Seven, said Lindsay, was "a tawdry judicial parody." He added, "After that dubious exercise, a disaster for all concerned, it is harder to believe that the system is open, fair-minded and humane. Something," said Mayor Lindsay, "is very wrong with America."

The mayor was absolutely right. Something *was* very

wrong with America, and you wouldn't have had to travel ten feet from New York's City Hall to find it.

Whenever a young American began to suspect that it might be better to obey the rules than to flout them, there was always Supreme Court Justice William O. Douglas to set him straight. In 1971, the Supreme Court refused to consider the case of a male student who had been ejected from his high school for failing to abide by the code governing hair styles. Justic Douglas, needless to say, filed a dissenting opinion. *The Washington Post*, also needless to say, thought so highly of it that it reprinted excerpts, including the following:

"It seems incredible," said Justice Douglas, "that under our federalism a state can deny a student education in its public school system unless his hair style comports with the standards of the school board. Hair style is highly personal, an idiosyncracy which I had assumed was left to family or individual control and was of no legitimate concern to the state."

This was pure poppycock, as Justice Douglas must have realized. If hair style were of no legitimate concern to the state, what would the eminent jurist do with a boy who decided to wear his hair in six-foot-long pigtails, color it bright green and soak it in essence of skunk? Choice of clothes is also highly personal. How would the Justice deal with a male student who elected to attend school in an evening gown? Or a loin cloth? Or in nothing at all? And one can't help wondering what the reaction of Justice Douglas might be if one of his colleagues or a practicing attorney were to show up at the Supreme Court some morning clad in hot pants and wearing his hair in purple-dyed braids.

It must have been obvious to Justice Douglas that every institution has the right to prescribe standards of dress and behavior for those using its facilities. Without that right, there would be an open invitation to chaos.

Unfortunately, the Douglas viewpoint was a popular one in the Age of Unreason. School after school abandoned dress codes and hair codes and smoking codes and eventually only one code remained. It was the "anything goes" code. Universities began permitting men and women to share the same dormitories and, in February of 1972, a cooperative housing unit for University of Michigan students announced that its male and female tenants could, if they wished, share the same rooms.

The breakdown of codes and standards for young people extended into the classroom. John Holt, one of the period's most popular and highly respected writers on education, stated that the college of the future would be one with no entrance requirements, no formal curricula, no tests, no grades and no rules for the hiring of faculty members. Anyone who wanted to teach would be permitted to do so.

In a magazine article outlining his blueprint for this type of institution, Holt admitted that it would not be suitable for medical students. Doctors, he said, should receive a more conventional kind of training. However, he apparently was willing to see candidates for other professions get their education in that rather casual, slapdash manner. Under the Holt plan, for example, ninety-story skyscrapers might be designed by untested architects who had been tutored by drop-in teachers and then built by engineers without any specialized schooling at all. The question that suggests itself is whether John Holt would care to occupy an office on the nineteeth floor of such a skyscraper—or even to walk past the structure when a stiff breeze was blowing.

But as preposterous as the Holt concept was, there were educators who applauded it and, worse yet, put it into practice. In February of 1972, a state supported college opened for business above a Walgreen drug store in downtown St. Paul, Minnesota. It was called Metropolitan State College and, true to the Holtian vision, it had no lecture halls, no dormitories, no semesters, no required courses and no grades. David Sweet, its 38-year-old first president, nicknamed it "Wing-it U."

According to *Newsweek*, Wing-it U represented "a radical idea" in education, an idea known as the external-degree system. In an external-degree institution, said *Newsweek*, "students of any age and almost any background can work out an individualized college program to suit their personal interests and responsibilities. So dramatic are the possibilities of the external-degree system that Samuel Baskin, who heads an external-degree consortium called University Without Walls, predicts: 'This plan will change the entire face of U.S. higher education'."

Some educators agreed with Baskin, but they doubted that the new face would be an improvement. The most skeptical were the teachers actually involved in external-degree programs. "I don't teach," said one instructor at a New York State external-degree college. 'The interests of the students are so diverse that I am just an educational broker."

The students were even more dubious. "We don't know what we're doing," a Metropolitan State matriculant told *Newsweek*. "And the staff doesn't know what it's doing. There are kids who walk in here and want a degree without fulfilling any requirements."

Chances are the kids at dear old Wing-it U will get their degrees. They won't get much of an education, but they'll get the piece of paper crediting them with having attained an education. In that respect, they will resemble millions of other American boys and girls of the period. For in some of the school systems that emerged from the wave of protests of the 1960's, a solid education was as rare and elusive as a peaceful individual at a peace rally.

In their protests, the youth of America had demanded the right to select their own curricula, to have a say in the hiring and firing of teachers and to determine the ground rules under which the colleges were to be run. It was their misfortune that they got pretty much what they wanted. University after university caved in under their pressures. Across the nation, sexagenarian college presidents with strings of degrees after their names and half-column listings in *Who's Who* held meetings with fuzzy-cheeked students and succumbed to the outcry that the students really knew more about operating the colleges than they did. If the youngsters wanted courses in contemporary trashing taught

by alumni of Federal prisons, then that's what the youngsters got. If they wanted English and history and science
courses dropped, these courses *were* dropped—or at least
made noncompulsory.

Then the ripples began to spread out. In many towns
and cities, self-appointed community leaders saw how successful the college protesters had been and they began to
stage their own protests. They demanded the right to run
the local public schools without interference from government agencies or professional educators. They too got what
they wanted. In many metropolitan-area high schools and
junior highs and elementary schools, amateur teachers were
recruited to replace qualified teachers and heavy stress was
placed on curricula downplaying the traditional studies in
favor of "relevant" studies, such as "Consumerism and Supermarket Shopping" and "Public Demonstrations and the New
Society."

One of the first school systems to make the switch was
that of the heavily black Ocean Hill-Brownsville section of
the borough of Brooklyn in New York City. For several
years, there had been complaints that children in the area
were not getting a satisfactory education. They consistently
tested lower than the average New York City student in
reading ability. Ocean Hill-Brownsville leaders recommended, as a means toward rectifying the disparity, that
control of the schools in the section be turned over to them.

At first, the recommendations came in letters and petitions. Later, they took the form of street demonstrations and
riots. Ultimately, the City and State authorities surrendered,
and in mid-1967 Ocean Hill-Brownsville became a Demonstration District in which a new scheme would be employed
"to solve educational retardation in the ghettos."

For the next three academic years, from the fall of 1967
to the spring of 1970, a decentralized system put the Ocean
Hill-Brownsville public schools squarely in the hands of the
Ocean Hill-Brownsville residents. They exercised their new
powers with determination and vigor. During the three
years, scores of incumbent teachers were fired or transferred

out of the District. Old curricula were jettisoned in favor of those championed by local leaders. Traditional teaching methods were scrapped and untested new ones were installed.

The experiment, as might be expected, received effusive praise from just about every new-breed liberal within a radius of 250 miles. Editor-columnist I. F. Stone said a trip to the Demonstration District was "like waking from a nightmare. The visit was therapeutic. It would be a tragedy if this experiment in community control were shut down... Their focus is on the child."

Literary critic Alfred Kazin wrote, "The flame [of learning] burns hotter than ever... The intentness all over the place audibly vibrated in my ears."

Social commentator Nat Hentoff wrote, "I would expect a substantial rise in achievement in those schools because of the staff that has been there from the beginning of the school year. I have no idea how many of them are fully licensed, and I don't think it matters in view of their attitude toward the children."

The Hentoff rationale was typical of the times. It implied that anybody could do anything if his heart was pure and if society would just give him a chance. Another liberal visitor, Dwight Macdonald, made the same point when he said, "Ocean Hill reinforced the prejudice I've always had in favor of amateurs who don't know how to do it but, as the etymology suggests, love doing it."

From the New York Civil Liberties Union came the statement, quite premature as it turned out, that "the experiment in local community control is bringing about substantial improvements in education in Ocean Hill-Brownsville."

Fred Ferretti wrote in *New York* magazine, equally prematurely, that the new system in Ocean Hill-Brownsville "has succeeded in raising the reading levels of many children in the district in a remarkably short time."

And New York City Environmental Protection Administrator Jerome Kretchmer, whose qualifications on education were no better than his qualifications on the environment, provided evidence of his inadequacy when he declared, in quoting an official of the Ocean Hill-Brownsville school system, that "by February 1, 1970, every youngster in that system will be classified as a reader. There will no longer be any students in that school system, in that district, classified as non-readers."

Kretchmer was wrong. Stone was wrong. Kazin was wrong. Hentoff was wrong. Macdonald was wrong. And so were all the well-meaning but unqualified community leaders who thought they could transform nonreaders into readers by junking the tested and proved techniques and getting rid of professional teachers.

Diane Ravitch, a fellow of the Institute of Philosophy and Politics of Education at Teachers College, Columbia, made a detailed—and objective—study of the Ocean Hill-Brownsville project and pronounced it a dismal failure in terms of its stated objective, which was to improve the children's reading capabilities. She based her conclusion largely on a series of standardized Metropolitan Reading Achievement Tests given to all New York City public school pupils in the spring of 1971, less than a year after the Ocean Hill-Brownsville experiment had been discontinued.

"Every school in the [Ocean Hill-Brownsville] district reported poor reading scores—as compared with other schools in the city, with other schools in the borough of Brooklyn and even with other ghetto schools generally," Miss Ravitch reported. "The highest-scoring school in the district, an elementary school, had only 24.5 percent of its pupils reading on or above grade level."

She noted that the results of the 1971 tests in Ocean Hill-Brownsville were even lower than those for similar tests given in the same schools in 1967, before the experiment began. No school in the district recorded a higher score in 1971 than it had in 1967.

She then made this observation: "After all the publicity and conflict, after all the bold rhetoric and revolutionary expectations, after all the money spent, jobs allocated, new machinery and programs introduced, the children of the district cannot read as well today as they did five years ago."

Because many schools and colleges in the United States were experimenting with new educational programs as a result of campus and community protests, the level of student achievement began to decline on a national scale. On February 2, 1972, the Federal government made public the results of a major study entitled "National Assessment of Education Progress." In compiling their data, the researchers had interviewed 86,000 children aged nine, thirteen and seventeen in 2,500 schools in various sections of the country, and had also spoken with 8,000 young adults. Dr. Henry Slotnik, author of the 150-page report, expressed shock and amazement at what the interviewers had found. "Only four or five people in the whole assessment had a really good command of the English language," said Slotnik.

That's "four or five" out of 86,000 children and 8,000 young adults. And the language under analysis was English, the native tongue of the vast majority of them.

College students fared just as badly when tested. A 1972 survey at Arizona State University revealed that one-fourth of the undergraduates there were unable to identify Saigon as the capital of South Vietnam or locate South Vietnam on a map. Similar studies at other universities uncovered similar deficiencies.

Perhaps the most striking irony in all of this—and there are ironies galore—is that at a time when achievement test scores were plummeting all over the place the youth of America had somehow acquired a reputation for being the most intelligent, best educated generation in history. At thousands upon thousands of luncheons and dinners, silver-haired speakers would arise to pay tribute to, as one speaker put it, "these wonderful young people of today who are so much smarter than we were at their age."

One prominent educator who had reservations about the nation's young people, especially those leading the protest movements, was Dr. Nathan M. Pusey, then President of Harvard. After eighteen years as head of the nation's oldest and most prestigious university, Pusey retired on June 30,

1971, and in his last speech to the student body, he denounced the "power-hungry revolutionaries" on campus who had been creating so many disturbances. He termed them "grievously, even malignantly deluded."

Said Pusey: "In recent years, campus revolutionaries, here and elsewhere, have held that a debilitating and dehumanizing contagion, allegedly springing from the interests and arrangements of the world outside, has so deeply penetrated and widely infected the activities and structures of academic societies, and has so controlled them, that the only acceptable attitude toward them must also be one of hatred, denigration and attack. I cannot see any significant correspondence between the world which I have experienced and come to respect and the world they describe."

He then went on to rebuke those who "amplify their rhetoric in public parks, shriek their calls to action over bullhorns and sound tracks within the Groves of Academe, repetitively spreading private—and usually very inane—doctrines . . . It is hard to discern in all this just who is kidding whom, but surely something is sadly mixed up, and there is room in our society for serious doubts about motives and behavior."

"Something is sadly mixed up." These five words of Harvard's Nathan Pusey epitomized an entire era. For something *was* sadly mixed up. And it bubbled to the surface in all of of those public protests and demonstrations for which the era was famous. Consider, as a prime example, the protests and demonstrations connected with the Women's Liberation movement.

As in most movements, there was a shred of validity to Women's Liberation. Women *had* been second-class citizens for a long time. They had not been permitted to vote or enroll in certain colleges or patronize certain establishments or join certain clubs, and they usually received less pay than men for equivalent work.

But long before Women's Liberation reared its lovely head, most of the inequities had been abolished. And many others were being abolished. Throughout the land, bastions of male exclusivity were toppling one by one. Then came the Betty Friedans and the Gloria Steinems and the Ti-Grace Atkinsons and the whole of the male-hating, bra-burning, logic-spurning Women's Lib brigade, and what had been a sensible crusade for women's rights turned into an antic side-show worthy of the Brothers Ringling.

A basic problem of the Libbers was one they shared with other placard-wavers of the Age of Unreason. They embraced the philosophy that regards everybody as being precisely the same as everybody else, with the same abilities and the same qualifications and the same desires and ambitions, and that holds that each person is therefore entitled to have exactly what every other person has.

Thus the Women's Liberation folks adopted a rather novel position. It was their view that women not only should be treated the same as men but that women essentially *were* the same as men. If you accept that thesis, you have little difficulty in accepting the Libbers' belief that women should hold down all the jobs once considered to be men's work, such as serving in frontline combat forces, and that the tasks traditionally reserved for women—housework and child care and the like—should be assumed by both sexes on a fifty-fifty arrangement. One outgrowth of this argument was a demand by women athletes for pay scales equal to those enjoyed by male athletes.

The problem here is that women are *not* the same as men. For one thing, they are a bit shorter on the average. They are also a bit lighter, a bit less muscular and considerably less hairy. They have somewhat higher voices than men do and, unlike men, they bear children.

For some of the above reasons, women are not as good at professional sports as men are. The best male tennis player in the United States would mop up the courts at Forest Hills with the best female player. The best male golfer in the United States would clobber the best female golfer. And you could gather together the eleven fastest, biggest and toughest women in this country and the Dallas Cowboys would still outscore them by at least a dozen touchdowns. It is for this reason—not bias, not hypocrisy and not male chauvinism—that women athletes are not paid as much as men athletes. In those pursuits where women excel—the theater is a good example—they have almost always received at least as much money as their male counterparts.

The physical differences between men and women have also determined other life-style patterns objected to so strenuously by Women's Libbers. Through all of recorded history, the women in civilized countries, because of their child-bearing nature, have tended the children and taken care of the home. Men, because of their superior physical strength, have gone out of the home to do the work that calls for superior physical strength.

It is interesting to note that even the lesser animals assign separate roles to the male and the female. In virtually all warm-blooded species, there is a sharply defined distinction between the activities of one sex and those of the other. Of course, this distinction is made possible by the fact that there are relatively few Women's Libbers living among the chickens and the mountain lions.

To support their contention that the women of America are persecuted by the men, the Lib folks engaged in some of the zaniest capers since the break between Dean Martin and Jerry Lewis. In the spring of 1972, for example, the New York City chapter of the National Organization for Women filed a petition with the Federal Communications Commission asking that the American Broadcasting Company's flagship television station, WABC-TV, be taken off the air. And why did NOW want WABC-TV stripped of its franchise? Because, NOW charged, WABC-TV discriminated against women. And how did WABC-TV discriminate against women? For one thing, said NOW, on the day seven American women won gold medals at the 1972 Olympic games, WABC-TV reporter Doug Johnson led off his commentary with the words, "Thank heaven for little girls." A clear case of male chauvinism, according to NOW.

And how else did WABC-TV discriminate against the equal sex? The NOW complaint noted that in 42.6 percent of the commercials shown by the station, women were depicted inside the home doing household chores. This, said NOW, was a calculated affront to females since it implied that women were unfit to do anything but keep house.

Now there is the kind of logic that would start Aristotle spinning in his grave. The remainder of the NOW petition was equally sensible, but that's as much as you could say for it.

Television commercials featuring women as housewives also came under attack in a *New York Times Magazine* article entitled "TV Commercials Insult Women" and written by two members of NOW. Since most of the commercials they cited were for household products and since almost all household products are bought and used by housewives, the focus on housewives in the commercials would appear to be more or less mandatory. But not to the authors of the article. To them, "watching commercials is like being blasted by some casually malevolent propaganda machine dedicated to the humiliation of women." Furthermore, they said, the constant portrayal of women as housewives keeps women from seeking new and more rewarding careers. "People tend to imitate the roles they see, to become what is expected of them," the article said.

This must be true. That's why so many American men are hard-riding Marshal Dillons and butter-fingered Ozzie Nelsons and lady-killing Cary Grants. They keep imitating the roles they see.

The authors of the *Times Magazine* piece had not yet run down. "Despite the fact that insurance tables show that women have fewer [highway] accidents than men," they said, "the woman is still imagined as the mechanically inept hairbrain who manages to run over a suitcase twice in the middle of her own driveway."

Here the authors were on shaky ground indeed. Most women *are* mechanically inept in comparison with men. The reason they have fewer automobile accidents than men, as any actuarial expert could have explained, is that women don't drive nearly as many miles as men do and they are much less likely to drive at night, in bad weather or over long distances. If all of these factors are taken into consideration, men are revealed to be safer drivers.

One parting shot from the authors: they referred to a commercial in which a male announcer tells a female model how to apply makeup "until she finally gets it." In the opinion of the women who wrote the article, "she really ought to haul off and sock him, but the need for male approval, implicit in 33.9 percent of these commercials, stops her."

Actually, something else might stop her. She might be deterred by the knowledge that if she hauled off and socked the announcer, he might forget his male chauvinistic upbringing and sock her right back. And because he probably outweighed her by a good seventy-five pounds and had a fist twice the size of hers, he very likely would end up rearranging her features to the point where she might no longer be able to function properly as a model.

But it wasn't only TV announcers and their sponsors who infuriated the myrmidons of Women's Lib; it was just about every aspect of our society, including the English language. As a matter of fact, the English language was condemned as one of the worst offenders.

A pair of authors named Casey Miller and Kate Swift brought to light the defects in the English language in a magazine article entitled "One Small Step for Genkind." The trouble with our native tongue, they said, is that it is hopelessly prejudiced against women. Take the word "mankind." It reeks of male chauvinism. It should, in the opinion of the authors, be "genkind." Why should men get all that free publicity? In the new lexicon, boys and girls would grow to "genhood" and feminine endings in words like "poetess" and "aviatrix" would be abolished.

Of course, most reference books would have to be rewritten. Miller and Swift—the advocates of Women's Liberation were in favor of calling women by their last names and dropping all that Miss and Mrs. and Mesdames stuff—were especially peeved with the *Britannica Junior Encyclopaedia,* which had the audacity to state that "Man is the highest form of life on earth." The two women also had a bone to pick with arithmetic books that launched their problems with phrases like "If a man can walk 10 miles in two hours..."

The New York journalism review (*More*) hopped on the semantic bandwagon by suggesting that "the generic personal pronoun 'co' be used to replace 'he' and 'she'." And quite a few female heads of clubs and government agencies began to refer to themselves as "chairpersons", while the same women and others insisted on being addressed by the title "Ms.", which, unlike "Miss" or "Mrs.", indicated nothing about the addressee other than her sex. Eventually, it was hoped by some, even that element of classification could be done away with, and both sexes would use the same form of address.

(The war on English, together with the attacks on advertisements featuring housewives, cosmetics and "sexist" lingerie, pointed up one underlying purpose of the Women's Lib movement. It was designed, among other things, to obliterate the differences between the sexes and to create a climate in which the line of demarcation that separates men from women would begin to blur. All of this fit in admirably with other manifestations of the period, particularly the tendency of young men and women to wear the same kinds of clothes, sport the same kinds of hairdos and occupy the same bedrooms, regardless of whether they happened to be married, engaged or even mildly attracted to each other.)

Some satirists, with tongues firmly implanted in cheeks, offered up a few Women's Lib phrases of their own. Martin Levin, in *Saturday Review*, after noting that he had recently received a letter addressed to the "Chairperson" of his university's Department of General Linguistics, recommended that the letters "m", "a" and "n" be excised from words pertaining to vocations. Thus, said Levin, we would have firepersons, policepersons, milkpersons and first basepersons. The classics would have to be revised, with titles now reading *The Postperson Always Rings Twice, A Person for All Seasons, Death of a Salesperson* and *The Iceperson Cometh*. In geography, the capital of Jordan would become Amper-

son, while the country of which Bonn is the capital would
be West Gerpersony.

Other commentators were less indulgent. In an article in
The New York Times Book Review, author Joan Didion mar-
veled at the "invention of women as a 'class' for the purpose
of manufacturing a class struggle." Said Miss Didion, "The
notion that, in the absence of a cooperative proletariat, a
revolutionary class might simply be invented, made up,
'named' and so brought into existence, seemed at once so
pragmatic and so visionary, so precisely Emersonian, that it
took the breath away ... "

She noted that an article in *Ms.*—they even named a magazine after the new method of address—had suggested that
housework be divided between husband and wife, with the
wife stripping the bed and the husband remaking it, with
the children directing their questions to one parent one day
and to the other parent the next day.

"It seemed," said Miss Didion, "that the aversion was to
adult sexual life itself: how much cleaner to stay forever
children. . . . More and more we have been hearing the
wishful voices of . . . perpetual adolescents, the voices of
women scarred by resentment not of their class position as
women but at the failure of their childhood expectations and
misapprehensions."

In another article, Joseph Adelson, Professor of Psychology
at the University of Michigan, ridiculed statements by Wom-
en's Libbers that "human beings no longer need to repro-
duce", that "the penis is outmoded, a vestigial organ like the
appendix", and that "the ultimate revolution will come only
when men have babies." Such remarks, he said, reveal the
immaturity and peculiar reluctance to face facts of many
members of the movement. "They deal," he observed, "with
certain human givens—anatomy, parturition, gender—and
they wish them away in a spasm of the distended will as
though the will, in pursuit of total human possibility, can
amplify itself to overcome the given."

Adelson also zeroed in on the Libbers' attitude toward
children. He quoted one woman as having suggested that

if a reserve of "trained practical mothers" were available, a professional woman could go back to work a few months after giving birth, leaving her child under the care of a practical mother. At the age of two, the child would enter a day-care center. For a two-child family, such an arrangement would require only one year's absence from work for the natural mother.

"One might be led to wonder," said Adelson, "why the woman she describes feels she needs a child at all, let alone two; and one might also note, mordantly, that a movement devoted to femine equality rather casually assumes the existence of a class of female servants." He went on to state that in the thinking of Women's Lib members "the child is transformed from a creature to be nurtured and protected to a perplexing problem that a good managerial intelligence will solve."

In his analysis of the Women's Lib crusade, Adelson placed his finger squarely on the nub of the irrationality permeating not only Women's Lib but most of the other social upheavals of the Age of Unreason. He said there was a great similarity between the Lib philosophy and that of John Locke in that both advanced "the idea of human perfectability through social action." Unfortunately, noted the professor, there are certain human qualities, including purely physical ones, that simply cannot be changed. And that is where the trouble begins, for, said Adelman, "there is a darker version of the Lockean spirit, in which it becomes intense, visionary, messianic. The displeasure with inequality is transformed into an assault upon difference itself, so that the pluralisms of the social order, even those pluralisms based on choice, are held to be too unbearable to endure." At that point, the reformers, frustrated in their efforts to make this a perfect world, may resort to violence, even totalitarianism.

Anyone who ever witnessed from close up a Women's Liberation rally very likely saw the Lockean spirit in full fury and with all the stops wide open. The flushed faces, the savage appearing eyes, the profanity, the screams, the con-

demnation of men and of women who like men, all gave
testimony to the crossing of a threshold that separates
rational reform from quixotic ravings and ram-it-down-their-
throats pressure politics.

In the end, of course—for this was that time—the quixotic
ravings and the ram-it-down-their-throats tactics carried the
day. The Women's Liberation movement got much of what
it was protesting about. An Equal Rights Amendment to
the Constitution seemed, by late 1972, to be well on its way
to adoption. What it will do, if interpreted the way the
Women's Libbers want it interpreted, is destroy the legal
devices originally designed to protect women. It will do
away with alimony. It will do away with limits to the number of hours women will be allowed to work and with
restrictions on night work and other possibly hazardous du-
ties. It would make women eligible not only to be drafted
into the armed forces but to be drafted for combat duty.

It would, in brief, rescind all of the protective legislation
enacted on women's behalf during the past two centuries.
Since all of that legislation had the whole-hearted support
of America's liberals, it seems strange that so many persons
and institutions bearing the liberal label now endorse not
only the Equal Rights Amendment but the entire Women's
Liberation movement.

The Washington Post, for one, backs the Amendment all
the way. "Consider," it said in an editorial, "all those moral-
istic limitations upon women which keep them from working
in an atmosphere men consider too indelicate for them—as
bartenders, for example."

The *Post* need fear no more. The Libbers' protests, like
those of the trashers and the bombers and the draft-card
burners, have been successful. It appears most likely that, in
the not too distant future, women will be permitted to tend
bar wherever they want, at all hours of the day and night,
and carry full kegs of beer if that is their pleasure. They will
also be able to serve in the armed forces as draftees rather
than volunteers. They will even be able to die in combat, just
like the men. In fact, their combat role is already past the

planning stage. On August 8, 1972, Admiral Elmo R. Zum-walt, Jr., Chief of Naval Operations, announced the repeal of regulations prohibiting women from serving aboard warships.

As the members of the Women's Liberation movement celebrated that victory, tens of millions of other women might well have been contemplating the words of the warrior King Pyrrhus, who, after defeating the Romans at the cost of most of his own troops, declared, "One more such victory and I am lost."

TWELVE **The Closed Fraternity**

On November 13, 1969, Spiro T. Agnew, Vice President of the United States, delivered a speech to the Midwest Regional Republican Committee in Des Moines, Iowa, in which he charged that the news programs produced and broadcast by the nation's three big television networks were biased in favor of liberal politicians and liberal viewpoints and against conservative politicians and conservative viewpoints. This was the case, said the Vice President, because the programs were controlled by "a tiny and closed fraternity of privileged men" who were themselves liberals and who were unable or unwilling to divorce their personal prejudices from their professional output.

There was only one thing wrong with the speech, which stirred up spirited response throughout the country. It was too mild. It rapped knuckles where it could easily have fractured noses. And it limited its indictment to network TV where it could have demanded a true bill against all types of communications media, including most of the national magazines and many of the metropolitan-area newspapers. For at the time Agnew spoke, virtually all of the major media were dominated to such an extent by dedicated left-wing activists as to make their contents hopelessly one-sided and, for that reason, almost totally unreliable. Indeed, the era of the Disaster Lobby could never have dawned without the whole-hearted cooperation, and often the calculated incitement, of the so-called "news" media.

Although many newsmen privately admitted, and sometimes bragged, that they and their colleagues were less than objective, spokesmen for the media were publicly infuriated by the Vice President's remarks.

Dr. Frank Stanton, president of the Columbia Broadcasting System, accused Agnew of practicing censorship through intimidation.

Television news commentator Walter Cronkite said the Des Moines talk was "an implied threat to freedom of speech in this country."

Frank Mankiewicz, a syndicated newspaper columnist who, not surprisingly, went on to become a top campaign adviser to George McGovern, saw in the Vice President's statements a resurgence of Nazism.

Interestingly and significantly, few defenders of the media denied the basic charge of bias. Such a denial would have been futile anyway, since a majority of people in the country, journalist and nonjournalist alike, knew the charge was true. *The New York Times*, not one to encourage the likes of the Vice President, admitted several days after the Des Moines speech that its mail had been running twenty-four to one in Agnew's favor. The Louis Harris poll reported 52 percent of the population supporting Agnew with only 29 percent opposed.

Of course, the news media of the United States had never been without bias, and for an obvious reason. News reports are written by human beings and human beings have prejudices. *All* human beings. As staunch an apologist for the media as TV's David Brinkley once observed that "objectivity is impossible to normal human behavior." And by the mere process of deciding which elements in a political speech should go into the lead paragraph of his story and which should be further down or omitted entirely—for there must be a sorting and a winnowing out when a thirty-minute talk is abbreviated into a half-column news item—a reporter brings into play a complex tangle of prejudices. He may not do it consciously but he does it nevertheless.

The slanting of news, whatever its cause, has infuriated men in public life since the first news reports were scrawled out on papyrus. Newsmen dearly love to quote that famous "government without newspapers" line of Thomas Jefferson's —he once said that given a choice between a government without newspapers or newspapers without government, he would "not hesitate a moment to prefer the latter"—but Jefferson actually had little liking for the press of his day, and for the same reason enunciated by Agnew. He found the newspapers intolerably biased. In fact, Jefferson's comments about newspapers make Agnew's speech read like a love sonnet by contrast.

Some excerpts from letters written by Jefferson to friends reveal his attitude:

"Advertisements contain the only truths to be relied on in a newspaper."

"Nothing can now be believed which is seen in a newspaper. Truth itself becomes suspicious by being put into that polluted vehicle."

"The man who never looks into a newspaper is better informed than he who reads them; inasmuch as he who knows nothing is nearer to truth than he whose mind is filled with falsehoods and errors."

"Perhaps an editor might begin a reformation in some such way as this. Divide his paper into four chapters, heading the first Truths, the second Probabilities, the third Possibilities, the fourth Lies. The first chapter would be very short."

"It is a melancholy truth that a suppression of the press could not more completely deprive the nation of its benefits than is done by its abandoned prostitution to falsehood."

One can readily imagine the shrieks of "censorship" and "intimidation" that would have filled the air over the intellectual community if those words had been uttered by Spiro T. Agnew in 1969 instead of by Thomas Jefferson in the years 1802 through 1813. But then Jefferson was a liberal and was therefore entitled to express his views while Agnew, as a conservative, was expected to remain mute at all times. And of course Jefferson had been attacking newspapers that were biased toward the right while Agnew was denouncing those tilted toward the left. That does make all the difference. Just how great a difference it makes can be seen in a fascinating episode that occurred in the decade encompassing World War II.

From the beginning of Franklin D. Roosevelt's long occupancy of the White House, the nation's press, most of it owned, operated and *controlled* by conservatives, had been inflexibly antagonistic. Whatever Roosevelt did in office was likely to bring down the wrath of the William Randolph Hearsts and the Scripps-Howards along with the equally intense, if less far-ranging, anger of small-town publishers from coast to coast.

The liberal supporters of FDR were outraged. To them, the spectacle of a one-party press—and it was the wrong party—was insufferable. So a number of them got together in 1946 and formed what came to be known as The Commission on Freedom of the Press. Chairman of the Commission was the liberal Robert M. Hutchins, then chancellor of the University of Chicago. The membership roster was so heavily weighted down with other liberals that if the Commission had been a ship it would have rolled over to port and sunk in a matter of minutes. Among them were the historian, Arthur M. Schlesinger; the poet, Archibald MacLeish; the theologian, Reinhold Niebuhr; and George N. Shuster, president of Hunter College.

After holding seventeen hearings, taking testimony from fifty-eight journalists and studying 176 documents prepared by its own members, the Commission issued its report on December 10, 1946. During the following year, a book based on the report and entitled *A Free and Responsible Press* was published by the University of Chicago Press. From cover to cover, both the report and the book were awash with pejorative remarks about the news media. Nothing Vice President Agnew was to say two decades later in Des Moines would approach in range or depth the contumely heaped on newsmen by the champions of liberal thought responsible for that 1946 study. *A Free and Responsible Press* went beyond mere criticism to invoke a very real threat of government censorship—a threat never even implied by Agnew. "Those who direct the machinery of the press," said the book's authors in Chapter I, "have engaged from time to time in practices which the society condemns and which, if continued, *it will inevitably undertake to regulate or control.*" (Italics ours.)

Succeeding chapters are studded with scathing attacks on the press that appear anomalistic in a book turned out by leading liberals—anomalistic, that is, until one remembers that what they were talking about was a *conservative* press. Here are some sample comments of the Hutchins Commission:

"These instruments [newspapers, magazines and radio newscasts] can spread lies faster and further than our forefathers dreamed when they enshrined the freedom of the press in the First Amendment of the Constitution." (Another implied threat of censorship since it questions the continued validity of the First Amendment.)

"One of the most effective ways of improving the press is blocked by the press itself. By a kind of unwritten law the press ignores the errors and misrepresentations, the lies and scandals of which its members are guilty."

"The few who are able to use the machinery of the press as an instrument of mass communications have not provided a service adequate to the needs of the society."

"From a moral point of view, at least, freedom of expression does not include the right to lie as a deliberate instrument of policy."

"The news is twisted by the emphasis on firstness, on the novel and sensational; by the personal interests of the owners; and by the pressure groups."

If Spiro Agnew had made those statements, the liberals would have been demanding his severed head on a pike. But because the authors were liberals and their target was a conservative press, the Commission report elicited nothing but praise from the left-leaning intelligentsia.

By the late 1960's, things had changed, and drastically. Now the important national media were leaning toward the left, and were therefore sacrosanct in academic circles. Question their integrity, as Agnew did, and you were a tyrant, a censor, a would-be dictator and a ruthless enemy of free speech.

What caused that right-to-left swing that made the news media of 1969 so different from those of 1946? Any brief answer would have to be an over-simplification, but probably the chief reason for the metamorphosis was a shift in functions within the top echelons of the various communications companies. In the past, newspapers and magazines had almost always been a one-man or one-family operation. The owner, who tended to be a conservative, would watch over the editorial content of his publications with all the vigilance of a fire marshal at an arsonists' convention. To the extent he could do so, he would make sure the articles in those publications reflected his own opinions.

Then, in the years following World War I, control of the biggest publishing empires began to move out of the hands of individuals and into the asset columns of giant corporations. Giant corporations rarely have the time or the inclination to ride shotgun over news items. The few tycoons who retained personal dominion over newspapers and magazines gradually relinquished their day-to-day editorial chores in order to concentrate on the increasingly sticky problems of finances. As they turned their attention to the selling of advertising space and the floating of bank loans and the launching of stock issues, the decisions as to what went into the news columns were left more and more to the senior editors and the writers. And just as most owners and publishers lean toward the right, most senior editors and writers tilt toward the left. The news columns—and the newscasts, for what was true of print media applied also to their electronic brethren—soon reflected the ideological change at the helm. Magazines like *Time* and *Life*, which had been rugged bastions of conservatism, evolved into the cutting edges of a new liberalism. Newspapers like *The New York Times*, which had once carried the banner for middle-of-the-road Republicans, now were shouting the praises of far-out reformers. Even *The Chicago Tribune*, that favorite whipping boy of New Deal Democrats and once the archetype of conservative journalism, began in the late 1960's to espouse liberal causes.

And when the media of America swung left, they swung like Jack Dempsey in his prime. Even in the heyday of the Pulitzers and the Bennetts and the Greeleys, there had been a semblance of balance in the press simply because the most determined and energetic publisher could not actually write everything that appeared in his newspaper or magazine. He had to depend to some extent on his underlings, many of whom were on the opposite side of the fence politically. They frequently managed to make some of their views known in print.

The old *New York Herald Tribune* was a case in point. Some of us who worked in its editorial department in 1952 recall the almost comic tug-of-war that took place during the Eisenhower-Stevenson campaign. The *Trib* was owned and published at the time by the widow and sons of Ogden Reid, and the Reids were strongly pro-Eisenhower. They kept saying so on the newspaper's editorial page. However, the writers and middle-to-lower-echelon editors of the *Trib* were, almost to a man, fanatically enamored of Adlai Stevenson. Result: when you read the news columns of the *New York Herald Tribune* in the late summer and early fall of 1952, you came away with the conviction that the newspaper was in Stevenson's hip pocket.

Significantly, it was primarily the editors and writers, and not the publishers, who denounced Vice President Agnew after his Des Moines speech. And even more significantly, many editors and writers agreed with Agnew, some of them publicly.

There was James Keogh, with an impressive list of credentials as a working journalist. Keogh had been, successively, a reporter and city editor of *The Omaha World-Herald* and a senior editor, managing editor and executive editor of *Time* magazine. In his 1972 book, *President Nixon and the Press,* Keogh endorsed the key element in the Agnew thesis: the complaint that news was being slanted toward the liberal left.

"There was a condition . . . of conformity," wrote Keogh about newsmen's treatment of President Nixon, "in which the most important and influential of the news media in the United States tended to report and comment on the news in a way which favored one political-philosophical point of view." That "point of view," Keogh made it clear, was not that of President Nixon.

The existence of bias was also noted by the National Broadcasting Company newscaster Douglas Kiker, who took the tack that total objectivity in reporting was too much to expect. "Today's politics has become so complicated," he said, "that the people who report politics are being forced to take a role beyond the old role of total objectivity, that we are, in effect, becoming a party to the action and we might as well admit it."

James Bormann, director of community affairs for wcco Radio, Minneapolis-St. Paul, said many of today's journalists and journalism teachers "are so intent on demolishing the establishment . . . that they would blindly destroy the credibility of the media in the bargain. Whatever else the new journalism may be called, the accurate name for it is 'dishonest reporting'." Bormann noted that one newsman at a meeting of Columbia Broadcasting System affiliates had said that "a good reporter should not be afraid, when covering a riot, to throw a few bricks himself." Stated Bormann: "It seems to me this kind of advice gives a clear clue as to what has gone wrong in our craft."

John Madigan, of Station wbbm, Chicago, had much the same opinion. "All these young newsmen and newswomen coming along these days . . . are being trained apparently to become participatory journalists, rather than reporters,"

Madigan said. "They want to make moral and political and social judgments on their assignments and then take sides. Never mind getting the facts straight and writing a strong, fair lead and striving for compactness and balance. Just get out there and participate."

One of the most outspoken critics of the 1960's brand of journalism was Robert Novak, a syndicated newspaper columnist specializing in political reportage. "The journalist working for the television networks, the big news magazines and the important metropolitan press [has] now become part of the liberal establishment, both in his manner of living and in his ideological commitment," Novak wrote in a paper for the Public Affairs Conference Center at Kenyon College. "These journalists [are] increasingly advocating causes of the moment rather than functioning as neutral observers." Novak cited as an example of bias in the press a *New York Times* article headlined "U.S. Says Hanoi 'Invaded' South, Keeps Reprisals Options Open." The first paragraph of the article stated that "The United States accused Hanoi today of launching an 'invasion' of South Vietnam and said Washington was leaving open all retaliatory options, including renewed American bombing of North Vietnam." The words "invaded" and "invasion" were in quotation marks, Novak noted, although at the time there were entire divisions of North Vietnamese troops inside the borders of South Vietnam. By enclosing the two words in quotes, the *Times* was telling its readers that, in its opinion, the existence of an invasion was open to doubt. The *Times* never did get around to acknowledging that an invasion had taken place, preferring instead to refer to the massive presence of North Vietnamese troops in South Vietnam as "an offensive" or simply as "a military operation." Thus the *Times*, with bias and prejudice, had adopted the liberal left position that what was going on in Vietnam was, despite evidence to the contrary and despite the official United States government stand in the matter, nothing more than a civil uprising. As far as the *Times* was concerned, there was no North Vietnam or South Vietnam but simply Vietnam, which is how some newspapers in the Age of Unreason rewrote history to suit their own notions.

(It is interesting to note that the *Times*, which refused to describe North Vietnam's assault on South Vietnam as an invasion, had no compunction about using the word "invasion" in referring to American operations in Cambodia in the spring of 1970. The *Times* said flatly, and without quotation marks, that we had invaded Cambodia, ignoring the fact that the Cambodian government welcomed our forces and was actively cooperating with them.)

There must have been great consternation in the editorial offices of the *Times* when, in 1971, perhaps the best known of all *Times* journalists, Arthur Krock, wrote a book entitled *The Consent of the Governed,* in which he spoke of an infiltration of the press by "the new American liberals" and of the "highly subjective nature" of Washington news reporting. Krock, a Pulitzer Prize winner and a veteran on the Washington scene, left nothing at all in doubt when he said in his book, "There is considerable fire beneath the smoke of slanted journalism that impelled Vice President Spiro T. Agnew in 1970 to roll out his engine and his hook and ladder."

Most of those who corroborated the Agnew charge of media bias had depended on random observations, but there was nothing random about a book called *The News Twisters* that came out in 1971. Written by Edith Efron, a contributing editor of *TV Guide* magazine and a frequently quoted expert on television matters, *The News Twisters* was the result of two years of painstaking research conducted by Miss Efron under a grant from the Historical Research Foundation. Heart of her study was a seven-week examination of network television news coverage during the climactic period of the 1968 presidential race. She actually taped some 300,000 words telecast by the networks and analyzed them on the basis of which candidate was being favored. Her findings:

On the American Broadcasting Company, there were 869

words that could be construed as supporting Richard Nixon compared with 7,493 words denigrating him. The National Broadcasting Company had 431 words favoring Nixon, 4,234 against him. The Columbia Broadcasting System had 320 words on behalf of Nixon, 5,300 words in opposition.

Hubert Humphrey fared considerably better by being treated more or less fairly. On ABC, there were 4,218 words analyzed as pro-Humphrey, 3,569 words con. The score at NBC was 1,852 for, 2,655 against. At CBS, it was 2,388 for, 2,083 against.

Miss Efron also noted that during the seven weeks the three networks carried seventy-two different stories in which opinion was heard condemning United States policy in Vietnam and demanding an immediate, unilateral bombing halt. These stories involved statements from such public figures as Eldridge Cleaver, Dick Gregory, Paul O'Dwyer, campus radical Tom Hayden, Averill Harriman, actress Vanessa Redgrave, Indira Gandhi, Senators Fulbright, Javits, Morse and McGovern and assorted other black militants, socialist party leaders, liberal politicians and academicians. Against this bombardment from the left, the networks aired thirteen stories giving the government position. The ratio was six to one against this nation's official policy.

From all of this evidence, Miss Efron concluded that there was indeed bias in the electronic media and that it was deeply embedded and repeatedly exercised. "It is clear," she stated, "that network coverage tends to be strongly biased in favor of the Democratic-liberal-left axis of opinion and strongly biased against the Republican-conservative-right axis of opinion. The networks [during the seven-week taping period] actively slanted their opinion coverage against U.S. policy on the Vietnam war. The networks actively slanted their opinion coverage in favor of the black militants and against the white middle-class majority. The networks actively favored the Democratic candidate, Hubert Humphrey, for the Presidency over his Republican opponent."

Like others who found prejudice in the news media, including Vice President Agnew, she saw no conspiracy to slant the reports. What she discovered was "political uniformity of staffing," with hundreds of reporters, writers and editors sharing the same basic viewpoints and independently weaving these viewpoints into their newscasts.

While some network newsmen immediately accused Miss Efron herself of being biased—against network newsmen—no such charge could be leveled against a subsequent report that said virtually the same things Miss Efron had said. This one was based on a ten-day survey of national television news programs and was sponsored by the American Institute for Political Communications. Not only was the sponsor a nonprofit, nonpartisan organization, and classified as such by *The New York Times,* but the five recent college graduates who conducted the research were all McGovern supporters and opponents of United States policy in Vietnam. So when they found and reported "a significant degree of bias" in favor of McGovern during the Democratic primary campaign of 1972 and when they found and reported similar bias against the Nixon posture in Vietnam, their honesty could scarcely be impugned. According to their findings, NBC and CBS were each guilty of thirteen bias episodes in the ten-day study period while ABC was guilty of seven.

Preposterously, the bias in the media extended even into the area of movie reviews. Through most of the period under discussion, the authors of articles about screenplays were prone to judge them not as works of art or of entertainment, which is what most of them were designed to be, but as sociopolitical treatises. In the words of Arthur Knight, movie columnist for *Saturday Review,* "their orientation is more social than cinematic." And because the reviewers' prejudices paralleled those of their news reporter colleagues, they invariably condemned the movies they regarded as conservative in approach and applauded the ones that beat the drums for left-wing causes. Whenever Hollywood was rash enough to issue a film that not only followed a conservative story line but employed conservative actors, the fury of the reviewers knew no bounds. Noting the critical barbs attracted by *The Cowboys,* a picture starring John Wayne,

Knight wondered in print "whether, if the star had been George C. Scott instead of the politically controversial John Wayne, [the] response would have been the same."

For more than two years after the highly publicized Agnew speech, official spokesmen for the communications media kept insisting the charges of bias had been false. On April 23, 1972, Benjamin Bradlee, executive editor of *The Washington Post*, was asked the following question by a television interviewer: "Are you suggesting that it is untrue ... that you have a cadre of highly motivated, intelligent, skillful, young, liberal reporters who tend to slant their stories toward Democrats, liberals, as they write for the news pages?"

"Yes," said Bradlee, "I am very definitely denying that."

But at the very moment Bradlee was issuing his denial, a meeting was taking place in New York City at which hundreds of prominent newsmen, several of whose columns appear in *The Washington Post*, were not only acknowledging that they were indeed biased but were asserting that bias was an essential ingredient for conscientious newsmen.

The New York City event was called the A. J. Liebling Counter-Convention, "A. J. Liebling" in honor of the late critic of American journalism and "Counter-Convention" in recognition of the fact that the putatively right-wing American Newspaper Publishers Association was holding its convention at the same time in another part of the city. The Counter-Convention was sponsored by (*More*), an ultra-liberal New York City journalism review. In an article explaining the purpose of the meeting, (*More*) said, "A growing number of people who put out the nation's newspapers and magazines and splice together the nightly news are no longer going to accept the old ways of doing things." The Counter-Convention was to afford this "growing number of people" an opportunity to tell it like it was.

And what were "the old ways of doing things" that were falling into disrepute? The old ways involved an honest attempt at the factual reporting of stories, the telling of truth, the striving toward objectivity. That was the Old Journalism, and the New Journalists reviled it. The New Journalists, said (*More*), were "sensitive employes [who] turn their attention to the kind of journalism that might help improve the quality of life rather than objectively recording its decline." There was the tacit claim in that statement that the New Journalists were somehow endowed by their Creator with a divine, and exclusive, awareness of just what was needed to improve the quality of life—an awareness not shared by the rest of us mortals. With this knowledge, they were thus prepared to distort the facts and shade the nuances, all in the interest of making conditions better for their intellectual inferiors who were not privy to that knowledge.

A total of 2,500 or so persons attended the A. J. Liebling Counter-Convention and most of them seemed to agree with (*More*). And it should not be assumed that the conferees were a bunch of anonymous hacks from the rural hinterland. Not at all. Among them were such stellar writers and commentators as Murray Kempton, Dan Rather, Studs Terkel, Tom Wicker, Gay Talese, David Halberstam, Gore Vidal, Tom Wolfe, Calvin Trillin, Gloria Steinem and Jimmy Breslin.

On April 26, *The Washington Post*, whose executive editor had declared three days earlier that there was no bias at his newspaper, carried an article on the A. J. Liebling Counter-Convention and called it "the Woodstock of journalism." Said the *Post* report: "The new personal journalism was the only reason this whole thing ever took place. Could you see a convention taking place among the old objective journalists?" Again there was the pejorative reference to objectivity, this time in a newspaper that for years had been insisting that objectivity was the alpha and omega for all good journalists. While Ben Bradlee was pointing with pride to *Post* impartiality in his TV interview, the troops in the city room were rejecting impartiality as a cardinal sin exceeded only by the taking of payola.

The New York Times, not to be outdone by its liberal sister publication, also buried objectivity in its coverage of the Counter-Convention. "The tradition of tin-ear objectivity

—reporting, for example, two opposing points of view with the implication that both are valid, and that the truth necessarily lies in between—is under increasing attack," stated the *Times*.

And *Time* magazine, in its report, noted that "Tom Wicker seemed to be swimming against the tide [at the Counter-Convention] when he observed that news stories should not be editorials."

One of the most fascinating comments on journalistic standards came from NBC's David Brinkley, who with more candor than tact asserted that "News is what I say it is. It's something worth knowing by my standards." His statement fell somewhere in between the arrogant "L'etat c'est moi" of Louis XIV and the muddled "When I use a word, it means just what *I* choose it to mean—neither more nor less" of Humpty Dumpty.

In employing the New Journalism to show America the way toward a liberal Utopia, the newsmen of the 1960's and early 1970's dug deep down into the bag of tricks that had served so well the Mussolinis and the Goebbels and the other masters of the half-truth and the big lie. There were the delicately wrought descriptions that were literally factual yet devastatingly deceptive. Thus when Gary Wills wrote about the *persona non grata*, George Wallace, in *The Washington Post*, the columnist told how Mrs. Wallace "fusses with her husband's tie, brushes dandruff off, tilts shadow out of his bunchy grained face." On the other hand, when Marquis Childs wrote about the darling of the liberals, Florida Governor Reubin Askew, the subject emerged as "tall, lean with a quick sense of humor that relieves his seriousness."

Now it is within the realm of possibility that George Wallace also possesses a sense of humor and that Reubin Askew occasionally falls victim to the scourge of dandruff, but you would never get that impression if you depended on the New Journalists of the Age of Unreason.

While most of the bias encountered in the media was of the subtle, or keep-your-eye-on-the-adjectives, variety, it sometimes got heavy-handed to the point of vulgarity. On

April 19, 1972, Nicholas von Hoffman, a syndicated columnist whose home base is *The Washington Post*, by-lined a piece entitled "An Ad Hoc Committee to Keep Tabs on the Military." The article told about an organization headquartered in Cambridge, Massachusetts, that encouraged disgruntled American servicemen to supply it with information about United States troop movements. This information was then made public, apparently in an attempt to embarrass the Pentagon and hinder our military operations. In praising the group and its motives, von Hoffman not only listed its telephone number so that servicemen could call in and "say what's going on at their base or installation" but he went on to identify a number of American naval and air units that, according to him, were either being alerted for shipment to the Orient or were already en route. There is a name for the kind of thing von Hoffman did, and the name is not "journalism", new or old.

A passionate opposition to our involvement in Vietnam so colored the mental processes of liberals like von Hoffman that the articles they wrote often bordered on the ludicrous. The anonymous writers of *The New Yorker's* The Talk of the Town column fell into that category. For many years, The Talk of the Town had captivated the magazine's readers with its incisive and witty commentary on the foibles of mankind. These foibles, to the magazine's credit, were liberal foibles *and* conservative foibles, and the column exposed them both, without fear or favor. Then, in the late 1960's, a blight all but destroyed The Talk of the Town. A plague of New Journalists had apparently descended on *The New Yorker*, for the column began to read like a political tract for the National Liberation Front. Week after week, year after year, the lead item in The Talk of the Town was devoted to the abuse of Richard Nixon and an emotional assault on his Southeast Asia policies. Week after week, year after year, the same tired old left-wing cliches were rolled out and put on display. And, tragically, the cerebral cool and intellectual detachment that had made The Talk of the Town the talk of the literary world now foundered under a wave of mindless rhetoric. For example, a month after Hanoi abandoned all pretense of merely aiding an insurrection and launched an all-out, tank-led invasion into South Vietnam, The Talk of the Town began with these astounding sentences: "Our current bombing campaign in Indo-China is something new in the history of warfare. The Nazis' and Fascist Italians' bombing in support of Franco's forces in the Spanish Civil War . . . is the only other instance of a great power's supporting one side in a civil war almost exclusively through bombing." So in a few lines of type, *The New Yorker* rescinded the treaty dividing Indo-China into separate countries, recombined those countries into a single unit and determined that Hanoi's invasion of South Vietnam was not an invasion at all, since it was really one big country out there, but simply a civil war. The magazine also cleverly linked the United States with Nazi Germany and Fascist Italy, implying that there was no substantive difference among the three powers. Like others of their persuasion, the New Journalists of *The New Yorker* could never seem to understand the dissimilarity between a country that coldbloodedly eradicates human beings by putting them into gas ovens and a country that accidentally kills human beings in the course of bombing military targets for the purpose of defending the victims of an invasion.

Only marginally successful in their attempts to influence United States foreign policy, the practitioners of the New Journalism scored a stupendous victory in whipping up public and government support for environmental reforms. In a few short years following the publication of *Silent Spring*, the American news media were able to convince a majority of this nation's citizens that the world was in imminent danger of succumbing to an ecological cataclysm. The methods employed in spreading this nonsense ranged from slight exaggeration to shameless lies.

Consider, for example, the report circulated through the nation's capital that "a ton and a half of poison" passes through the lungs of every man, woman and child in Washington, D.C., each year. What the newsman who originated the report had done was divide the weight of the contaminants in Washington's air by the population. The scary statistic was being quoted everywhere, including the cloakrooms of Congress, when someone wrote a letter to the editor of the newspaper involved pointing out that an average person doing light exercise moves about two-thirds of a cubic foot of air in and out of his lungs per minute. In one year, this would amount to fourteen tons of air. Application of the average contaminant load would result in a figure of four-and-a-half *ounces* of poison per year—rather a long way from "a ton and a half."

Throughout the period, the major newspapers and big national magazines never let up on the constant drumbeat of environmental alarms. In just one issue taken at random, the issue of March 26, 1972, *The New York Times* carried thirteen feature stories on the environment, stories large enough to be listed in the paper's news index. The articles covered subjects as disparate as the defoliation of Java, pollution in the Great Lakes and the growing menace to harbor seals off the coast of New Jersey.

Like most of the other news media, the *Times* refused to believe the reports of environmental improvement, even when those reports appeared in the *Times*. On the same day the newspaper published a story about the lessening of air pollution in New York City—the city had just announced that the air quality in the preceding twenty-four-hours had been the purest in this century and that average air quality was getting better all the time—it ran an article containing the following sentence: "The [environmental] meeting in Stockholm will be the first at which the nations of the world assemble to deal with the deterioration of the air, land and water." *Times* editors were seemingly weaned on the statement that the air, land and water were deteriorating, and nothing—literally nothing—could dissuade them.

(In view of the *Times'* almost obsessive preoccupation with the environment and its habit of accusing everybody in sight of being a polluter, there was a certain piquant irony in a series of public statements made in 1970 and 1971 by

Jerome Kretchmer, New York City's Environmental Protection Administration chief. In the statements, Kretchmer singled out *The New York Times* as the city's single biggest source of solid waste pollution. Each Monday, explained Kretchmer, the New York Sanitation Department has to pick up some 50 million pounds of refuse. Eight-and-a-half million pounds of it—or more than one-sixth—consist of discarded copies of the Sunday *New York Times*. Five hundred collection trucks are needed to haul the copies to city incinerators. When they are burned, the *Times* copies send more than 87,000 pounds of particulates into the atmosphere, some of which settles to the ground and must be carted away in 100 residue trucks. Cost to the city for all this is $7.5 million a year—and that is just for the Sunday *Times*. The weekday issues deliver additional tons of pollutants into the air and account for additional millions of dollars in Sanitation Department expenditures. The conclusion is obvious: the greatest contribution *The New York Times* could make toward a cleaner environment would be to suspend publication.)

The devices used by the news media to convert sows' ears into silk purses—and, of course, vice versa—were many and varied. A popular method involved the imaginative and creative juggling of words and word meanings. Nothing illustrates the genre better than *The New York Times* stories about Dr. Daniel Ellsberg, the gentleman who, by his own admission, copied secret Pentagon documents taken from secret files and, in violation of the rules he had agreed to obey, turned them over to the *Times* for publication. Reluctant to describe Ellsberg in the terms he so richly deserved, the *Times* resorted to verbal gymnastics. One article reporting on the Ellsberg trial is especially noteworthy. Said the *Times* account: "Dr. Ellsberg, a defense analyst, and Mr. Russo, a social worker, are alleged to have arranged for the release of the Pentagon Papers when they were associates at the Rand Corporation, a think tank that does research for the Pentagon." How delightful. How absolutely ingenious. "Alleged to have arranged for the release of the

Pentagon Papers." That's like saying Babe Ruth is alleged to have arranged for the propulsion of several baseballs into the right-field bleachers at Yankee Stadium.

Another common device for manipulating public opinion was less devious and even more effective. It took the form of simply playing up those news items that favored the liberal cause and burying those items that didn't. The most casual reader of newspapers will remember the story of the Watergate Caper. It broke one June night in 1972 when five men were arrested on charges of having broken into Democratic National Committee headquarters in Washington's Watergate complex for the purpose of gathering information through electronic listening devices. While the case was pending, the news media had a field day establishing what they called "links" between the arrested men and various high-ranking Republicans. A record of a telephone call between one of the suspects and a Nixon aide was regarded as "a link." The name of a GOP leader in a suspect's address book was another "link." A headwaiter's recollection of having once seen a suspect in the company of a White House employe was "a close link." By revealing these "links" one at a time, the newspapers, particularly *The New York Times* and *The Washington Post,* and the TV networks managed to come up with a Watergate story almost daily during the critical period of the 1972 presidential campaign. Day after day, the same tenuous allegations were dredged up and hung out on public display. When a Republican spokesman suggested that the news media were keeping the Watergate story alive for no other reason than to try to swing some votes from Nixon to McGovern, media executives were indignant. They insisted that their only motive in perpetuating the Watergate story was to keep the public informed about a serious crime in the interest of justice. Then came the election and the Nixon landslide, and suddenly the word "Watergate" disappeared. The week before the election, it was all over the front pages and the 11 o'clock news. The week after the election, you couldn't find it with the Mount Wilson telescope. For now the Watergate Caper could no longer hurt

Richard Nixon, so the media had no further use for it, justice or no justice.

One of the most curious, yet revealing, aspects of the New Journalism was its handling of the nation's drug problem. The media attitude toward drugs went through two distinct phases.

Phase One, which encompassed the years from 1965 to 1969, might be described as The Turn-On Phase. During this period, many of the major newspapers and magazines carried articles glamorizing illicit drugs and their advocates, such as Timothy Leary. Publications as highly respected as *The New York Times* kept referring to certain drugs as "mind-expanding"—an adjective that did little to discourage experimentation by teenagers, most of whom were understandably in favor of having their minds expanded.

The stories that appeared in the late 1960's implied that there was nothing dishonorable or dangerous about drug usage. *Newsweek* dismissed the fears about LSD by saying, "In truth, LSD lives up to neither the scare headlines nor the glowing tributes of believers."

Time magazine reassured its youthful readers with the words, "Pop drugs hardly portend anything as drastic as a new and debauched American spirit." *Time* quoted a user as saying, "Acid has taught me a new way" and concluded its report by stating that "adults must get used to . . . a separate youth culture, or counterculture."

The *Times* contributed the remarks that "Many youths say a trip [on LSD] has been a valuable experience . . ." and "LSD . . . has produced enormously pleasurable and seemingly illuminating mental states for thousands of persons."

Look magazine devoted an entire issue to drugs, with one article describing the benefits accruing to LSD users. "They claim feelings of insight, of the unit of things, of seeing into people, trees, walls, music . . . It is an ultimate religious level, perhaps a vision of God. The light, they say, is complete ecstasy, the end and the beginning."

After making drugs almost irresistible to young Americans, the media entered Phase Two, or The Turn-Off Phase.

Starting in 1970, they professed to be appalled by the increase in drug usage, which they attributed to youth's disenchantment with American foreign policy, the materialism of their elders and other facets of our society.

During the period, there emerged a media language that could be called New Journalese. A favorite word in New Journalese was "immoral." It was used to describe any activity with which the writer disagreed. Thus our participation in the Vietnam war was immoral. Our bombing of North Vietnam was exceptionally immoral. So, of course, was the government of South Vietnam.

The adjective "immoral" was never applied to North Vietnam or the Viet Cong, even when they engaged in pursuits more heinous by far than those of the United States. There was nothing immoral, in the eyes of American journalists, in North Vietnam's invasion of South Vietnam. There was nothing immoral in the massacre by North Vietnam of civilians in Hue. And there was nothing immoral about the government of North Vietnam, which according to reliable witnesses, was responsible for the slaughter of thousands of its own citizens and which never made even the slightest pretense of being a democracy.

Another popular word in the New Journalese vocabulary was "racist." The word "racist" was freely applied to those who criticized the actions of any person whose skin happened to be other than white. Denigraters of the convicted criminals known as the Soledad Brothers were racists. So were those who questioned the practices of Malcom X, Rap Brown and Eldridge Cleaver.

So distraught did the New Journalists become about imagined affronts to nonwhites that the most innocent happenings were transformed in their minds into racial incidents. Typical of the syndrome were the contents of a speech delivered by the best-selling novelist Fletcher Knebel while he was an editor of *Look* magazine. In the spring of 1968, Knebel told a Chicago audience about an occurrence that had taken place several weeks earlier at the start of an airplane trip. On boarding the airliner, he had sat down one seat away from a Negro clergyman. It was in a row of three seats, and the clergyman was next to the window, while Knebel had the seat on the aisle. They had just begun a conversation when another passenger, a white man, approached. Knebel, wishing to continue his conversation, got up and started to move into the vacant middle seat, but the white passenger stopped him.

"Don't bother moving," he told Knebel, and he pointed to the seat next to the black man. "I don't mind sitting there."

Knebel was furious. "What kind of country is this where people go around saying they don't mind sitting next to a black man?" he asked his Chicago audience.

After the speech, someone pointed out to Knebel that, in all probability, the other white man simply meant that he didn't mind sitting in the middle seat, since there is a fairly universal preference for the window and aisle seats. Knebel was unconvinced. "It was a racist remark," he insisted.

Eventually the bias of the New Journalism overflowed the news media and seeped into the supposedly inviolate pages of standard reference works. One of these was *The New York Times Encyclopedic Almanac,* a popular source of factual information for millions of school children and adults. But some of the *Almanac's* "factual information" had a familiar slant to it. The presidential biographies contained in the 1972 edition, particularly those of John F. Kennedy and Richard M. Nixon, are worth noting.

Some excerpts from the *Times Almanac's* Kennedy biography: ". . . Kennedy was diligent and ingenious in advancing civil rights policies . . . Kennedy emerged from this [Cuban missile] crisis as a well-poised, rational, and resolute leader . . . A master of irony, both keen and gentle, he directed it at himself as well as at others . . . A capacity for self-criticism helped Kennedy maintain exceptional composure in crisis . . ."

Some excerpts from the Nixon biography: "President Nixon was elected with a minimum of support from black voters and his civil rights policies have not altered their attitude . . . He has recommended legislation to protect consumers against deceptive sales practices, but critics belittle the proposal as hamstrung with restrictions . . . The administration has . . . distressed civil rights interests by nominating to the Supreme Court unfriendly Southern jurists . . . Led by Vice-President Agnew, the [Nixon] administration has dealt out rough rhetoric to those who displease it . . ."

During their years as officers of *Look* magazine, the authors of this book had many opportunities to observe firsthand and close-up the application and effects of bias in the production of news reports. This is not to imply that *Look* was especially culpable in that respect. The amount of bias in its editorial department was about average for the period. Nor do the authors mean to convey the impression that there was at *Look* a conspiracy to slant the news. Not at all. There were no meetings at which editors and photographers plotted to destroy the Establishment. There were no instructions handed down from senior editors to junior editors to tilt a story one way or the other. Each author wrote his articles according to his own values and judgments. What created the bias in the finished product was the fact that most of *Look's* editorial people thought pretty much along the same lines and those lines skewed to the left. With only a handful of exceptions, the men and women who produced *Look* detested big business, worshipped the ecological and consumerism reformers and abhorred Richard Nixon.

Those who wonder why the owners of *Look* permitted bias to seep into its pages probably do not know the conditions that now prevail in the publishing world. No longer does the proprietor or board chairman have the last word—or even the first word. Today the hired editors set the policies. They do this under the always effective threat that if management interferes the editors will quit, taking with them the writers, artists, photographers and technicians. And so financially precarious is the publishing business these days that such a threat will cow the most dictatorial of owners.

At *Look*, the editors not only controlled everything that

got into print but exerted considerable influence over the activities of business office personnel. When in 1970 *Look* Publisher Thomas R. Shepard, Jr., began making conservative speeches to business organizations—in the interest of clarity, the authors of this book are referred to in the third person—a group of *Look* editors drafted a petition demanding that Shepard be muzzled. The petition was presented to Gardner Cowles, chairman of the parent corporation, and although Cowles, to his credit, resisted the pressure and upheld Shepard's right to say whatever he damn well pleased, the implied threat of an editorial department mutiny had an inevitably chilling effect. There were fewer Shepard speeches in the wake of the petition. (One of the most fascinating aspects of the confrontation was the anti-free-speech stance adopted by *Look's* ultra-liberal editors. In the pages of the magazine, they had been clamoring for zero restraints on freedom of speech—for the right of every individual to speak up loud and clear, even when what he said might lead to civil disorders or to a breach in the nation's security mechanism. But now, when someone dared to express a viewpoint contrary to their own, they insisted that he be gagged.)

A similar situation developed a year later at *Life* magazine. Toward the end of the 1972 presidential campaign, the *Life* management put together an editorial supporting the candidacy of Richard Nixon. Ninety-one *Life* employes, including forty-two members of the 150-member editorial department, drew up a petition attacking the editorial and endorsing George McGovern. The petition was handed to *Life* managing editor Ralph Graves, and the offending editorial, set to run in the October 20, 1972, issue, was lifted. However, a week later there was a stiffening of top-echelon backbones, and the editorial did appear in the October 27 issue.

Although the authors could cite many examples of editorial bias at *Look*, there were three episodes that stick in their minds and that should serve to indicate the kind of shenanigans going on behind the scenes in magazine publishing at the height of the Age of Unreason.

Episode One. In July of 1967, there was a tragic race riot in Newark, New Jersey, in the course of which twenty-six persons died and 1,100 were injured. For many months after the riot, the city teetered on the brink of bankruptcy and open warfare between blacks and whites. The underlying causes of Newark's problems were numerous and highly complex, but in the opinion of Charles Mangel, the *Look* senior editor assigned to research and write the Newark story, there was no mystery at all. To Mangel, as he stated in an article in the September 9, 1969, issue of *Look*, Newark's troubles stemmed from the fact that white suburbanites in the area surrounding Newark weren't contributing enough money toward the welfare of the black families inside Newark. Wrote Mangel: "Because New Jersey—fourth among states in per capita income but dead last in per capita aid to its residents—has irresponsibly turned its back on its urban problems, Newark has to get 70 cents of each budget dollar from local real estate tax."

At *Look*, as at other magazines, photostats of articles were customarily distributed to executives well in advance of publication. When stats of the Mangel piece arrived at the desk of Melvin J. Grayson, *Look* promotion director, he almost choked over that sentence about aid to residents. Grayson lived in New Jersey and he knew that, in matters of public welfare, New Jersey was exceptionally open-handed. So he did some checking in the *Statistical Abstract of the United States* and he discovered immediately what Mangel had been up to. It was another clear case of data juggling to make a point. The point Mangel wanted to get across was that riots are the natural result of an insufficient sharing of wealth. If you want to avoid riots, he was in effect saying, you had better spend more money on welfare. New Jersey didn't do it, and look what happened in New Jersey.

The only trouble was that, according to the *Statistical Abstract*, New Jersey ranked *first* among all the states in the Union in welfare payments *per welfare family*. In 1969, the average monthly aid to dependent children in New Jersey was $266 per family receiving such aid. New Jersey easily topped New York State, with $248; Connecticut, with $240; and California, with $186. Average for all states was $176, with Mississippi's $47 putting that state at the bottom of the list.

What about Mangel's charge that New Jersey ranked "dead last in per capita aid to its residents"? The statement was factually correct but shamefully misleading. New Jersey ranked last in aid to *all its residents* because, as a prosperous state, New Jersey had relatively few residents in need of aid. Divide the total aid figure by the total population and you were bound to come up with a quotient lower than those for less affluent states. When it came to taking care of *those families in need of help,* New Jersey, as the aid to dependent children statistics revealed, was uncommonly generous. The evidence pointed only one way. If Mangel wanted to pinpoint a reason for the Newark riots, he would have to look elsewhere.

In a politely worded memo, Grayson apprised Mangel of his findings and suggested that the piece on Newark be altered. Mangel just as politely declined to change so much as a word. He noted that every figure he had used was literally accurate, the implication being that if people misinterpreted his data, that was their business. The principle of *caveat emptor* was a good deal more popular in liberal circles than might be suspected.

Episode Two. In the spring and summer of 1970, a *Look* senior editor named Jack Shepherd was collecting material for what was to be a major article on the peaceful uses of atomic energy. Shepherd—no relation to Publisher Shepard—had several qualifications for the job of producing the article. He was young, bright, talented and deeply concerned about the future of the United States. He also had one outstanding liability. Like most of his colleagues on the *Look* editorial staff, he had a built-in antipathy toward big corporations and the Republican Administration in Washington. Since no atomic energy plant was being built or operated in 1970 without the active involvement of both big corporations and the Republican Administration, Shepherd started out on his assignment with the conviction that somewhere, some-how, something had to be wrong.

Because of these preconceptions, Shepherd put together a rather curious interview schedule as he toured the country gathering information. As reflected in the article, he talked frequently and at length with scores of persons opposed to nuclear power plants on safety and environmental grounds; he had few conversations with persons who favored the plants.

The article that emerged from this one-sided research was what might have been expected. Entitled "The Nuclear Threat *Inside* America" and featured in the *Look* issue of December 15, 1970, it took the position that money-hungry private corporations had teamed up with power-hungry Atomic Energy Commission members to construct and operate nuclear plants that, as a result of corner-cutting to save a few dollars, posed a grave threat to the health of the American public.

A key source of Shepherd's data was Dr. John Gofman of the AEC's Lawrence Radiation Laboratory at Livermore, California. Gofman detested the so-called military-industrial Establishment even more than Shepherd did. His hatred of the AEC was of such magnitude that he seemed to lose all sense of balance in describing its members. As quoted in the Shepherd article, Gofman made this incredible statement about those who served on the Commission: "There is no morality . . . not a shred of honesty in any one of them—none. I can assure you, from every bit of dealing I've had . . . there is absolute duplicity, lies at every turn, falsehood in every way, about you personally and your motives."

And this was the man, this Gofman who could find no morality, honesty or truth in an entire government agency, who imagined himself the victim of lies and persecution, upon whom *Look* Senior Editor Jack Shepherd relied for much of the material that went into his article.

On the surface, that material seemed to constitute an ironclad case against nuclear plants and the people behind them. Sentence after sentence in the Shepherd article hammered home the idea that the plants represented a serious health menace through radiation leaks and the possibility of explosions. Here are just a few of the statements made by Shepherd:

"In 1966, there were 42 accidents at nuclear plants around the world, 37 in the U.S. Six U.S. plants had more than one accident."

"Over 200 fires have occurred at Rocky Flats (an AEC plant near Denver) since 1953."

"A 1957 AEC study, WASH-740, shows what would happen to a hypothetical reactor of 100-200 megawatts, near a large body of water and about 30 miles from a major city of about 1,000,000 if it became super-critical and all safety devices failed. WASH-740 predicted an explosion that would kill 3,400 people up to 15 miles away, injure 43,000 up to 45 miles, contaminate up to 150,000 square miles . . . and damage property to $7 billion."

"By the end of 1966, 98 uranium miners had lung cancer."

"Some 325 workers [at Rocky Flats] have been contaminated by . . . radiation since 1953. Fifty-six workers got cancer; 14 have died."

The picture painted by Jack Shepherd appeared to be a grim one indeed. Without saying so in so many words, he had implied that nuclear power plants were already causing cancer in human beings and that, what with all those fires and accidents, you could expect one or more of the plants to blow up at any moment.

But a careful examination of the statements quoted above reveals that, in actuality, Shepherd had not said any such thing. In fact, he had not really said anything of any importance whatsoever. What he had done was toss out a dozen or so unrelated, and largely irrelevant, figures and, through careful innuendo, he had conveyed a good deal more than he had stated.

Take that remark about "42 accidents at nuclear plants around the world." All plants have accidents. A truck backing into a loading dock is an accident. How many of those forty-two accidents were trivial and how many constituted a major health hazard?

The same thing is true of those 200 fires at Rocky Flats. How many, if any, involved a substantive danger to fissionable material, and how many were papers smoldering in an office wastebasket?

And that WASH-740 study was a concoction of the sheerest gossamer. As Shepherd himself noted, the researchers had merely wondered aloud what *might* happen *if* a long string of very unlikely events were to occur. They might just as easily, and with just as much import, have contemplated the dire consequences if the State of California were suddenly to break loose from the mainland and sink into the Pacific Ocean.

Then there were those allusions to cancer. The word "cancer" is in itself sufficient to generate a certain amount of hysteria, as the Disaster Lobbyists knew. And here were ninety-eight uranium miners down with it, along with fifty-six workers at a nuclear power plant. But those figures are, in themselves, totally meaningless. How many uranium workers were there altogether? How many years had they been working in the mines? And how did the incidence of cancer among uranium miners compare with the incidence in the population as a whole?

It was this latter consideration that intrigued *Look* Promotion Director Grayson when he saw the stats of the Shepherd article. Specifically, he was somewhat puzzled by the fourteen cancer deaths among the Rocky Flats workers. There were hundreds of workers at that installation and the plant had been in operation for seventeen years; the total of fourteen fatalities appeared to be on the low side from an actuarial standpoint.

So again Grayson did some checking. And what he found, to his utter lack of surprise, was that the *cancer death rate at the Rocky Flats nuclear plant was lower than the cancer death rate for all American adults.* In other words, you stood less of a risk of acquiring a fatal malignancy if you worked at

Rocky Flats than if you worked in, let us say, the editorial department of *Look* magazine. Of course, Shepherd had never indicated otherwise in his article. He hadn't said that the fourteen cancer deaths at Rocky Flats were an unusually high number. He hadn't said that a worker in an atomic energy plant was particularly susceptible to cancer. He had merely cited the fourteen deaths and let the reader draw his own erroneous conclusion.

This time, Grayson didn't bother sending a memo to the author of the article. He went directly to Vernon C. Myers, president of the *Look* division of Cowles Communications, Inc., and, after pointing out the many flaws in the Shepherd piece, suggested something be done to correct them. Myers agreed and, in the next few days, exerted all the pressures he could, but to no avail. The editors, with total dominion over the editorial content of the magazine, prevailed, and the Shepherd article went to press in its original form. Not unexpectedly, it aroused a storm of protest from scientists, businessmen and government officials involved in atomic research and nuclear power production. They focused on the same errors observed by Grayson, submitting irrefutable evidence that, while the figures in the article were technically correct, the implications were entirely false.

Ultimately, so many obviously knowledgeable men and women complained about the Shepherd article that the *Look* editors belatedly interviewed someone *in favor* of the nuclear power program. He was Dr. Chauncey Starr and his credentials made Shepherd's "experts" look like first-year medical students at a brain surgeons' convention. Starr, a physicist and engineer, was dean of the UCLA School of Engineering and Applied Science, as noted in an earlier chapter. He was also former president of the North American Rockwell Corporation's Atomics International Division, founder and past president of the American Nuclear Society, a past vice president of the Atomic Industrial Forum and a former member of California's Advisory Council on Atomic Energy Development and Radiation Protection. In a subsequent *Look* article based on the interview, Starr, as related earlier, categorically denied that the nuclear plants then in operation or on the drawing boards constituted a threat to the health or safety of the American public. His remarks demolished, one by one, the nuances and innuendos and half-truths that were the substance of the Shepherd article.

Episode Three. As stated previously, *Look* Publisher Tom Shepard had begun in 1970 to make public speeches. The speeches hewed to the theme of this book. Shepard took the position that the United States was *not* on the brink of ecological disaster, that the American consumer was *not* the victim of some sinister plot to defraud him in the market-place, and that whatever problems this nation did have were *not* the exclusive fault of the business community. This stand of Shepard's deeply offended the *Look* editorial staff, which believed that the nation *was* going down the drain and that it was the businessmen who had pulled the plug.

A few days after *Look* suspended publication in the early fall of 1971, Joseph Roddy, a *Look* senior editor, showed up at the office of Promotion Director Grayson. Roddy said he was preparing an article on the demise of *Look* for (*More*), the journalism review, and he wanted to get some information about those Shepard speeches, which Grayson, in his promotion director's role, had written.

The Roddy-Grayson dialogue follows:

Grayson: "Look, Joe, I know you hated those speeches, and I know how bad you can make Shepard and me look in print if you want to. I used to be a reporter myself."

Roddy: "Oh, no. Nothing like that. I just want to get a few things straight."

Grayson: "Well, o.k., but I'm asking you as a fellow *Look* employe to play it square. After all, we all have enough problems right now."

Roddy: "Oh, sure. Sure. Tell me, does Shepard really believe all those things he says in his speeches?"

Grayson: "You'd have to ask him that, but since he's an honorable man, my assumption is that, yes, he believes what he says or he wouldn't say it."

Roddy: "But how about those ridiculous things he's been saying about the environment?"

Grayson: "What ridiculous things? The only ridiculous things I've seen on the environment lately have been in *Look*. The stuff in Shepard's speeches is absolutely accurate. I researched it myself. I can show you unimpeachable sources for every word."

Roddy: "What about that statement on drugs? Shepard said there's less drug addiction in the country today than there was sixty or seventy years ago. Some of the editors checked that out in Washington and it wasn't true, so Shepard cut it out of his speeches."

Grayson: "Where the hell did you get that from? The statement Tom made about drugs is absolutely correct. It's— wait a second, I have the source right here—it's from the 1968 edition of the *Encyclopedia Americana*. The *Americana* says there was a study in 1914 and it turned up 200,000 narcotic addicts, which would mean a rate of addiction of about one addict per 500 population. Today's rate is estimated at about one per 1,000 population. In fact, the Bureau of Narcotics and Dangerous Drugs put it at one in 3,000 in 1969. And Tom never deleted that drug reference from his speeches. He's still using it. I can show it to you in a speech he gave just a week ago, and if you have a couple of minutes, we can go down to the library and I'll show you that article in the *Americana*."

Roddy: "Oh, that won't be necessary, Mel. I believe you."

After a few desultory remarks, Roddy got up to go. Grayson accompanied him out of the office and as they passed through the anteroom, they were joined by Frank Frontera, a friend of Grayson's who had been waiting there throughout the Grayson-Roddy discussion. Grayson introduced Roddy to Frontera, and Roddy departed down a staircase leading to the editorial floor.

"I shouldn't have talked to that guy," Grayson told Frontera. "He's writing an article about *Look* and he's going to do a hatchet job on Tom Shepard and me. He's going to screw up everything I told him."

"But how can he do that?" Frontera asked.

Grayson shook his head. "I don't know how. I just know he'll find a way."

Roddy did indeed find a way. His article appeared in the November 1971 issue of *(More)*. It stated in part:

"Mike Land, an assistant managing editor [of *Look*], asked Shepard where he came upon the remarkable information reposing in a speech . . . that there was less drug addiction in the U.S. now than 70 years ago. The publisher, after checking with his ghost, *Look's* advertising promotion director, Mel Grayson, referred his doubter to a doctor at the U.S. Public Health Service. Land read Shepard's claim to the doctor who contradicted it. From then on Shepard dropped the decline in addiction lines from his speech and counted on his claim that the air is getting better all the time in Manhattan for the same consoling effect."

To Joe Roddy and to far too many of his fellow journalists of the Age of Unreason, facts were like ants at a picnic. If they got in your way, the best thing to do was ignore them.

THIRTEEN

Sic Transit Bill Kunstler et al

It's almost over. The pendulum is swinging back. Like other periods of aberration that preceded it, the age of the Disaster Lobby has run out of steam. Logic and reason, long absent, are returning to their throne. Wherever you look, the signs are as unavoidable as a nonnegotiable demand at a meeting of the s.d.s.

On October 17, 1972, for example, Richard Nixon vetoed the $27.3 billion Federal Water Pollution Bill of 1972, having accurately described it as exorbitant, inflationary and ecologically unnecessary. The salient point here is that the veto came only three weeks before the presidential election and left Nixon wide open to the inevitable charge that he was "anti-environment." Two or three years earlier, such a charge could have put an end to a political career. The President obviously felt that this was no longer the case, and his smashing victory on November 7 proved he was right. With Disaster thinking on the wane, Americans no longer believed that they had to bankrupt themselves in order to achieve zero pollution through a program of cleanup overkill.

To be sure, Congress ultimately passed the measure over the President's veto, but quite a few Senators and Representatives voted to sustain his move. The Congressional tally showed that, while there was still a great deal of residual nuttiness extant in the United States, it had ceased to be a raging epidemic.

In its issue of May 1, 1972, *Barron's* cited a number of recent developments that could be construed as harbingers of a new era of sociopolitical sanity. Among them: the out-of-hand dismissal by President Nixon of Canada's proposal for a bilateral agreement to ban the use of phosphate detergents in areas bordering the Great Lakes; the defeat of an amendment that would have made the Federal water pollution bill even more onerous and less reasonable than it was; the financial troubles that forced the Sierra Club to shut down its New York City offices; the political eclipse of Senator Edmund S. Muskie and Mayor John V. Lindsay, each of whom had made ecology his personal crusade; a statement by a Federal hearing examiner giving DDT a clean bill of health; and the abject failure of Earth Day 1972, which came and went virtually unnoticed in sharp distinction to Earth Day 1970, "when a flood tide of flower children surged through the streets of Gotham, jamming traffic and leaving in their wake monumental heaps of rubbish and debris."

To *Barron's*, these were all "signs that 'the winter is past, the rain is over and gone' and the still small voice of reason again is heard in the land."

Ad Daily, a New York City-based trade paper, came to the same conclusion a month later, offering its own list of encouraging symptoms. It observed that most of the consumerism bills deposited in state legislatures three or four years earlier on the crest of Nader-inspired, anti-business lobbying were still languishing in the hoppers. The sponsors had lost their enthusiasm, which would indicate that their constituents had lost theirs. Reflective of the new public apathy toward consumerism was the response to a Federal Trade Commission ruling that all companies making claims in their advertisements must document those claims upon request. In the first six months after the ruling went into effect, the total number of requests from consumers for such documentation was less than 100. And there had been massive efforts by consumerists to swell the figure.

Also noted by *Ad Daily* was the failure of pressure group campaigns to encourage the purchase of aspirin by its generic name (Bayer's sales were booming); to boost the sale of unleaded gasolines (lead-free gasoline still accounted for less than 2 percent of gasoline sales); to spur the sale of private-label merchandise in supermarkets (the national brands were holding on to their share of the consumer dollar); to abolish detergents containing phosphates (phosphates were coming back); to stamp out cigaret smoking (cigaret sales were climbing out of sight); to get more people to use seat belts (no more people, as a percent of the total, were using seat belts); to discredit First National City Bank, Du Pont and other companies attacked by Ralph Nader (all these companies were doing just fine); to depopularize brassieres, feminine deodorants and other products reviled by the Women's Lib movement (such items were proliferating rather than disappearing); and to turn consumers on to the unit-price method of shopping (in a major study sponsored by the Consumers Research Institute, only 1.5 percent of the shoppers interviewed said unit pricing solved one of their shopping problems).

A sure sign of movement from left to right has been the surge in public support for capital punishment. The attitude of Americans toward the death penalty in murder cases is one of the most accurate barometers of the political climate, since the New Left, with its belief that society is to blame for most crimes, has made the abolition of capital punishment one of its chief goals. In 1953, according to the Gallup Poll, 68 percent of all Americans favored the death penalty for persons convicted of murder, while 25 percent were opposed. By 1965, after several years of Disaster Lobbying, the ratio was 45 percent in favor and 43 percent opposed, and by 1966, it was only 42 percent in favor and 47 percent opposed. Then in 1969, the return swing began, with 51 percent supporting capital punishment and 40 percent rejecting it. And in November of 1972, the tally was 57 percent for the death penalty and only 32 percent against it.

Not even the most enthusiastic and dedicated Disaster Lobbyist could disregard the evidence. It was a rueful William M. Kunstler who submitted to an interview for the

March 6, 1972, issue of *Time*. "Nationally, the pace of and interest in the left has dropped way down," said the left-wing lawyer who had represented scores of leftists in their clashes with government agencies. "I think there is a feeling that the movement is dead. There just isn't the same furor."

Contributing to the discomfiture of the anti-Establishment forces was the fact that, one by one, their claims were being refuted by highly respected authorities. There was that warning of theirs about the gradual accumulation of solid, nondegradable wastes to the point where man would have to compete with beer cans for room to exist. This was the prognosis that led to the almost hysterical attacks on the container industry and the pressures to replace cans and bottles with containers that were "biodegradable." Then, in early 1972, Dr. Edward L. Owen, a specialist in corrosion of metals and a member of the faculty at Pennsylvania State University, punctured that particular balloon by observing that everything made by man was biodegradable. In time, said Owen, nature recycles everything. The old-fashioned tin can is absorbed into the earth in about 100 years, while the aluminum beer can makes the round trip in 500 years.

Then some of the world's most universally esteemed social commentators—genuine liberals of the caliber of British novelist-scientist-statesman C. P. Snow—began chipping away at the bedrock thesis of America's new-wave liberals: the concept that all human beings are created absolutely equal at birth and that any differences that show up later on must therefore be the result of societal favoritism and injustices. It was Snow who first stunned the Disaster crowd in the early 1970's by announcing that, in his opinion, the Jews were a genetically superior people. Since you cannot have a genetically superior people without also having a genetically *inferior* people, the pith of the Snow declaration came through loud and clear, and to many American intellectual leaders it was utterly devastating. On October 25, 1972, Snow elaborated on his earlier remark. Speaking to a group of doctors at the opening of a new hospital wing in New York City, he ridiculed the leftist theory that each individual is a blank sheet of paper at birth, with the spaces to be filled in subsequently by parents, teachers and other instruments of society. "Each of us," said Snow, "is born with a different endowment, a realization which brings home that there are certain things that we could never have done and can never do."

At the same time, almost as if they had a secret death wish, the environmentalists and consumerists and other units of the Disaster Lobby made the grave mistake of overplaying their hand. In California, they got a state Supreme Court ruling that required local government agencies to complete an environmental impact report before approving each private construction project. In effect, the decision made it possible for any citizen to file suit to stop any building project on the ground that the building permit had been issued without due regard to environmental effects. The results of the court action were cataclysmic. Huge companies shelved their plans for putting up new factories, homes and office buildings. The cities of San Francisco and Santa Barbara stopped issuing any building permits at all for fear they might violate the new edict. According to one *Wall Street Journal* report, "the housing and construction industries are in a state of shock—as are many leaders in construction unions and lending institutions." That shock would soon be transmitted to the general public of California as new homes and apartments became relatively scarce and as the curtailment of building activity sent the state's economy into an ever-accelerating tailspin.

But the Disaster Lobby had not yet finished with Californians. Having deprived them of places to live and work, it now moved to immobilize them. On January 15, 1973, the Environmental Protection Agency formally proposed an 80 percent reduction in automobile travel in the Los Angeles Basin, to be made effective by the rationing of gasoline. Only through such a stringent measure, said the EPA, could the city conform to Federal air quality standards by the legal deadline of 1977. Los Angeles air was already cleaner than it had been in decades, but the ecology buffs were going to make it totally impeccable, even if it meant legislating Angelenos back to the stagecoach.

While the citizens of California took to regarding environmentalists with a certain ambivalence, if not outright distaste, a similarly rude awakening was in progress in the nation's capital. From the outset of Ralph Nader's career in consumerism, members of Congress, with few exceptions, had supported his efforts. Some Congressmen genuinely believed in what he was doing. Most Congressmen were somewhat skeptical, but felt, with considerable justification, that to oppose him would be political suicide. So any piece of legislation that had Nader's endorsement was sure to get respectful attention on Capitol Hill.

Then Nader committed the same error as the California environmentalists. He went one step too far. He conducted an investigation of the members of Congress, and he compounded his folly by publishing the results. Great was the wailing and the gnashing of teeth in the Senate and the House as the country's lawmakers suddenly found themselves on a griddle once reserved exclusively for America's businessmen. For Nader had tried to vilify the Congressmen in much the same manner as he had tried to blacken the names of First National City and Du Pont and General Motors and the other corporations, and he had done so with the same shoot-from-the-hip irresponsibility. Overnight, Congressional leaders who in the past had venerated Mr. Consumerism spotted the feet of clay. No longer would a Nader endorsement carry all that weight at committee meetings and hearings. The hands that had fed Ralph Nader had been bitten, and the owners of those hands had lengthy memories.

To add to the growing disenchantment, the cost of all those far-out, clean-it-up, shut-them-down projects began to surface in retail sales outlets across the country. When they first broached their ideas for the projects, the Disaster Lobby had hypnotized millions of Americans into believing that the manufacturers or the retailers or Big Daddy in Washington would pay for everything. They would pay the scores of billions of dollars for antipollution devices, for safety controls, for new insecticides to replace DDT, for all of the packaging and labeling and pricing gimmicks. But they didn't. They never do. Despite what some good-natured newspaperman once told Virginia, there isn't any Santa Claus. When the cost of doing business shot skyward as a result of the agglomeration of new rules and restrictions, the nation's entrepreneurs passed the increase on to the consumer in the form of higher prices. And whenever the government got stuck with the tab, it simply raised taxes, which had the same effect.

Occasionally in the slaphappy Sixties, someone would make a half-hearted attempt to let the public know that the piper would have to be paid. But the cost mentioned in these instances was always laughably low. As late as the summer of 1971, the Louis Harris organization was asking the man and woman in the street if they would be willing to pay $15 a year more in taxes to finance a Federal program to control air and water pollution. *Fifteen dollars a year!* By 1975, according to the Environmental Protection Agency, the average American would be paying *$140 a year* for environmental cleanup. And that was reported to be a very conservative estimate. Some experts were predicting that by 1975 a family of four in the United States would be shelling out more than $1,000 annually as its share of the colossal purification program.

But long before 1975, the American consumer, who was supposed to benefit from all of those visionary schemes, began instead to pay for them. Household electric bills were up sharply in 1972 because of emission controls mandated for utilities. Car prices were substantially higher as a result of compulsory antipollution and safety devices. Family expenditures for gasoline were climbing because the gadget-loaded new cars gulped gasoline in prodigious amounts. Food prices kept rising in the wake of shortages attributed by farmers to the ban on DDT and certain other insecticides. (There was a 30 percent hike in the price of honey, for example, after 250,000 bee colonies in California were wiped out in a single year by a new pesticide introduced as a substitute for DDT.) And the cost of cotton goods was similarly affected for similar reasons.

Tired of shouldering the blame for price increases and defective merchandise, farmers and businessmen started at last to let their customers know who the real culprits were. In the summer of 1972, one roadside produce stand in New Jersey displayed a sign bearing the following message: "We have stopped using DDT. Result—corn worms."

There were other side effects of the DDT ban that the public hadn't anticipated. In Oregon, 500,000 acres of timber were threatened by an invasion of tussock moths, and in December of 1972 Governor Tom McCall sent an urgent plea to Washington for permission to use the proscribed chemical. It was DDT or no more forests, said McCall, and without forests the birds and the animals would die out anyway.

Also militating strongly against the Disaster Lobbyists was the dearth of disasters. This is always one of the most serious problems faced by the prophets of doom. If you go around telling folks that the world is coming to an end at 1:25 p.m. on Easter Sunday, 1971, and then it gets to be 1:26 p.m. on Easter Sunday, 1971, and no end of the world, there is likely to be a disposition on the part of your audience to question your reliability. So it was with the Disaster crowd. For years, they had been warning about an impending catastrophe in the form of oxygen depletion, water contamination, DDT poisoning, billboard clutter, overpopulation and sundry other perils, but when the chips were down they couldn't produce a single catastrophe worthy of the name. Not even a minor tragedy. So the public became bored with them, and when the American public becomes bored with you, the best thing you can do is fold up your pitchman's case, stow it away in your wagon and retire to a seaside cottage in Asbury Park.

In years to come, there will be those who will argue that the Disaster Lobby was sincere and meant well and actually did some good. In those assessments, we must concur. But then we feel impelled to point out that Caligula was sincere, that Attila the Hun meant well and that Ivan the Terrible did some good. Not much, but some. However, each of these persons, despite the best of intentions, did infinitely more harm than good. And so it was with the Disaster Lobby. No sane person would deny the need for protection of the environment. But by exaggerating the dangers and demanding the impossible, the environmental activists of the 1960's impeded this nation's progress toward meaningful and worthwhile ecological reforms. Nor would anyone dispute the fact that some businessmen are out to cheat their customers. But by tarring all businessmen with the same indictment and by insisting on regulations that would have crippled the free enterprise system, the leading consumer advocates hurt the very people they were supposed to be protecting.

As 1972 drew to a close, there was a growing awareness that, despite its faults, the United States is a good country . . . that, as a consequence of mankind's quest for a longer, healthier existence, some animals may have to perish . . . that zero pollution is neither attainable nor necessary . . . that the consumer is much better off making his own mistakes in the marketplace than having an expert make the "right" buying decisions for him . . . and, above all, that the real danger we face is not too much scientific and technological progress but too little. For if mankind is to survive and flourish, he must find new ways to supply himself with the necessities of life and new challenges and rewards to make that life more worthwhile.

The Disaster Lobby failed because it was made up primarily of elitists, and a distrust of elitists has been ingrained in the American character from the time of Alexander Hamilton to the time of Adlai Stevenson. Perhaps it is a vestige of the pioneer and rebel spirit that makes the average American bridle when some self-anointed know-it-all tells him to do something for his own good.

It was no coincidence that one of the most resoundingly defeated presidential candidates in American history was the one heavily supported by the intellectual and cultural elite of the Disaster Lobby. The superior quality of George

McGovern's constituency was alluded to in a newspaper column written by Harriet Van Horne just two weeks before the 1972 election. Miss Van Horne described a scheduled Madison Square Garden rally for McGovern that "will feature the most glittering names in show business" and she added this statement: "If George McGovern doesn't make it, at least he'll know that the best and brightest people in the land gave him their hearts, their strengths and their faith."

George McGovern didn't make it. He lost out, as did the Disaster Lobby, because, in a democracy, "the best and brightest people in the land" have only one vote apiece, just like the rest of us. And, thank God, there are so many more of us than there are of them.

Index

Hazardous

Fish CYCLAMATE

Chap Stick

wild animals endangere

safe QUOTAS

Pollution board Mercury

an-made Chemicals

OIL SPILLS

TUNA

Strip Mining

drip

Phosphates

clean-water

SACCHARIN

Nuclear

POLLUTION READIN

Zer

Health Hazard

safeguards urc

sue

est

POWER

SAFETY BELTS Hex